Shifting Currents

A Memoir

by

Paula Dunning

Embajadoras Press

Cataloging data available from Library and Archives Canada
ISBN 978-1-988394-00-8 (paperback)
ISBN 978-1-988394-01-5 (ebook)

Cover photo by Jack Dunning

Published by Embajadoras Press
www.embajadoraspress.com

For Jack

whose love and enthusiasm have made both the living
and the writing of this story possible

and

For Morley and Gloria

who welcomed us and mentored us and taught us
that friendships can blossom in unexpected places.

Acknowledgements

Thank you to fellow writers for their encouragement and suggestions: Gregg Friedberg, Elizabeth Creith, Mary-Lynn Murphy, Peggy Lauzon, Angie Gallop, Earl Blaney, Jeff Hinich, Ted Fryia, Annie Smith, Miriam de Uriarte, Lee Gould.

Thanks, also, to the many friends who have read and commented on this during years of revisions and who have helped me recover shared memories. I am especially grateful to those who have allowed themselves to appear in these pages.

And of course, thanks to my three children—Erica, Robin, and Galen—from the bottom of my heart, for being characters in this book and for enriching my life in ways that go far beyond the limits of this story.

Finally, I am grateful to the Ontario Arts Council for its support.

Memory is our only route to the past. Its flaws and ambiguities bleed into its certainties to create a life in retrospect. The characters and events in this memoir are consistent with my memory. The people depicted here are real people; I have changed the names of some in the interest of privacy or at their request, and I have invented the names of some minor characters because memory has failed me entirely. In a few cases, characters and events are composites of several people or multiple events. In all cases, the story is mine.

• • •

"The Dunnings were not farmers and during the first year or so some of the neighbors watched with interest and wondered how they would manage. However, by trial and error they are learning."

From the *Tweedsmuir History of the Echo River Valley,* compiled by the Echo Valley Women's Institute, 1976.

CHAPTER 1 • FLOWING BACKWARDS

I am standing on the edge of the Echo River, watching it flow up-stream, seemingly determined to find its way back to its beginnings, to retrace its steps and revisit where it's been. The locals here say, with understandable pride, that this is one of only two rivers in the world to flow in both directions. On most days, it flows from Echo Lake toward its ultimate destination, Lake Huron. But sometimes, when the winds, the currents, and the water levels align themselves just right, it reverses itself to flow back toward its source, the tiny Upper Echo River that trickles into Echo Lake at its northern shore. I've never been able to confirm this local myth, and nobody seems to know which other river purportedly shares this retrospective inclination. But I've seen it happen here. In the end, of course, there is no stopping the forward flow from hills to river, river to lakes, lakes to the sea. As I watch the Echo River in one of those rare moments, I find myself thinking about flowing back-wards, and wondering how far back I would have to go to understand how I got here and what it means.

• • •

Maybe it was Laura.

When I was eight, my father brought home a copy of *The Little House in the Big Woods*. He and Mom took turns reading it aloud to me, a chapter a day, but I couldn't wait, so I rushed ahead and fin-ished it on my own. It was the biggest book I'd ever read, and Laura became my idol. By the time I was ten, I'd read the whole series, following the Ingalls family from the big woods of Wiscon-sin to the prairies of Kansas and north to the Dakotas, always

1

imagining myself as Laura, milking a cow in tall grasses, tramping down a haystack in the sweltering sun, enduring the hardships of bad harvests and worse weather. By twelve, I knew the Ingalls family as well as my own, and usually liked them better. At fourteen, I'd read *Gone with the Wind, Jane Eyre,* and *Grapes of Wrath.* But I still retreated to the *Little House* books and Laura whenever I needed an escape from adolescent angst. At eighteen, I re-read them secretly — they were for children, after all — imagining myself as the older Laura now, wholesome, adventuresome, in love, and still farming.

Or maybe it was when I first baked bread, or when I first harvested tomatoes from my own tiny vegetable garden, or when I began to make yogurt. By the time I read Adele Davis' *Let's Eat Right to Keep Fit* in 1970, the dominoes had begun to fall. From brewer's yeast to organic vegetables, from organic vegetables to goat's milk, from goat's milk to — well — goats, and finally to this northern Ontario farm, three hundred acres of field and forest stretching from the edge of the Echo River to the rocky hills of the Precambrian Shield.

Or maybe it was Jack the enthusiast.

• • •

It was summer 1964, on a Lake Michigan beach. I was standing beside a tall, blond guy in cut-off wheat jeans and a rumpled green shirt, seeing who could spit watermelon seeds the farthest. I was eighteen. He was nineteen.

"Gotcha this time," he said and took another bite of watermelon, chewing carefully to separate the fruit from the seeds in his mouth. His arms and the backs of his broad hands were sunburned, and shiny from the dripping juice.

"Oh, no you don't. That's mine. See it? Just past the rock."

He looked down at me and grinned. "Call it a draw?"

"No way," I said, trying to be both flirtatious and independent.

The lake was quiet; except for a faint lapping of water on sand, the only sound was music and the buzz of voices from the party in the house back off the beach behind us, a party for Grinnell College students with summer jobs in the Chicago area. I was working as an au pair girl in a suburb north of the city.

Looking skeptically at this guy's solid build, deep-set blue eyes, and ruddy complexion, I said, "I thought Jack Dunning was a tall, dark-haired guy with glasses who plays the guitar. I guess not." I laughed, hoping I'd kept the disappointment out of my voice. Jack seemed nice enough even though he wasn't the tall, dark guitar-player of my imagination.

"You're thinking of Andy Hand. He's in my dorm. I hang out with him sometimes. And I think five-eleven is pretty tall. I've got six inches on you, I bet!" He straightened up.

"More like seven" I said.

After an awkward silence, when I feared he would wander away, I asked, "So, what are you doing in Chicago?"

"Houseparent at a home for screwed up kids. Three days on, three days off. I'm not going back to Grinnell."

"You're just gonna quit?" I couldn't imagine.

"I'm sick of school. I'm gonna stick with this job. For now, anyway."

"What do your parents think?" I asked.

"Who cares?" he said. I looked away and bit my lower lip, hoping he couldn't tell how much I would care.

He tossed the last of the watermelon rind over his shoulder into the shrubs lining the beach and placed his sticky hand tentatively on my shoulder. I felt a tingle go up my spine. Jack grinned again, fingered my shoulder-length, straight brown hair for a moment, and settled his hand back on my shoulder. We moved toward the house where the party was in full swing; the smell of grilling hamburgers and the sound of Mick Jagger drifted toward us.

3

"Want a beer?"

"Sure." I didn't actually drink beer, but this seemed a good time to start.

"Wait here," he said, halfway between the beach and the party. I sat down and leaned back on my elbows. The coarse grass tickled my bare legs. Jack came back quickly, handed me a bottle of Old Milwaukee and took a gulp of his own. As he settled onto the grass beside me, I noticed his fine blond hair was thinning on the top of his head. Definitely not the dark-haired guitar-player.

"Hey!" He turned toward me. "Want me to analyze your handwriting? I just did a project on handwriting analysis last semester."

"Nuh-huh. Not my thing." I said. *Stupid*, I thought.

"Really, I bet I could tell a lot about you." He leapt to his feet again. "I'll find a pen."

"No thanks," But I was too late. He'd already gone. Did he ever sit still? A wave of anxiety rose from my stomach to my chest. I stretched my legs out on the grass and took a sip of beer. Foul. I made sure no one was watching, then poured half of it onto the ground; it left the bottle with a pleasant gurgle and disappeared silently into the sandy soil.

At last, Jack came bounding back with a pad of paper, a pen, and two hamburgers. He handed one to me and took a bite of the other, dripping grease onto the paper, which he shoved into my free hand. I bit into my hamburger, eager for the familiar flavours of meat and ketchup to erase the last of the beer taste from my mouth.

"Write a sentence," he said, shoving the pen toward me. "Any sentence."

Tricky. My mouth was full. So were my hands. Chewing, I put the hamburger beside the nearly empty beer bottle on the grass, tipping the bottle and spilling more beer into the sand.

4

Jack set it upright before it was quite empty. "Want another one?"

I shook my head, finished chewing, and took the paper and pen. My handwriting wouldn't tell him anything about me at all; I was sure of that. But the sentence might. Okay, play it safe. Trying to be both careful and unconcerned, I wrote "Now is the time for all good men to come to the aid of their country" and handed the page back to Jack. I picked up my hamburger, brushed the bits of grass off the bottom, and slowly took a second bite. As he studied my sentence, Jack's thick blond eyebrows nearly met above his nose, and a hint of a smirk formed on his face. I looked down and noticed he was wearing a pair of sandals fashioned from an old pair of desert boots; in front of the laces, his toes poked out through crudely cut holes. My turn to smirk. He took a breath and dropped a bombshell: "You are basically conservative."

I choked on my hamburger, coughed, and wiped a large blob of ketchup off my shirt with the back of my hand. "Well, hardly. I'm about as liberal as you can get! Actually, I'm radical. I've been in freedom marches and peace rallies. My parents are *Quakers*. My dad's a *theatre prof*. I bet I'm a lot more liberal than you!" I knew his dad was a wealthy Connecticut businessman and his mom's family tree included Louisa May Alcott. New England upper crust.

Jack put the last of his hamburger into his mouth and chewed slowly. He finally swallowed and said, "This is about your deeper personality. See how you close your 'b's' and cross your 't's'?"

"Ridiculous," I snorted.

He was grinning again. "You're also a pessimist."

• • •

On our first date we played tennis, sailed on a small lake, ate a picnic lunch on an island, and rented a little motorcycle. I had never played tennis and couldn't hit the ball; I cowered in fear at the tippiness of the little sailboat; I spilled mayonnaise on my blouse; and I fell off the back of the motorcycle. When he kissed me at the end of the day, I knew none of that mattered.

Two weeks and four dates later, in the small bedroom I occupied as an au pair girl—the servant's quarters—I sprawled on the bed, tuned the radio to Chicago station WCFL, and listened to Ray Charles singing "Hit the road, Jack, you're never comin' back no more, no more..." Should this be my song? But I was having fun, and something about this guy's energy and enthusiasm made me smile and kept me from singing along.

I returned to school in September, and Jack regularly drove his little black VW from Chicago to Grinnell College in the middle of Iowa, pedal to the metal for five hours, to spend weekends with me. In between visits, we wrote long letters—his passionate, mine repressed, which was, as he pointed out sadly, further evidence of my conservative nature. Every time he stepped on the gas pedal, I applied the brakes, until we reached an understanding that if we were to move forward together, we would have to both temper his enthusiasm and loosen my repression.

• • •

Less than two years later, on a rainy April evening in 1966, I stood beside the phone in the basement apartment Jack shared with two friends in Grinnell. He had returned to school after all and was about to graduate. He stood beside me, his arm around my shoulders, as I dialed my parents' number.

In the middle of Pennsylvania, Mom answered: "Hello."

She must have been in the kitchen; I could hear water running; she would be stretching the phone cord on her end to reach the faucet without dropping the receiver. I could see the last of the sunlight coming through the window over the sink, the copper-bottom pots hanging on the peg-board, and Mom leaning against the counter, ready for a chat.

"Paula! We were going to phone you this weekend about the summer. We're booking a house at the shore for August. Will you be coming home?"

"That's what I called about, Mom." Why was my throat so dry? Jack took a deep breath and pulled me closer; I shrugged him away. "Can you get Dad on the other phone?"

Jack picked up his black cat, Gasman, and dropped onto the worn maroon sofa. The ancient refrigerator began to hum; just a hint of evening light made its way through the tiny, dirty basement windows; I could still smell the bacon we'd cooked an hour ago.

"Warren!" I heard Mom call.

Jack was still on the sofa, holding the cat against his cheek. Maybe I shouldn't have shrugged him away, I thought, but I needed to do this myself. I twisted the black spiral of the phone cord around my finger, shifting my weight from foot to foot, blood pounding in my ears.

"Warren, it's Paula. Pick up your phone." I heard a few last taps of the typewriter keys and knew that Dad had shifted from his typewriter table to his oak desk. His glasses would be in one hand while he rubbed the bridge of his nose with the other, tucked the phone under his chin, and stretched his legs out in front of him.

"Hi, kiddo." Dad's voice was warm, a bit raspy. "What's up?"

Jack leaned back, then forward, his elbows on his knees. The cat ran across the floor and jumped up on the counter.

I gulped a deep breath and just said it: "Jack and I are going to get married. In June."

Silence.

I blurted, "I'm not pregnant, just in case you wondered."

Silence. They knew Jack. They liked him. Why wouldn't they speak?

Jack stood up, moved toward me, then back to the sofa.

I was about to speak again when Mom found her voice, businesslike, already planning: "Will you get married here? In the Meetinghouse? Do you have a date?"

I telegraphed Jack with a tense smile and a nod; it was going to be fine. He leaned back again, patting his hand on the sofa, inviting the cat to re-join him.

I said, "Of course. In the Meetinghouse. A Quaker wedding. We're thinking June third. My exams are over the last week in May, so I can come home for a week ahead of time to get ready."

Dad had taken a moment, planned a final statement. I could hear him clear his throat, and I could see him tilting back in his wooden desk chair. "Well, gal, this is big news. It's a big step. But you're an adult, and we trust your judgment."

Mom coughed. Or was it a sob?

Dad said, "Jack's a good guy. You'd better phone your mom in a few days to talk about details. She's a little emotional right now."

"I'm fine, Paula," said Mom in a steady voice. "Just a little surprised." She paused. "But happy."

When they hung up, Jack reached for me. I turned toward him and buried my face against his shirt, still holding the phone. "I guess we're getting married," I said.

It didn't go quite so well with Jack's family. They wanted more than a simple wedding and an afternoon reception at home. His mother was annoyed that we'd limited the number of guests to the capacity of the small Quaker Meetinghouse. When she phoned from Connecticut to press for a bigger event, more guests, a larger venue, she also asked me about my choice of silver and china patterns.

"I'm not really the silver and china type," I said. "I'd rather have stainless and stoneware."

"That's unusual, Paula," she said. "The relatives will want to know what to get you."

I stood my ground. "They can get me stainless and stoneware."

• • •

Mom read up on wedding etiquette. She made sure my younger brothers, ten and seventeen, had suits and ties. She bought a pale green dress that fit her perfectly. She got a really good haircut and a fresh perm. A few days before the wedding, she set up two card tables in the dining room to display the gifts that were pouring in.

Jack's aunt and uncle gave us service for twelve in the Dansk stainless pattern we'd chosen. My aunt and uncle gave us a frying pan. Another of Jack's aunts gave us service for eight in blue and white stoneware. Jack's grandmother gave us a silver pitcher and serving tray; mine gave us an ironing board. Jack's parents gave us a brand new, red Volkswagen Squareback; mine gave us a sewing machine. Mom pretended it didn't matter.

Dad took me aside, in his study with the revolving oak bookcase and the Victorian settee, and we talked about my future. I would finish up my bachelor's degree at Western Michigan University in Kalamazoo, where Jack was going to grad school in experimental psychology. Maybe I'd go on for my masters in history the next year.

"I know it's not as good a school as Grinnell." I apologized; Dad would care. "We could have waited another year. We just, you know, we just didn't want to."

He surprised me, shook his head. "I do know. Relax, gal. Your education is supposed to be a *part* of your life, not *instead* of it. Jack's a good guy, and you seem happy." When he hugged me, I pressed my face against his thin chest, breathed the familiar scent of home and security, mopped my tears on his rough sweater.

The day before the wedding, Mom and I took a walk on the mountain roads surrounding the home I'd lived in all my life. "I'm afraid we won't impress the Dunning clan much," she said. "The Meetinghouse wedding. The reception at home. We could have done more."

"It's what we want, Mom."

"But Jack..."

"Jack's fine. He doesn't much care what his parents think."

We walked for a long time and talked about things we'd never talked about before—her own decision to marry young, to a man thirteen years older; her feeling of inadequacy about her lack of a college education; her idea about what made a good marriage: "Sharing meals, sharing a joke, sharing a bed." And then, she took a deep breath and said it: "Will you go on the pill?" I knew what she was really asking, and I'd been dreading it.

"Yeah," One foot in front of the other. "I'm already on it."

"I thought so," she said. Another pause. Then, "You know about the penny jar?"

"What penny jar?"

"Well. They say that if you put a penny in a jar every time...every time...every time you have *intercourse* during the first year of marriage, and take one out every time after that, you'll never empty the jar." She blushed. "But it's not true."

• • •

We married each other in State College, Pennsylvania, in a traditional Quaker ceremony, without the aid of priest or pastor. Light poured through tall sash windows on two sides of the room. Friends and family sat on stern grey pews facing the fireplace in front. Jack and I sat on a front pew. After a few moments of silence, we stood. Jack spoke first. When it was my turn, my voice quavered. "In the presence of God and these our friends, I, Paula Mae Smith, take thee, John Alcott Dunning, to be my lawful wedded husband, promising to be unto thee a loving and faithful wife so

10

long as we both shall live." We exchanged rings, kissed, and sat down.

In the silence that followed, members of my family and family friends, accustomed to this tradition, rose and spoke of marriage, shared memories, and wished us happiness. Jack's family sat quietly, puzzled by the strangeness of it all.

The only wedding photos we have are a handful of slides taken by Jack's uncle. When I look at them, I realize we were children. In one, Jack is shoving a piece of wedding cake into my mouth; I am leaning away from him, and we are laughing. We both look fifteen. In another, Jack's grandmother is seated at a table, adding her signature to the traditional, poster-sized Quaker wedding certificate. Then, we are lined up in front of the Meetinghouse, with our parents on either side of us, everyone looking very ill at ease, saying "cheese" as instructed. On a final slide, we are leaving my parents' house, my childhood home, by the front door—the only time I remember using that door. Jack is still wearing his black wedding suit and blue tie. I have changed from my knee-length, off-white wedding dress to my "going away" outfit, a green dress of shantung silk that I tried to sew myself, but at the last minute handed over to Mom. The dress is beautiful, my smile is bright, but what stands out for me, as I look at this photo nearly fifty years later, is the large, thoroughly scuffed leather purse slung gracelessly over my right shoulder, and I want to ask that child-bride—was it a fashion oversight or a fashion statement?

Chapter 2 • Navigating the Sixties

We rented a sprawling apartment above a drugstore on West Main Street in Kalamazoo, a fifteen-minute walk from the Western Michigan campus. The eighty-five dollars a month was more than we wanted to pay, but we had an upper-crust New England nest-egg propping us up; Jack's dad had recently sold his business for more than a million dollars, and since each of his children held five percent of the shares, we were, in my mind, embarrassingly well-off for students. Jack wasn't embarrassed; he was used to having money. His dad had started his sand and gravel business on a shoestring in the thirties, but by the time Jack came along, his parents had stopped worrying about price tags.

My parents always worried about price tags, and I didn't think Jack worried about them enough.

"What's the big deal?" he asked. "It's not like we're throwing money away." He was taking the new Dynakit stereo components out of the box.

"Here's the big deal," I said. "Nobody else drives a new car. Nobody else can go to school without working on the side. We've got this nice apartment. You just bought a stereo. Your parents gave us their cast-off furniture—the red chair, the sofa. And the dining room table—it's nicer than anything my parents ever had. It just doesn't feel right."

"For Christ's sake," said Jack. "What's everybody else got to do with it?" He turned back to the stereo, leaving me to wonder if this would work.

• • •

As the discontent of the sixties escalated into more and larger anti-war demonstrations, louder voices calling for equality, ritual burnings of draft cards and bras, assassinations, and racial violence, I hovered at the edges of protest. I attended a few anti-war rallies in downtown Kalamazoo and reassured myself that I was a radical at heart, just waiting for the right moment to take my stand. Students for Democratic Society, Peace Marches, Women's Lib, Freedom Marches, Free Love — emblems of the New Left. I nodded my head in agreement, and prepared for the next day's classes.

We built big desks out of concrete blocks and lumber-yard reject veneer doors; we combined our books and arranged them alphabetically on brick-and-board shelves; we argued over who took out the garbage and emptied Gasman's kitty litter; we debated whether we should trade the Volkswagen in on a sports car (we did — a dark blue MGB, used); and we made frequent stops in the bedroom to build up our penny supply.

In the kitchen, we hung a black-and-white poster of two hippos mating, with the words "Make Love Not War" beneath them; in the dining room Andy Warhol's tomato soup can with blood pouring out of a bullet hole; in our bedroom, the framed marriage certificate. And we let the politics of protest unfold at a safe distance.

I graduated with a B.A. in history in the spring of 1967, and by the winter of 1968 we were both working on our Masters theses. Mine was on the anti-republican right in France, 1871-1893, a subject that must have inspired in me some enthusiasm at the time. My favourite source book was a cheery volume entitled *The Sense of Decadence in Late Nineteenth Century France*. Jack was looking into Ph.D. options in experimental, behavioural psychology. His choice of universities would come first; then I would consider my own options. Maybe a Ph.D. as well. Or maybe a job. I was only twenty-two. No rush.

While we toiled at our desks and quietly seethed at our country's politics, Jack's draft board in Connecticut was running out of fodder for the war in Vietnam. The ranks of the poor had been decimated; all eligible married men without children, single non-students, and non-essential workers had already been drafted. In recognition of this nation-wide supply problem, Congress removed the automatic student deferment that protected fulltime students, the children of the wealthy, from the draft.

On a February afternoon, Jack picked up the mail at the bottom of the steps, and began sifting through it. I followed him upstairs to our apartment, my book bag slung over my shoulder. What should I make for supper? How was I going to get my Philosophy of History paper written before the weekend?

"Uh-oh," I heard Jack mutter. "Something from the draft board." He dropped the rest of the mail on the sofa. I held my breath.

"Okay," he said. "It's just a form letter. Student deferments are being withdrawn...blah, blah. When the effective date is set, my status will be reviewed. Blah, blah." He slammed his fist against the wall. "Motherfuckers! I won't go."

He slumped into the red chair. I dropped onto the sofa and sat there, head in hands. An ambulance whooped its siren on Main Street, then roared past.

"You could apply for C.O. status," I said. Conscientious Objector.

Jack shrugged. "I'd have to lie. And they'd catch me at it." He was a firm atheist, and one of the conditions for C.O. status was religious conviction. Very few men received C.O. status unless their families belonged to one of the peace churches--the Quakers, the Mennonites, the Bretheran. Jack's were Congregationalists. Mine didn't count.

"We could have a baby," he said. "Or go to Canada."

"A baby?" I said. "So soon?"

• • •

Though I felt like a traitor to the women's movement, I was thrilled, the very next month, to learn that I was pregnant. We would begin our family, and Jack would be safe from the draft. All around us, young people were making life-altering decisions based on their draft status, a status that could change with little warning. By the time confirmation of my pregnancy reached Jack's draft board, in April 1968, Congress had removed the fatherhood deferment. Even fathers of infants could now be required to kill and die in Vietnam. *No,* we promised our still embryonic child. *Not your father.*

That left Canada. Jack applied for the Ph.D. program at McMaster University in Hamilton, Ontario, and was accepted with a teaching assistantship and a small salary.

That summer, in the midst of our growing excitement about the pregnancy and the move to Canada, Jack's mother phoned to tell him she'd left his father. She'd waited, she said, until Jack, her youngest, was married and settled. She would be filing for divorce. I'd never seen Jack cry before; it frightened me. I pulled him close and held his head against my breast. Like a mother, not like a lover.

"It's not that we were ever a close family," he said. That was an understatement. From the age of five, he'd been left with another family so his parents could winter in Florida, from the age of six he'd spent all summer every summer at summer camp, and he'd attended boarding schools from eighth grade on.

"I hardly spent any time with them growing up; I don't think they actually cared that much about me. So why am I so upset?" he groaned.

"Because they're your parents," I said, and silently promised the child growing in my belly that it would never doubt our love.

• • •

15

A month before we moved, Jack saw an ad in the paper for an old school bus. "Wouldn't it be fun to have a bus?" A rhetorical question. Who wouldn't want to own a school bus?

"We could use it to move. Then, it'll make a great camper. Fun to fix up, with a crib for the baby and everything. We can go camping in Canada."

Huh? I looked up from my coffee, stared at him in disbelief. "You're serious? A school bus? You want to buy a school bus?" Jack the enthusiast. I was beginning to sense this ride would not end with a bus.

He started by removing all but two front seats to turn it into a moving van. That's what he was driving when we pulled up to the Canadian border at Windsor, Ontario, on the afternoon of August 2, 1968. I was driving the MG with the top down. Jack carried a folder with his acceptance to graduate school, our birth certificates, and the lease we'd signed several weeks earlier for an apartment in Dundas, a short drive from the university.

We marched together into the border station, Jack in his usual jeans and t-shirt. His hair—even sparser than when I'd first met him—hung almost to his shoulders; it occurred to me that maybe he should have washed it. Or even cut it. At least he'd shaved that morning. I was wearing an orange cotton dress that hung loosely over my six-month pregnant belly and ended several inches above my knees. My long hair was pulled back in a ponytail at the nape of my neck. I carried a large woven purse with a Navajo theme.

The man behind the counter was tall and clean-shaven, with a military haircut. He wore a white shirt with a red maple leaf on the pocket. He smiled. "Good afternoon, folks. Heading off for a holiday?"

"Nope," said Jack. "We're moving here." He put his arm around me. Family man.

16

"I'll need to see your papers." His smile had faded a bit, but his tone was still friendly. He studied the contents of our folder with a deepening furrow between his brows.

"This will entitle you to temporary student resident status," he said. "You'll have to fill out the proper forms here."

"No, we want to have permanent immigrant status," I said.

The officer glanced at me, but continued speaking to Jack. His smile was gone now. "You can apply for landed immigrant status later. For now, if you are admitted, it will be on a student visa." He finally looked at me. "As the wife of a student, you will be eligible for a work visa if you can get a job."

Jack and I looked at one another. What was this "if you are ad-mitted...if you can get a job"?

The officer ushered us into a small office with two wooden chairs in front of a large metal desk, took his seat on the other side, and began asking questions: Where were we born? Did we have proof of marriage? How long would Jack's graduate program last? Any criminal record? We filled out forms itemizing all the goods that we were bringing into the country. An hour later, we signed on the dotted line and the officer followed us outside, holding the list in his hand. "Let's see what you've got here." That's when he saw the bus.

"You're importing this vehicle?" he asked, making it sound like a contagious disease.

"Yes. Well, yes. It's on the list. Um, it's for a, um, camper." Jack didn't usually stumble over his words.

"A camper? I see. You'll have to register both vehicles here. I'll need proof of insurance, ownership. While you're finding those, I'll be checking through the contents."

He did. Very carefully, opening every box in the bus, checking under the seats and in the glove compartment of the MG. Finally, apparently satisfied we weren't running drugs, the officer present-ed us with our temporary student visas. He stood at the door shaking his head as Jack climbed onto the bus and I slid my thickening body behind the wheel of the little sports car. We drove out of the parking lot and continued east toward Hamilton and our new lives.

We settled into our basement apartment, smaller than the rambling apartment we'd left in Kalamazoo. Jack met with his advisor, began preparing for classes, and found a place in the country to store the bus. I signed up with an obstetrician and discovered that, even with temporary student status, we were eligible for the Ontario Health Insurance Program. This baby would be coming into the world without a price tag.

The draft board drama continued; within a month we learned that Jack's date of birth fell just before the cut-off for reclassification; he would retain his student deferment after all. The pregnancy made no difference; neither did the move to Canada. Jack was not, technically, a draft-dodger, but we had no regrets. We would be having a Canadian baby.

I spent the last three months of my pregnancy preparing for the birth: we bought and painted a used crib, I made room-darkening curtains for the high basement windows in the baby's room, and Jack built an over-sized change table and storage unit out of plywood and dowels, which we painted orange and filled with diapers, rubber pants, tiny undershirts and sleepers. In late October, just weeks before the baby was due, Jack reluctantly agreed that the MG was not a family car.

"You can't have everything," I said.

"Why not?" He really wondered.

We traded it in on a Volvo station wagon.

My obstetrician wasn't keen on natural childbirth, but I was. And so I read *Thank You, Dr. Lamaze* and, in lieu of classes, did breathing exercises at home. How hard could it be? Exactly one week before my twenty-third birthday — after twenty-four hours of labour and all the drugs on offer — our seven-pound, four-ounce daughter, Erica, was coaxed and tugged into the world with forceps.

I took her home five days later, ready to commit myself to full-time motherhood for a few months. That was my plan: breastfeed for three months, stay home for another three months, then find childcare and look for meaningful work. Motherhood for a liberated woman.

Leaning over the bassinet, gazing at my week-old daughter, I shared my six-month plan with Mom, who'd flown in from Pennsylvania to help out with her first grandchild. She looked up from the little green sweater she was knitting and said, "There are lots of good reasons to go to work, Paula. And, of course, if you need the money you don't have a choice. But then, you have to understand that someone else will be playing a big part in raising your children — maybe bigger than you."

As though objecting, Erica began to stir, her little face puckering into a cry. I lifted her gently and nestled her against my shoulder, where she began to nuzzle and suck at the skin on my neck. I joined Mom on the couch, and put the baby to my breast.

"I do have a choice," I said. "It's just that I want to do something that feels *important*."

Six months came and went; I weaned Erica to a bottle as planned, but postponed the job search. One day in June, when she was almost eight months old, she was sitting on the living room floor, her little back straight, her fine blond hair just reaching her forehead, her chubby legs stretching out in front, her gaze locked on the block in her right hand as she slowly moved it toward the plastic bowl in front of her.

"Yes, you can do it!" I said. "Put it in the bowl!"

She dropped the block on the floor and looked up at me. Her toes wiggled madly, and a smile — just for me — pushed her chipmunk cheeks up far enough to squint her eyes. The smile exploded into a laugh, and in her excitement she tipped over onto her side. I picked her up, laughing with her, and hugged her tight.

I would not be giving these moments to anyone else.

• • •

That summer we moved from the apartment building into a two-story, three-bedroom house in a real neighbourhood, where children walked back and forth to school and played road hockey on the street, where we could chat with neighbours over the back yard fence and, most importantly, where we could keep the bus in the driveway.

I was sitting in the back yard with a book, watching Erica play on the grass and trying to keep our new German Shepherd puppy, Shastek, from licking her face. She was working hard, trying to fit a red plastic donut on a yellow spindle. Mrs. Swackhammer was hanging out wash next door. She took two clothespins out of her apron pocket and added a pair of green workpants to the line that was already sagging with jeans, bright-coloured blouses, and over-sized ladies' underwear.

She glanced over at me and sighed. "A woman's work is never done, that's what they say. But you look relaxed." She looked at Erica. "Now's the time to enjoy them. When they're as old as mine, they're trouble, trouble, trouble." She'd moved from work clothes to striped boys' t-shirts and ruffled girls' blouses. When her basket was empty, she came over to the fence.

"That yard of yours used to be pretty. Sweet peas all up the hill." She gestured toward the back of the yard, a steep bank, overgrown with vines and wild raspberry canes. "Of course, it takes work. We were hoping someone would rent who'd take care of it." She was looking at my book with an accusatory eye. I jumped off my lounge chair to push the puppy away from Erica's face and said, "I like it wild. And we won't be here that long."

"You'll want to wash her up good now. You never know what a dog's been into," said Mrs. Swackhammer. "By the way, we've been meaning to ask you. How long will that bus be parked in your driveway?"

"It's ours. We're converting it to a camper."

"It's an eyesore," she said, pursing her lips and shaking her tightly-curled head. "Ugly, ugly, ugly."

There were days when I agreed with Mrs. Swackhammer. The bus occupied most of the driveway, and almost as much of Jack's time. It really was an eyesore, and this wasn't my idea of how a Ph.D. student should spend his spare time — measuring, sawing, drilling, hammering.

Erica was in bed and we were both in the bus looking at the overstuffed chair Jack had just brought home in the back of the car. "Five bucks at the Sally Ann." He was placing it just inside the door of the bus, opposite the driver's side. He angled it a bit toward the back to create a homey feel, then drilled into the floor to bolt it down and attach seat belts.

He looked up at me with a grin. I responded with a shrug. "I just don't understand how you can you take this much time from your real work."

The grin disappeared, his shoulders slumped, and he rubbed his chin, where the beginnings of a blond beard were barely visible. "I work at school all day, you know — and quite a lot here, in case you haven't noticed. What's wrong with having a project?"

"This isn't a project. It's an obsession. It might be nice if you came into the house now and then. Read a book or something."

He turned, walked to the back of the bus, and slammed a wrench on the countertop he'd salvaged from a demolition site, cracking the formica surface. "Something intellectual, you mean. To show I'm as smart as you? I'm just not what you figure I should be, am I?"

"You've got that right," I muttered and headed back in to the house, not quite sure why I was so angry. Sometimes the bus seemed like a good idea; but sometimes it was just an embarrassment.

With Erica's first birthday approaching, Jack shifted his enthusiasm away from the bus to the woodworking shop at the university, where he was building home-made gifts: a bus made from a chunk of four-by-four with holes for the passengers—a multi-racial group of dowel-people, beige, red, and black; a hinged shape-box with round, square, and triangle holes on the top and blocks to fit through them; and a set of building blocks that he never finished, because two days before the birthday he ran his left hand through the table saw. He lost the end of one finger and the mobility in two more. The only thing that prevented further damage was his wedding ring, which deflected the saw away from the palm of his hand and was found in a pile of blood and sawdust the next day. He spent almost a week in the hospital, and missed both Erica's first birthday and her first steps.

• • •

This was the decade where the personal became political. Individual preferences and personality traits floated on the surface of the violent currents and side-eddies of protest and rapid social change. My own personal decisions—to shy away from activism, to marry early, to have a baby early and stay home with her—left me feeling out of sync with the prevailing cultural drift, and I began to fear that Jack's diagnosis that I was "basically conservative" might be true.

Our brief encounter with "consciousness raising" didn't do much to reassure me. I've buried the details, but here's what I remember.

Eight of us were sitting in the living room of the house where two couples had established a mini-commune in the country near Hamilton. James, who had organized this gathering, tilted his chair on its back legs and looked around, seeming to take stock of each of us. "Since this was my idea, I'll get things started," he said, lowering his chair, crossing his long legs, and leaning into the circle. James was an intense man, the only one of the group working on his degree in clinical psychology. The other men were, like Jack, lab-rat types in the Psych Department's Ph.D. program.

"I've been reading about consciousness raising groups, and that's what I have in mind here. We all know each other pretty well. The idea is to get to know ourselves and each other better. To sort of let go of our inhibitions."

"Which inhibitions are those?" said Jack, trying to lighten the tone. He looked like he belonged, with his beard — now full and bushy — his hair hanging down the back of his neck, his jeans appropriately faded. But I knew he was skeptical.

We were skeptical.

James said, "We'll just be totally open and honest, and talk about our deepest feelings." He lit a joint and began passing it.

"Tonight, let's just go around in the circle and tell the group something about yourself, something you've never told any of us before."

I felt a sensation akin to panic as revelation followed revelation — admissions of youthful indiscretions, sexual fantasies, violent tendencies. What's wrong with me that I hate this, I wondered. These people are my friends. Now they were all looking at me. My turn.

I squirmed, then blurted out, "I sucked my thumb until I was in college." James' wife, Liz, raised one eyebrow and shrugged.

Jack's turn. "When I was a kid, some friends and I beat up on another kid and he passed out. Scared me to death. The story hit the *National Inquirer.*"

The discussion that followed suggested I was orally fixated and seriously insecure, and Jack had a barely repressed violent streak.

Two weeks later, we began the in-depth consciousness-raising of individual members of the group. First up was Jan.

"We'll go around the circle and each person has to say one good thing about Jan and one thing she should do to improve," said James. "Remember, the idea is to help her understand herself better."

Jan was sitting on the floor. She dropped her forehead onto her hand and said, "I'm ready."

She couldn't have been ready. One friend after another spoke up, bombarding Jan with trivial praise and soul-destroying criticism. This was no-holds-barred truth-telling, which should have been exhilarating.

"Jan is a good friend," I said. "But I don't think she realizes how condescending she can be." When my eyes met Jan's, I saw tears welling up, and I knew at once. She had counted on me to rescue her from this hell, and I had let her down. I had sacrificed kindness at the altar of self-serving group-think. I dropped my gaze, ashamed.

When it was Jack's turn, he shook his head. "I like Jan. I guess she's got some problems, but no more than the rest of us." I smiled at him. Good for you, I thought. It's what I should have had the courage to say.

I was silent on the way home.

"That was appalling," said Jack. "It might have been true, but what was the point of it?" He was right. And yet I was secretly pleased that, when it came my turn, I'd probably come out better.

At the next meeting—Jan was absent—we went around the circle again, a little less honestly. When we'd all had our say about Liz, we lingered over beer and agreed that maybe this was doing more harm than good to our friendships.

"Not everyone is at a level of self-awareness to take advantage of this kind of openness and honesty," said James. Jack and I rolled our eyes at each other from opposite sides of the room.

I sighed as we got into the car. "I'm glad that's over—and that they never got to me!" I was no longer confident I'd have emerged unscathed.

"We should never have agreed to it in the first place," said Jack. "I think I like everyone less than I did before."

"Jan thinks James wanted this consciousness-raising thing to end up with group sex. "

"Didn't work out that way, did it?"

I stared out the side window and watched the scattered lights of rural southern Ontario become denser as we got closer to the city.

"James and Liz have friends coming to visit next week," I said.

"Yeah? More victims for James's hocus-pocus?"

"Liz says they're planning to swap partners."

Silence.

"Would you want to do that?" I asked.

We were almost in Dundas—almost home. I held my breath, afraid of his answer.

He took his eyes off the road and turned to me briefly. "It's a turn-on to think about, I guess. But no, I don't think so."

I let my breath out slowly.

• • •

We were beginning to feel like Canadians, ending our sentences with *eh*, listening to CBC radio, talking endlessly about the weather, and following Canadian politics. The summer after Erica turned one, we strapped a canoe on the roof of the bus, now fully outfitted inside and painted in brilliant primary colours outside, and took it on its maiden voyage to see more of the country first-hand—a trip north to the forest and lakes of Algonquin Park. We walked on hiking trails, picked blueberries, and paddled the canoe with Erica between us, her blond head just emerging above her bright orange "boat coat". I cooked bannock over a campfire, spread clothes out to dry around the campsite, fried the fish Jack caught, and imagined that I was Laura, the bus a covered wagon en route to an unsettled land.

We were now officially landed immigrants, on track for citizenship, but the U.S. continued to hold its grip on us. Before we'd left Kalamazoo, Jack's master's thesis had been approved by his department and sent on for final approval to the Dean of Graduate Studies, a chest-thumping patriot. This normally routine finalization hit a snag when the Dean got wind that Jack had left for Canada. He assumed that this degree candidate was a draft dodger, and he told the head of the Psychology Department, "No draft dodger will get a degree from this university as long as I'm Dean."

"He can't do this," I fumed. "You're not a draft-dodger. And even if you were…"

But he could, and he did.

At first, Jack clung to his principles and insisted his draft status was irrelevant to his degree status. The more pressure the department put on the Dean, the more objectionable he became, even harassing Jack on the telephone about his decision to move to Canada. Once he phoned late at night asking in a slurred voice for money to buy "smokes for the boys in 'Nam.'" Eventually, to end the harassment and receive his degree, Jack swallowed his pride and sent a copy of his draft card to the Dean's office, proving that, although he was in Canada, he was not a draft dodger. His diploma arrived in the mail two weeks later.

Jack's grad school commitments were intensifying, absorbing most of his day with course work, lab work, and his teaching assistantship. Between housewifely and motherly tasks, I read the Tolkein Trilogy and immersed myself in the fantasy world of Hobbits and orcs, dragons and ents. But I was also discovering a very different world where the threats were not imaginary. I read Rachel Carson's *Silent Spring*, planted a small garden, and began hauling bottles and cans to the recycling depot. I read Adele Davis' *Let's Eat Right to Keep Fit* and *Let's Have Healthy Children*, and began searching out organic food, baking bread, and mixing batches of Tiger's Milk. I read *Diet for a Small Planet* by Frances Moore Lappé, and began balancing amino acids to form complete proteins without meat. I read Paul Erlich's *The Population Bomb*, and joined ZPG—an organization dedicated to zero population growth. Finally, I was taking a stand for a better world.

Jack hadn't had any trouble convincing me to become pregnant two years earlier, and I didn't have any trouble convincing him we should adopt our second child. In the fall of 1970, we sat in an office of the Hamilton Children's Aid Society. I wore a modest skirt and blouse, and my hair was done up in a French twist. Jack wore a button-up shirt, tucked into khakis. His beard—now a full and permanent fixture on his face—was trimmed and brushed. Our social worker, Mrs. Polk, leaned across her wide desk and said, "We need to know why you're choosing to adopt. Are you unable to have more children of your own?"

I answered. "No, we could have more. We're worried about overpopulation."

She looked at me quizzically. "I've never heard that reason before." Then, "Would you consider an older child?"

"No," said Jack. He'd been reading the research on parental bonding and was convinced those first few months, even weeks, were critical. "We'd like a baby as young as possible—right out of the hospital. And we have a girl, so we'd like to adopt a boy."

Mrs. Polk shook her head. "I can't make promises. The birth mother has the legal right to change her mind for three months, so we don't like to place babies in adoptive homes until then. Would you take a hard-to-place child? That might make an early place-ment easier."

"Oh, yes," we said in unison.

We left the interview with a list of conditions that make babies hard to place. Mental disabilities? We'd have trouble with that, we agreed. Physical disabilities? Depending on how severe, maybe. Mixed race? That would be no problem.

In November Mrs. Polk phoned to tell us about a child, due to be born around Christmas, who could be placed immediately from the hospital. The mother, a woman of mixed race – Black, White, Native American – was very firm about her decision to put the child up for adoption; the odds of her changing her mind were minimal.

The baby boy was born on December 22. On the last day of 1970, Jack and I called a trusted babysitter and left Erica in the house patting her hands together and singing, "Baby brother come to my house, pretty soon, pretty soon." We drove the fifteen minutes to St. Joseph Hospital in Hamilton and walked out half an hour later with Robin – a long, gangly baby with big feet, a swarthy complex-ion, and a head of dense, almost-black hair.

I consulted Adele Davis and found a recipe for baby formula that included condensed milk, brewer's yeast, lecithin, sunflower oil, and blackstrap molasses. Robin grew rapidly, demonstrating what we began to call hybrid vigour. But within a few months he was congested most of the time, sometimes struggling to breathe. After batteries of tests and a three-day hospital stay, the doctor, who knew nothing about the brewers' yeast and blackstrap molas-ses, decided the baby was probably allergic to cow's milk.

"Try him on soy milk. Or goats' milk, if you can find it." Cans of soy formula replaced the Adele Davis concoction, and Robin gradually improved.

That spring, the owners of our rented house stopped by with a "For Sale" sign. We had a month to find somewhere else to live.

Some friends knew of a farmhouse for rent in the country. It had a barn and a huge space for a garden.

"Great," said Jack the enthusiast. "We can get goats."

"Yes, let's!" I said. Or was that Laura?

CHAPTER 3 • MILKING THE FANTASY

Beeforth Road no longer exists. Jack and I tried to find it a few years ago with our son Galen, who wasn't yet born when we lived there. At first, we assumed we were suffering from one of the inevitable memory lapses that plague those of us who insist on travelling upstream. "Maybe it was the *next* crossroad?" But no. Sometime in the last forty years, the entire square mile of farmland surrounding Beeforth Road morphed into a gigantic greenhouse complex. No physical evidence remains of the place that ushered us into the world of farming.

It was the largest house we've ever lived in, and we lived there for only fifteen months. The brick farmhouse, just outside the little town of Waterdown, Ontario, had five bedrooms, a big country kitchen with a summer kitchen attached, a dining room, and two living rooms separated by etched glass doors. The house sat almost alone on a mile-long stretch of road. Only the spruce windbreak along the north side of the driveway and one small bungalow to the south interrupted our view of the flat fields that stretched as far as the next crossroad in every direction.

• • •

It was April when we moved in. Robin was only a few months old; he slept in the baby buggy or was passed from one pair of arms to another as friends, carrying furniture and boxes, clamoured through the house. Erica was old enough to be excited. She lugged small boxes of toys from the car, through the long hall, and

30

up the steps to her new room. And she took responsibility for Gasman the cat and Shastek the German Shepherd, making special beds for them so they could be happy in the new house, too.

By early evening, everything was unloaded, we had celebrated the move with plates of spaghetti and glasses of chianti, and our friends had driven away. I fed Robin his last bottle of soymilk for the day and carried him up the broad front stairs to his spacious bedroom. Some previous inhabitant had decorated it with drab beige and rust-coloured wallpaper featuring cowboys wearing sombreros, riding bucking broncos, and swirling lariats in the air. I leaned over the crib and passed my hand over his curly, dark hair. His eyes opened and he started to whimper. I put the soother back in his mouth and tiptoed out the door and down the narrow back stairs that led into the kitchen.

Jack was reading to Erica in the living room. "One fish, two fish, red fish, blue fish," the two of them were sprawled out on Jack's childhood trundle bed, which had served as our sofa since the apartment in Kalamazoo. Somewhere in the piles of boxes were the madras spread and cushions that made it look more like living room furniture. I dropped onto the red armchair in the corner, propped my feet up on the leather-covered footstool, pulled the rubber-band off my pony-tail, and leaned my head back. The house smelled of spaghetti sauce and cardboard boxes.

For the first time, I noticed the quiet. A slight breeze moved through the spruce trees, providing a background hum to the Dr. Seuss story. That was all. Through a sleepy haze, I heard Jack carrying Erica upstairs, heard him speaking softly to her, then her cry, "Don't turn off the light!"

When he came back downstairs he was chuckling. "Monsters. But the hall light's on, and she's got her special blanket and her Teddy. She'll be fine."

"Right," I said, shaking myself awake. "I thought maybe we'd left the monsters behind."

He came over and pulled me out of the chair. "Tired?" He held me close and rubbed his beard against my face.

"Mmm." I collapsed into his arms, then reached up and rubbed the back of his neck. He leaned down and kissed me.

"Not too tired," I said. "We can finish unpacking tomorrow."

•••

A few weeks later, Jack was in the stable area of the old barn a few hundred yards behind the house, hammer in hand, a copy of *Mother Earth News* propped against the edge of the stone stable wall. The smell of damp soil and spring growth drifted through the open door. At Jack's feet were a box of nails, a measuring tape, a pencil, a hand-saw, and a stack of one-by-six spruce planks. Erica was jumping on and off a bale of straw in the corner. "I'm helping," she said, as she landed with a bang and her short blond pigtails flopped up and down. "Daddy says I'm helping!"

Jack picked up the measuring tape and ran it along one of the planks. "It says here, each hen needs a two-foot by two-foot box. If I make twelve, that should be plenty."

I shifted Robin on my hip and leaned over the edge of the stall we'd designated as a henhouse. "I thought we were just getting six. That's what I ordered. Six laying pullets."

"Well, six to start," he said. "But I can imagine wanting more. I've got the stuff here. Might as well be prepared."

"Right," I said, remembering the bus, now parked behind the barn, out of sight.

With chickens came chores. Every day, Erica and I made our daily trip to the barn. With her little hands on mine, we raised the old pump handle up and down to fill a pail with fresh water. I poured the water into the flat watering pan and scooped the mixture of crushed grains from a burlap bag in the corner while Erica picked up the eggs, slowly and methodically, counting as she

32

placed them in her special egg pail. "One…two…mommy! This one's still warm!…two, three. Mommy! The chicken flapped me! She won't let me have it!"

One Sunday afternoon in May, Jack and I left the kids with a babysitter to attend a meeting of the regional goat society at the University of Guelph's College of Agriculture, a forty-five-minute drive from home. A goat specialist, a bulky man with round glasses, red hair, and a British accent, talked about protein quality in hay. Second-cut alfalfa was best, he said, whatever that was.

That's where we met Ingrid Johnson, a wiry woman in her mid-fifties who lived near us and had goats' milk — and goats — for sale, and Peter and Margo, a couple our age who rented a farmhouse not far from us and had recently acquired a goat. We bought a copy of *Goat Husbandry*, a serious-looking manual by David McKenzie with a picture of a white goat on a blue background, and picked up a pile of pamphlets on goats' milk, goat care, goat nutrition.

"Just in case," said Jack.

The next day I scrubbed out a large glass jar, put the kids in the car, and drove the back roads in search of Ingrid Johnson. When I found her, she filled the jar with milk in the kitchen and then took us to the barn so Erica could pet the kid goats. I held Robin up so he could see too, and chatted with Ingrid. "The milk's for your little one, here?" she asked, tickling Robin's tummy. "I raised all mine on goats' milk. It's the best thing for them. Easy to digest. Hardly ever allergic."

That was Monday.

On Tuesday, between changing diapers, entertaining Erica, feeding Robin, washing clothes in our portable washer-spin-dryer, and hanging them to dry on the pulley clothesline, I began reading *Goat Husbandry* — which turned out to be as British as the goat expert, and as highly technical — and leafed through the pamphlets.

"I think we should," I said when Jack got home that afternoon.

33

"I'm game," he said. "But milking might have to be your thing." He held up his injured left hand. It had healed completely after its encounter with the table saw nearly two years earlier, but it was badly scarred, and even with regular exercise and therapy, three fingers refused to bend.

For the rest of the week we pored over *The Whole Earth Catalog* and copies of *Mother Earth News* and *Organic Gardening and Farming*. Jack found a design for a milking stand and came home from school on Thursday with a stack of lumber hanging out the back of the station wagon.

"I'm not going in to school tomorrow," he said. "We have to get the barn ready."

Erica spent another morning helping Jack, handing him nails and taking a turn with the hammer. By mid-afternoon, the barn smelled of fresh-cut lumber and Jack's milking stand looked impressively like the illustration. It stood eighteen inches off the floor with space for a person to sit beside the goat while milking. Two hinged wooden bars formed a stanchion to hold the goat's head in place; a small shelf in front held a pan of grain to keep her content.

For the rest of that afternoon, Erica marched around the house and yard, with Shastek at her heels, chanting, "A goat, a goat, two goats, two goats. And we have chickens. And a cat. And a dog."

"Just one goat, Erica!" I said as I jostled Robin on my lap and read the section in *Goat Husbandry* on how to milk a goat.

"Grip the teat lightly in one hand and press the hand gently upwards towards the base of the udder, so filling the teat with milk. Then close the index finger tightly around the neck of the teat, with the hand still pressing gently upwards...Now close the other fingers in succession tightly around the teat, so forcing the milk down and out. Release the grasp of the teat, and relax the upward pressure. Then repeat the process with the other hand and the other teat."

I was reading this over and over to myself, trying to imitate the hand action, when Jack stuck a magazine in front of me.

"Look at this," he said. The article instructed us to practice milking on a balloon half-inflated with water, squeezing our fingers gradually from top to bottom, moving the liquid toward a pin-prick opening at the bottom. It was harder than it looked. Just as the bulge of liquid approached the bottom, if the first fingers loosened their grip at all, up it popped to the top again. After an hour of practice, my hands ached but I was directing a thin stream of water into a cup. Jack could do it with his right hand; he'd obviously be an occasional, one-handed milker.

Just six days after the goat association meeting, we buckled an excited Erica into the station wagon, strapped Robin into his car seat, and drove to Ingrid Johnson's farm to shop for a goat.

We examined three milking does and settled on a sleek, aristocratic Nubian with a Roman nose, long, drooping ears, and doleful eyes. She was black, with a white crescent on her side, and her udder hung low between her back legs. We had already decided to name her Eowyn, after the princess-warrior in Tolkien's *Lord of the Rings.*

"This is her daughter," said Ingrid, rubbing the forehead of a mottled brown goat, about half the size with the same haughty look. "They're social animals. You really should have two."

"Pippin?" said Jack, ever the enthusiast.

The two goats were surprisingly docile in the back of the car, baaing occasionally and lifting their tails to drop brown berries on the floor. Erica stood, facing backward, chatting with the goats and stroking their noses.

That evening, when Jack urged Eowyn onto the brand new milking stand, in the clean barn, with the chickens clucking around, with Erica bouncing up and down beside the goat and me holding Robin in my arms, I felt like an advertisement for country living. A snap-shot advertisement; when the action began, the euphoria

35

ended. The udder that hung heavy between Eowyn's back legs didn't feel much like a balloon; the teats were stiff and hard, and neither Jack nor I could express more than a few drops of milk. By the time we had each taken several turns, Eowyn had finished off the grain in her feed pan and decided enough was enough; she first began a tap-dance on the milking stand, and then lifted a back leg and placed it firmly in the pail.

"Leave her 'til morning," I said. "She probably just needs to get used to the new place."

"But I wanna drink it!" said Erica.

"We will," I promised. "Tomorrow."

The next morning was worse. Jack had to hold Eowyn still as she tried to escape my useless attempts to get milk from an udder that was tight and distended and clearly tender. Pippin was crying from inside the stall. Erica hovered close to the milking stand.

"Isn't there any milk? Why isn't there any milk?"

Jack snapped. "Get away!" He flung his arm toward Erica.

She burst into tears and ran into an empty stall. Robin began screaming from his stroller. Eowyn was baaing and kicking. Chickens were clucking and skittering around. My forearms were exhausted.

"*You* get away!" I said. "Take the kids to the house and leave me alone here!"

"You really think you can do this alone?" Jack challenged me.

"I really don't know. But we're not doing it this way, are we?"

Alone in the barn, I unhooked Eowyn from the milking stand and let her walk back to the stall to munch hay with Pippin. I pressed my arm against my breasts, remembering the pain and pressure of too much milk, and then ran my hand over Eowyn's wiry, pointed spine.

"It's okay, girl. Just settle down a bit."

She looked at me with sad eyes, thinking, I was sure, *These people don't know what they're doing.*

"You're right," I said. "We don't."

When I put her back on the milking stand in the now-quiet barn, her hind legs stepped up and down, but she didn't kick and she didn't try to get away. I put the pail under her udder and tried again. Slowly, drop by drop, I managed to get a cup of milk.

I returned several times that day until the pressure in Eowyn's udder began to subside, and as it did the milk came more easily. That evening at supper we each had a small glass of milk from our own goat—whiter than cow's milk, a little sweeter, a little richer.

"It tastes good," said Erica, grinning under her milky mustache.

Within a few weeks, we'd decided that if two goats were good, three goats would be better, so we added another Tolkien character to our flock—Gloin, a white Saanen doe, less elegant than Eowyn, but with more milk. We now had all the milk we needed for Robin's bottles, all we wanted to drink, and enough left to make quart jars of yogurt.

That summer, chore times became the bookends of my days. After Jack left for school in the mornings, I took the kids on the short walk to the barn to collect eggs, feed the hens, milk the goats, and let them out into the small pasture area behind the barn. We were homesteaders. It felt good.

In our garden, reclaimed from a plot that had been abandoned for years, we grew lettuce, cucumbers, squash, beans, peas, tomatoes, carrots, corn, and an enormous number of weeds. That was fine, though, because we'd also discovered Euell Gibbons, and it turned out many of the weeds were more nourishing than the food they were choking out. Gibbons' book, *Stalking the Wild Asparagus*, became Jack's entrée into the world of natural food. While I harvested lettuce and broccoli, he harvested lambs quarters and pigweed between the rows, trout lilies from the roadsides, and dandelion greens from the yard. As the summer progressed, he turned his attention to the red sumac berries and cattails growing in abundance along the roadsides. Sumac made a beautiful and

37

mouth-puckering drink; the young, firm tops of the cattails—
boiled and dipped in butter—tasted remarkably like corn. According to Gibbons, the roots of the cattails, when dried and ground,
make a "nutritious white flour with an analysis very similar to
grain flours," and he described the resultant biscuits as "perfectly
edible." We found them barely edible.

• • •

My high school friend, Carolyn, came to visit in July. We hadn't
seen each other for several years, not since I had re-defined a
"meaningful life" to be one of parenthood and self-sufficiency.
Carolyn had done no such thing.

She arrived after her drive on a hot August afternoon looking
crisp and well-groomed, with a short, unisex haircut that empha-
sized her narrow face, rimless glasses, and broad smile. I greeted
her in my usual attire: cut-off jeans, tee shirt, shoulder length hair
pulled into a ponytail at my neck. She chatted with Erica and held
and played with Robin. She visited the goats and chickens, and listened to me extol the virtues of homesteading. Then she began to
fill me in on her own life plans, her marriage to a scientific re-
searcher, her decision to return to school for a Ph.D. and make a
life in academia, her uncertainty about parenthood. She pulled me
back to a time when that path lay open to me, too—when it had,
indeed, seemed my most likely path. By the time she left two days
later, I was looking at the goats, the garden, even Jack and the
children, as signs of my failure to live up to my intellectual potential, which was surely almost as great as Carolyn's.

• • •

We were spending more and more time with Peter and Margo,
the couple we'd met at the Goat Association. Margo was a slim,

38

athletic woman, with a pixie-like face framed by soft brown curls, who didn't suffer from second thoughts about her choices. Like me, she stayed home with children, baked bread, milked goats, planted and harvested a garden. She also rode horses—when she wasn't studying dance. "You can't do both," she explained. "The muscles are totally different. My dance teacher doesn't want me to ride...so for now, I'm not dancing." She grinned at me. "Peter likes it better when I ride. Strengthens the thighs." She raised and lowered her hips provocatively.

Margo and I were sitting under the lilac tree outside the house they rented, not far from ours, sipping iced tea and sharing goat stories. Robin was crawling on the grass in his overalls and picking up pinecones. Erica and four-year-old Emilie were playing restaurant in the sandbox. Food was Erica's passion, and restaurant was her favourite game. The two little blond girls were making sand-cakes and sand-hamburgers and squealing in delight.

"You really should get a horse," said Margo.

"I've never ridden. Well, once when I was about ten." I jumped up to take a pinecone out of Robin's mouth.

"I can teach you," said Margo. "And I know a beautiful horse that's for sale. Wanna look?"

Karma was a big strawberry roan mare, part quarter horse, part workhorse. We brought her home in a plywood horse trailer we bought for a song, put her in one of the empty stalls in the stable, and parked the trailer behind the barn with the bus.

Margo taught me to approach the horse with confidence, clean her hoofs with a hoof pick, brush and curry her, put a bit in her mouth, and saddle her up with the old military saddle I'd found. She taught me to lunge before riding; I stood trembling, a long lead rope in my hand while she showed me how to get Karma moving in a gradually widening circle as I let the lead rope out, little by little, until the horse was trotting around and around at the end of the taut rope, burning off energy, walking, trotting, and cantering on command. Sometimes.

I learned to love the feel of Karma's soft mouth when she picked up an apple or a carrot from my open palm, the smoothness of her forehead, and the massive warmth of her flank when I groomed her. I even learned to ride her with some confidence, but she was too much of a horse for a beginner. I never relaxed on her back, and I never mounted without help; she shied away the moment I lifted my foot to the stirrup. And so Karma spent most of her time in the pasture, or escaping from the pasture to roam the back roads until someone figured out she was ours and phoned. That set off a flurry of activity as we piled children into the car, gathered halter, lead rope, and a bucket of grain and headed off to a neighouring farm or garden to coax the wayward animal home.

"Not the greatest idea you ever had," said Jack. This enthusiasm had been all mine.

"Yeah, it was probably a mistake. But isn't she beautiful?"

• • •

That fall, we discovered the local farmers' market and supplemented our small garden harvest with bushels of produce. Jack and I spent Saturday afternoons canning peaches, pears, apricots, cherries, tomatoes. We gathered apples from abandoned roadside trees and had them pressed into cider. We prepared for winter in the barn by stocking up on hay — second cut alfalfa as the goat expert had recommended. We took the goats to visit Ingrid Johnson's smelly billy goat so they'd give birth in the spring. As the cold weather set in, they gave less milk, and the chickens laid fewer eggs. And because the goats and the horse were inside all the time, we spent more time shoveling manure. I didn't remember Laura doing that; I supposed she must have, and wondered what else she'd kept from me.

Jack discovered that Euell Gibbons wasn't just about food. He piled heaps of cattails in the attic just as their heads were bursting into fluffy down. When the weather turned nasty, I set my sewing machine up on the kitchen table, arranged bright yellow and orange squares of cotton fabric, and constructed a queen-sized bag. I held it open while Jack poured in the down by the pail-full, both of us sneezing as it wafted in the air; then I sewed the big bag of fluff shut and tied yarn through both layers every several inches to hold the down in place. A comforter for Mom and Dad.

We invited my family to spend Christmas with us — Mom, Dad, Rod, and Selden. They arrived in the late afternoon two days before Christmas. We'd hoped for a snowy Canadian Christmas, but barely an inch of snow covered the ground. Mom and Dad walked to the barn with us to meet the animals, Mom wearing jeans and running shoes, Dad wearing galoshes over his leather shoes. Erica held Mom's hand, dragging her along. "Grandma Mae, Grandma Mae! Come see the goats! And we have a new kitten in the barn. Her name is Giga. I named her!" I walked with Dad, and Jack carried Robin, who had just celebrated his first birthday and showed no interest in walking. My brothers brought up the rear. Rod, just a few years younger than me, was sporting a beard and looked like a stranger. Selden, my cute baby brother, had become a sullen fifteen-year-old cursed with a bad case of acne.

Erica took the lead in introducing each of the animals by name. While I milked, Dad stood beside me and recollected that his mother had grown up on a farm in eastern Pennsylvania in the late eighteen hundreds.

"But I never spent any time there," he said. "And I certainly never expected my kids to become farmers." There was something about the way he said "farmers" that made me turn away. I looked to Jack for help, but he was leaning over the goat stall with Rod and Selden, letting Robin pet Pippin.

"We're not exactly farmers, Dad. We're just doing this for fun," I said, suddenly needing to distance myself from the very thing I'd been so excited about sharing. I heard Malvina Reynold's voice singing in my head: *Somebody else's measuring scale of win or lose doesn't tell the tale, so I don't mind failing in this world.* I hoped it was true, but Dad's measuring scale had been with me all my life.

I turned my attention to the others. Erica was showing Mom how to hold the apple flat in her hand for Karma to pick up with her soft lips.

"Grandma! See how it tickles!"

Mom and Dad may have been ambivalent about the farm, but they were thrilled on Christmas morning when I presented them with the comforter—especially so because, as it turned out, they knew Euell Gibbons, who lived in a central Pennsylvania town not far from them. Two months later, Mom phoned to say they'd told Gibbons about the comforter, and also about the insects that had hatched inside it in the warmth of their bedroom. "Next time," said Mom with a chuckle, "He says you should bake the down in the oven first to kill the larvae."

By the spring of 1972, Jack had completed everything in his graduate program except the thesis, so he could apply for teaching positions indicating "Ph.D. pending." His advisor wanted him to stay on for another year to finish up, but Jack wanted to test the waters. "I've been in grad school for six years. That's enough."

And our commitment to homesteading had grown; we wanted our own place.

Together, we pored over job postings in Psychology journals, looking for university teaching positions in remote places. His applications led to three interviews: one in Vermont; one in St. John, New Brunswick; and one in Sault Ste. Marie, Ontario. Vermont was first, and they offered him the job.

"I'd like to stay in Canada, too," he said, looking at my downcast face, "but the job's a good fit for me, and there's no reason we can't go back." The draft was no longer a threat. "It's beautiful country. Lots of little farms, probably job opportunities for you. And I can't afford to burn bridges." I thought we'd already burned that one, that we were going to become Canadians, but I knew he was right.

Jack held the Vermont people off for ten days, until after the other two interviews. St. John didn't look as promising, and nobody had ever heard of Algoma College in Sault Ste. Marie. I was bracing myself to move back to the States.

A week later, the kids and I were at the Toronto airport waiting for the return flight from Sault Ste. Marie. Robin stood at the glass wall, watching the airplanes take off and land, barely touching the wall for balance but still refusing to walk. "Truck," he said. "Truck" — which meant anything that moved and made a noise.

"There's Daddy!" shouted Erica as Jack bounded from the arrivals gate toward us. After he hugged me and tickled Erica with his beard, he lifted Robin from my arms and we headed to the parking lot.

"It's a tiny little college, just one building that used to be an Indian residential school, and a couple of portables." He dug his keys out of his pocket and slid behind the wheel of the Volvo while I buckled the kids into their car seats.

"So far, it's mostly part-time students, all local, lots of mature students, teachers coming back for their degrees." Algoma College had only been in existence for two years, he explained, and its small, young faculty was trying to build a liberal arts college on the U.S. model. That was the kind of education we'd both had at Grinnell College in Iowa, but it was a rarity in Canada.

"Small classes. They want teachers, not researchers," he said. Sunday afternoon traffic was light; we were moving steadily along the Queen Elizabeth Way between Toronto and Hamilton. He took his eyes off the road for a moment to look at me.

"It's risky. The place might fold. But we could go for a few years, anyway, and then look around if we want to move on."

He was on a roll. It was a nice little city, he said, right on the edge of the St. Mary's River, really close to Lake Superior. His interview had been weird, with two other candidates at the same time. They'd ended up at a party at someone's cottage. The people seemed nice. I interrupted him long enough to learn they'd already offered him the job.

"Can we take Shastek? And Gasman? And Giga?" asked Erica. She was almost four, aware that change was afoot, excited because we were.

I turned around, and Jack looked at her in the rearview mirror. "You bet," he said. "And the goats, and Karma."

44

"Jack," I said. "Don't make promises."

"No, I mean it. Listen. It's beautiful country. You'll love it. Rugged. Real wilderness. And I'm sure we can find a farm. We can have a whole herd of goats, maybe sell milk, raise our own hay, maybe work the land with a team of horses, grow our own wheat to make our own flour."

Jack the enthusiast was back.

I had no idea how to make flour. But we were going to stay in Canada, and we were going to find a farm, and we were thrilled. The current was taking us just where we wanted to go.

• • •

In June, we phoned a "farm wanted" ad into the *Sault Star* classifieds, left the children with Peter and Margo, and arranged with a neighbour to do the chores for a week. The trip took us north along the rocky, pine shore of Georgian Bay, then west on the Trans-Canada and over the north shore of Lake Huron. Among the rocks, hills, and small lakes, little towns appeared every now and then—often just a row of houses on both sides of the highway, sometimes with a few side streets veering off at right angles until they ended abruptly at rocky outcroppings or petered out in dense forest. Perched on the edge of the wilderness, these towns signaled our departure from the beaten path. Also from the prosperity of rural southern Ontario.

Picturesque, I thought. Depressed, said Jack. We were both right. These little towns sprang up at the end of the nineteenth century with healthy economies based on mining, logging, and the newly constructed Canadian Pacific Railway. By the mid twentieth century, the homes and businesses visible from the highway showed little sign of those earlier boom times.

As we approached the Sault, we saw more cleared farmland but not much evidence of prosperity until we reached the city, itself. In 1970, Sault Ste. Marie, a city of ninety thousand, had the highest average income of any city in Canada, due not to pockets of great wealth, but to its reliance on a single industry, the Algoma Steel Corporation, and its population of well-paid union workers.

We stayed with one of Jack's former grad student colleagues, who had been teaching at Algoma College for just a year and was moving on to a *real* university. He had agreed to be a local contact for our ad. When we arrived, he handed us a stack of names and phone numbers and said, "You're nuts."

The next morning, road map in hand, we headed out of town. "Look at this place!" I said, staring at the map. "Sylvan Valley. Wouldn't you just love to live in a place called Sylvan Valley?"

The first house we looked at was, in fact, on the edge of Sylvan Valley, a broad, slightly rolling valley east of the Sault, several miles north of the village of Echo Bay. We pulled into the driveway of an unfinished bungalow. Its owner, a man of about forty with two days' growth on his face and a cigar in his mouth, invited us in. "There's still some work to do," he said, gesturing at the rough chipboard floors and taking a puff on his cigar. The two small bedrooms had insulation stuffed between the studs, but no interior walls. The kitchen counters were bare plywood. A wood stove, the only heat source in the house, dominated the small living room.

For the rest of the day, we drove from one run-down rural property to another. Some had septic systems, some had central heat, some had level floors, some had exterior finishing, some had enough land for a small farm; none had them all.

The next day, we contacted a real estate agent. She did her best, she really did. But along with our homesteading fantasies we carried a burden of middle class expectations. We'd been imagining a spacious southern Ontario farmhouse on northern Ontario scrub farmland. Those were few and far between and apparently not for sale. We'd have settled for small and snug, but we did insist on plumbing and central heat. Over six days of touring the rural areas east and north of the Sault, we watched the dream drift away. We would sell the animals and rent an apartment in town.

When we went back to thank our friend for his hospitality, we found one last message from the real estate agent. She knew we'd given up, but did we want to look at one more place? It was on our way out of town.

Jack looked at the map. "It's not *in* Sylvan Valley, but it's close. Looks like the next valley to it. On Echo Lake Road. Could be nice." I shrugged. I'd given up on nice.

We drove through the little village of Echo Bay — general store, post office, church, school — and made a left turn onto Echo Lake Road. For two miles, we drove through trees and swampland, passed a few houses, and made a couple of sharp turns until the Echo River appeared on our left.

Elmer White came out to meet us, a lean man of about sixty, wearing work pants and a green work shirt. His white clapboard house was well built and close to the road with a deep yard that ended at the riverbank. It *was* nice. But there was not enough land to pasture goats and a horse and no barn to house them.

"What a waste of time," I grumbled as we started backing out of the driveway. Jack stopped when he saw Mr. White flagging us down.

"If it's more of a farm you're lookin' for," said the old man, poking his head in the car window, "my brother down the road's thinkin' of sellin'. Best farm in the township."

"Why not? We're here anyway," said Jack.

I shrugged again. "Not much point, but sure if you want."

So, instead of turning back we drove a mile farther, with the river on our left and a few small bungalows on our right, until we reached open fields with a rocky hill rising abruptly from the flat land.

The mailbox said "Fred and Gertrude White." Not far from the tidy, two-story brick house, the first brick house we'd seen, stood a huge grey barn, a long, red shed, and a tidy line of equipment. Peonies bloomed in a long flower garden that separated the freshly mowed yard from the barnyard.

"Look at this!" said Jack, a hint of enthusiasm creeping into his voice.

I sighed and shook my head. "Don't even bother. It'll be way too much."

"Ever the pessimist," he muttered.

A plump, grey-haired woman in her early sixties answered his knock, joined a moment later by a lanky man, who looked just like his brother, clad in blue and white striped overalls. They spoke for a few moments before Jack waved me to come in.

Mr. and Mrs. White led us through a small, enclosed porch and into the kitchen, a spacious room with a small window above the counter and sink looking out over the fields and toward the hill. On one wall, inset cupboards with glass doors held stacks of dishes and glasses. At the far end of the kitchen, one swinging door opened into a long, narrow pantry and another into the living room.

"Well, this here's the kitchen," Mr. White said. "The wife'll show you through the rest of the house, then I'll take you to the cellar."

Mrs. White took us through the downstairs first—a large living room with polished oak wainscoting and bay windows facing southwest, two tiny bedrooms (his and hers), and a sun porch that stretched the full width of the house with windows looking across the road to the river. Everywhere, yellow maple floors gleamed. We followed her up the narrow staircase with oak treads and an oak railing.

"Fred had a heart attack, and the doctor ordered him to slow down. He'll never slow down here, so if we can sell, we'll move to town," she said.

Upstairs, three small bedrooms and a bathroom opened off a narrow hallway.

"The bedrooms are tiny," I said. I was trying hard not to look or sound enthusiastic. Before we began this journey, Jack had warned me not to look too impressed. "You give yourself away all the time with your face," he'd said.

So far, it hadn't been hard.

"There's no upstairs over the kitchen or sun porch," said Jack. He would notice; I hadn't. "Makes for a pretty small upstairs."

"I guess it *is* small," said Mrs. White. "But big enough. We raised nine children here." Jack and I exchanged wide-eyed looks, and I thought about the separate bedrooms downstairs. "Do you have children?" she asked

"Two," I said. "And that seems like lots sometimes." She chuckled.

The cellar was as tidy as the house. Fred showed us the wood furnace, the wood storage room stacked with split firewood, the cold cellar with bins awaiting this year's crop of potatoes and turnips from the garden. Then he took us to the barn, much bigger than the Waterdown barn, leading the way along the short path with long, relaxed strides. The stable was empty; so were the haymows and the granary, both swept clean in anticipation of the summer harvest.

"I've been on this farm for thirty years," he said. "Grew up in this valley. But I reckon I'll be moving to the Sault now. Doctor's orders." He cleared his throat and blew his nose on a red handkerchief he pulled from the pocket of his overalls. "Well, I'll give you the tour of the property." He led the way across the dirt-packed barnyard to an old green pickup.

We began by driving back where we'd come from, where the small bungalows ended and the fields began. "This here's the beginning of the farm," he said, as he pulled into a laneway leading to a big storage barn—the lower barn, he called it—then turned around and headed back toward the house.

He drove past the house and the barnyard, then turned right, away from the river.

"School house acre there." He was pointing to a fenced plot with huge old willow trees at the road and a vegetable garden. "School's gone. School board deeded the land back to the farm when they moved all the kids into Echo Bay, maybe twenty years ago. Now it's my vegetable garden. Vegetables for the family and turnips to sell. Good soil. A good strawberry patch, too."

He kept driving, past fields shaded by groves of elm trees, past a herd of brown and white cattle grazing near a fence. "The farm'd be a full half-section, except the river cuts off the corner. There's a woodlot, too. More than three hundred acres in all. About a hundred-twenty cleared."

Three hundred acres was just a number to me, but I knew it was more than a homestead. "Is the hill part of it?" I asked.

"Yep. Almost to the top."

When we finally reached the far edge of the property, Fred pointed to the next farm.

"There's the farm I grew up on. Strange fella lives there now. Keeps goats."

Back at the house, standing beside our car, we asked about the price.

"I won't deal with the real estate people," said Fred. "They'll take you for a ride. So, I reckon it'd be fair to ask what it says on the assessment notice." He went into the house and came out after a few minutes with an official statement of the farm's assessed value for property tax purposes. It was more than we'd figured on spending, but we'd seen enough to realize that the property was worth that, and then some.

"How soon could we have it?" I asked. Jack glared at me. "That is, if we decide to make an offer," I added.

"There's a house we're looking at in the Sault now, and the family would help us move. We could be out by the end of August, but I'd need to come back for the grain crop." He paused and frowned slightly. "You folks been farming? You have livestock?"

Jack hesitated.

I piped in: "We have goats."

Fred glanced toward the farm where he'd grown up and where the strange fella now lived.

• • •

By the end of our ten-hour drive home, the boundaries of both my fantasy and Jack's enthusiasm had expanded to encompass three hundred acres. "We're buying a real farm," I said to Margo when we picked up the kids. "On a river. Tons of land. We'll get cattle along with the goats. Ponies for the kids. Chickens. Maybe pigs." We'd also decided to swallow our pride and approach Jack's dad to help us with the down payment.

That evening, Jack phoned Fred White to make the formal offer.

"I see," I heard Jack say. "When will you know?"

Silence. Endless.

"Can we call you in three days, then?"

Jack put the phone down slowly.

"What the hell is going on?" I was shouting. "We offered him what he asked!"

"His family wants his youngest son to have a chance to buy it." Jack's voice was quiet, sad rather than angry. "To keep it in the family. He doesn't think the son has the money, but he's going to give him a chance to come up with it. We'll call back on Wednesday night."

Jack went to school as usual on Monday, and Tuesday, and Wednesday. I had nowhere to go. I phoned Margo on Monday morning, filled her in, begged her to come visit.

"I can't today...dentist appointment. Maybe tomorrow. Hang tight."

She didn't come the next day either. Erica whined for a playmate.

"Why can't Emilie come? I want Emilie to come."

"She just can't." I snapped. "And stop clinging to me! Find something to do!" Erica retreated to a corner of the kitchen and began to sniffle.

I plunked Robin onto the living room floor. "And you," I said. "You're getting too heavy. For god's sake, why don't you walk?" The eighteen-month-old looked at me with his wide blue eyes and puckered up to cry. I knew I wasn't being fair. I didn't care.

Wednesday evening finally arrived. We put the kids to bed early. Jack hovered near the phone.

"We won't get it," I said. "I know we won't get it. If he wants his son to have it, his son will have it." I slumped onto the sofa.

"Why do you always assume the worst?" asked Jack.

I lifted one shoulder and gave him a half-smile. "Easier not to be disappointed."

"What a way to live." He stared out the window. "Well, we might as well find out."

My heart pounded sickeningly while Jack dialed.

"Fred? Jack Dunning here. I'm calling to see whether you can accept our offer."

I held my breath. What was taking so long on the other end? Then Jack finally spoke.

"We can send a certified cheque by the end of the week. And I'll get back to you soon about the cows and the equipment." When I let go of my breath, it came out as a sob.

Jack dropped the phone back on the hook and leapt up. "Yes! And he'll sell us as many cows and as much equipment as we want to buy!"

We hugged and shrieked and danced around the room. Erica came down the steps in her pajamas, rubbing her eyes. "Are we buying a farm?"

"We are!" I said, and picked her up to join us in the dance.

• • •

Flowing back with the river in reverse, I try to connect the streams and eddies that led to that unlikely decision in the spring of 1972. An energetic young man determined to live life differently from his wealthy, conventional parents. A financial legacy from those same parents. A dreamy young woman, less radical than she thinks, trying to find a comfortable place in the generation of protest. A war that threatens their security, challenges their convictions, and leads them to parenthood and a new country in their early twenties. A child apparently allergic to cow's milk. An emerging social movement heralding natural foods and homestead farming.

Travelling as far back as the reverse current will take me, I see no tributary that prepares them for life on a farm. Not a trickle.

• • •

On the afternoon of August 20, 1972, I waved goodbye to Jack and our friend Dennis, who was using this drive as a jumping off point for a trip farther west. Jack was driving the bus, packed for the second time with our accumulated possessions. Dennis sat behind the wheel of a six-year-old red Datsun pickup truck, a recent acquisition to celebrate our new status as real farmers. Its passenger seat was piled high with boxes, but its primary cargo was in the back under the cap, where Eowyn, Gloin, and Pippin shifted about restlessly. Behind them, in the plywood horse trailer, freshly painted bright blue, Karma stood quietly, apparently resigned to the coming journey. Shastek rode with Jack in the bus.

I settled the kids into their car seats — a new extra-safe design of heavy, molded plastic — in the station wagon. Erica clutched her "special blanket" and looked anxiously at the bus and truck as they pulled away. "We're going to the zoo, aren't we?"

"The Sault. Yup. To a new house on a big farm near the Sault. And Daddy will be there when we get there, with the goats, and Shastek, and Karma."

"And the chickens?

"No. We gave the chickens to Mrs. Johnson. Remember? We'll get new chickens."

"But I liked the old chickens."

"Chickens wouldn't like the long ride. You can help collect eggs when we get new chickens."

Robin squirmed in his seat and waved as the other two vehicles honked their horns — a quick toot-toot from the Datsun, a prolonged bugle blast from the bus — and drove down the road. "Bye, truck," he said. "Truck go goats."

"Atta boy, Robin. Off they go. We're going too. But first, we're sleeping at Emilie's house tonight." That was the plan. The slower vehicles would arrive at the farm late that night; the kids and I would leave in the morning and arrive mid-afternoon.

I picked up a cardboard box with the last of the cleaning supplies and stuffed it under the driver's seat, then loaded the two cats — the aging Gasman, and Erica's favourite, the calico Giga. Gasman cowered under the front seats. Giga charged from back to front until Erica grabbed her and held her on her lap. The house on Beeforth Road grew smaller and smaller in the rear-view mirror until it disappeared altogether.

Driving north the next day, between Erica's potty stops, Robin's car-sickness, mewing cats, and the usual litany of "are we there yets", I barely registered the rocky protrusions and pine-rimmed lakes that had captivated me just a few weeks ago. My mind vascillated between visions of the farm I'd seen only once and now owned, and images of a conventional suburban life, images I hadn't visited for a long time but that I was now finding oddly comfortable. I imagined myself living Carolyn's life, a scholar among scholars. Then I imagined picking up my children from daycare, harried at the end of a long workday. Back again to the homestead, where I saw myself churning butter to spread on home-baked bread. Laura is there. But now, it was a farm, I reminded myself, not really a homestead. Then to the lecture podium where I awed students with my eloquence and vast knowledge. To the goats, and back again at a dizzying, sickening speed.

Halfway, almost to Sudbury. Robin had dozed off and Erica lapsed into a bored stupor. I stopped at a pay phone to check in with Jack. Whites' phone was still in service; it rang several times before Fred White answered.

"Mr. White. Hello, it's Paula Dunning. Can I speak with Jack?"

"Not here yet."

How could he not be there yet? He left—what?—twenty-four hours ago. Weak-kneed, I walked back to the car, turned left onto the Trans-Canada Highway, and squinted into the afternoon sun. What could possibly have happened? Would I come upon them, maimed or dead by the side of the road, goat bodies and bus parts blocking the highway? How would I tell Erica? Robin would never remember his dad. Would I keep the farm? And then Jack's voice whispering in my ear: *Why do you always assume the worst?*

Four sweltering hours later I made a right turn off the highway at Echo Bay, drove through the village, and turned onto Echo Lake Road, my heart pounding. As we rounded the last bend, there was the bus. Relief cut through the adrenalin and, suddenly weak, I pulled into the driveway, *our* driveway, turned off the ignition and

55

dropped my head to the steering wheel. Tears ran down my cheeks.

Jack ran out to meet the car and pulled open the driver's door. "Just look at this!" he said, spreading his arms wide.

The Echo River sparkled in the late afternoon light. On its far side, reflections of trees on the water undulated with the slow-moving current. Acres of green, freshly cut hayfields stretched from the road to the hills, interrupted by fence lines and the occasional cluster of shade elms. The hill lorded over it all, patchy with many shades of green, imposing with grey rock faces looking sternly down from its peak. The air smelled of grass, sunshine, and excitement.

And here was Jack, holding out his arms for a hug, safe and sound and here.

"What happened?" I wiped my eyes on my sleeve as he helped the kids out of the car. "I phoned four hours ago and you weren't here."

"Lots happened," he said, sniffing Robin and crinkling his nose. "I got here right after you called. I'll fill you in later."

The four of us walked through the house, a bit dingier than I remembered, and smaller — much smaller — than the house I'd left just the day before. But the sun was shining through the bay windows in the living room, my living room, and reflecting off the yellow maple floor. On the other side of windows, the fields, the road along the river, a glimpse of the river itself, and the hill again. I turned to Jack with a weak grin. "Can you believe it?" He shook his head and took my hand.

With Robin riding on Jack's shoulders and Erica skipping ahead, we followed the short path to the barn, where Karma and the goats were munching hay and our two new brown cows, hand-picked by Fred for their easy dispositions, were standing in their stanchions, chewing their cuds. "Dual purpose. You can milk 'em or eat 'em," he'd said.

"He left us a dozen chickens in the henhouse, too," said Jack, and Erica shrieked with delight.

When we came back out of the barn, half a dozen neighbourhood children had gathered in the yard to welcome us, checking out rumours of the Partridge Family's arrival with their brightly painted bus.

"Partridge Family?" I asked a quiet eight-year old who stood apart from the others.

"You don't know the Partridge Family from TV?" I didn't.

And Fred was there, too, walking toward us from the red equipment shed in his farmer-striped overalls, an old man unable to turn his back on his life's work until he knew he'd left it in good hands. He looked at the bus with its psychedelic colour scheme and I wondered—I still wonder—what he was thinking. He didn't say, of course. Only, "I'll let you folks settle in," before he got into his truck and drove to his new home in the city.

I collapsed on the back steps while Erica ran around the yard and Robin, who was finally walking, toddled after her. Dennis had already left, hitchhiking his way farther west. Jack filled me in on their trip. The bus had blown a radiator hose just outside Toronto. By the time they got it fixed, it was too late to finish the drive, so they drove until late in the evening, after stopping to milk the goats at a gas station amidst a crowd of curious observers, and spent the night camped in a gravel pit by the side of the road.

Around a green-painted kitchen table the Whites had left behind, we ate a picnic supper of sandwiches. Digging through one of the boxes labeled "miscellaneous kitchen and books" to find a knife, I stumbled on a shiny new, hot-off-the-press copy of *Grow It!* "The beginner's complete in-harmony-with-nature small farm guide," by Richard Langer. I opened it to the Introduction.

"Of course, you alone cannot save the world. But you can do your part. Grow good rye and wheat for your bread and noodles, grow good corn and oats for your livestock. Live and breathe, enjoy your life as you plow the rich earth, as you watch crops rise from the earth to yield their bounty, as you celebrate Thanksgiving from a table groaning under the weight of your own fresh produce…Enjoy the fruits of your labors. The world will be a better place for them."

Chapter 5 • Settling In

I've been waking up in the same place for more than forty years, and what meets my eyes is home. Familiar fields with familiar names—the trefoil field, the far field, the barn field—farmed by someone else now but still mine and comfortingly familiar. A yard and garden that have evolved as yards and gardens do: old trees gone, new trees planted and grown tall; a vegetable garden beside the house, expanding some years, shrinking others; flower gardens ebbing and flowing as the mood strikes.

The hill, from a distance, seems immune to the passage of time, but I know it has undergone its own evolution over four decades: clearings grown in, poplar stands logged, the sugar bush matured. The river—even the river has changed, lower now, with tag alders grown up along the edge where doomed elms once thrust their branches up and arched over the slow-moving, brown water.

And of course the house, now nearly a century old, has seen old walls removed, new walls built, windows changed, decks added, bedrooms assigned, reassigned, and then converted to other uses as children vacated them.

It's all been so gradual that when I look at photographs from those early months and years, I am taken aback by the absence of the trees that now dwarf the house, by the dilapidated fence that for years separated the yard from the barnyard, and by the shabby wooden steps and laundry-stoop that pre-dated the spacious deck. These are the changes of a life lived in one place for a long time, and they only deepen the sense of belonging, of home.

It's hard to remember how strange it all was to the young woman who awoke to this place on an August morning in 1972:

the fields, random patterns of colour, some yellow with grain, others green with second-growth hay; the hill, a picturesque backdrop, an unreadable topographical map, painted in shades of green and grey; flowers, planted and cared for by others, blooming as if by chance; and the house, an empty shell to fill with furnishings and the yet-unimagined treasures and detritus of a lifetime.

• • •

I woke early that first morning. The children still slept soundly, but Jack's spot on the bed beside me was already empty. I rolled off the mattress we'd thrown on the floor the night before, rose awkwardly to my feet, pulled on yesterday's jeans and a t-shirt, and crept down the stairs. No Jack.

Quietly, I opened the back door, walked sixty paces on the narrow path across the freshly-mowed lawn, and unlatched the small wooden gate into the barnyard. I opened the corner door and stepped over the high sill into the stable area, greeted by the smell of fresh hay and the sound of Karma snorting in her stall. Small square windows, divided into even smaller panes, let light in on the south side of the stable. Jack perched on the milking stand.

"Good morning" he said as he stripped the last milk from Eowyn's udder, using an awkward two-finger grip with his injured hand. "Thought I'd get the chores done early." He looked up at me smiling, a piece of hay stuck in his beard, a thin strand of hair falling over his eyes. "I already put the cows out and cleaned the gutter. I'll put the goats out now. Maybe you can clean their stall."

"Can't stay," I said. "The kids are still sleeping."

He straightened up from the milking stand, walked to a door in the middle of the stable, and let the goats out with a little push from behind to urge them down the steep step to the ground. They hesitated for a moment, then began prancing around until Gloin spotted the pasture on the other side of the barn, where the two cows were already grazing. She took off at a lope, with the others close behind, udders banging against their back legs.

We watched, then turned to each other and grinned, sharing a moment of sheer joy at our luck, at the promise of this new life.

"Did you see how the manure bucket works?" He was heading toward a huge bucket, the size of ten wheelbarrows, hanging from a metal track that ran along the ceiling the full length of the stable, between the stanchions on one side and the stalls on the other.

"Later, Jack." I said. "I have to get back. We have children...remember?"

"No, look. Just for a sec. This is gonna make it so easy to keep the barn clean."

A pulley mechanism let the bucket drop to the floor for filling, then raised it to almost ceiling height to roll out the back door. There, the track continued, attached to a beam that swung between two vertical poles some forty feet beyond the barn, creating a wide arc. By swinging the beam to the left one day, to the right the next, you could distribute the pile over a broad area throughout the winter months. Jack had it all figured out. Before I left, he had to demonstrate, winding the chain, pushing the bucket, opening the door, swinging the beam, releasing a latch to dump the meager contents from the morning's gutter-cleaning.

All the way back to the house I could hear Robin singing— "Momma, momma, momma"—and I found him jumping up and down in his crib, his drenched diaper around his feet. Erica stood at her bedroom door, special blanket in one hand, Teddy in the other, tears running down her cheeks. "Where *were* you mommy? I'm scared."

I was wiping her tears and hugging her when Jack came bounding back in the house. "Hey, pumpkin," he shouted up the stairs. "I'm gonna check for eggs. Wanna come?"

"Remember, Daddy, that's *my* job!" she said, dropping both blanket and bear and running down the steps.

Eggs for breakfast.

• • •

We spent most of that first day arranging furniture, opening boxes, hooking up the stereo, and making a lumberyard list: bookshelves, toy shelves, pantry shelves.

I unpacked our assortment of glasses, dishes, and mugs, and arranged them in the recessed, glass-fronted shelves along the kitchen wall. I stood, bewildered, at the pantry door looking at the empty space and wondering how Mrs. White had used the space without shelves. Construction Job One.

In the living room, I smoothed the madras bedspread over the trundle bed and leaned cushions against the wall. The red naugahyde armchair sat in the nook created by the bay windows, the butterfly chair in one corner, and in another Jack hung the swinging basket chair, drilling his first hole in the house: sacrilege. We centered the long dining table against the wall nearest the kitchen.

We designated the tiny bedroom next to the kitchen as a playroom, and the larger downstairs bedroom as Jack's study. He rebuilt the door-and-cinderblock desk that had followed us all the way from Kalamazoo, unpacked boxes of psychology books and his thesis research notes, and hung a calendar on the wall.

"Two weeks," he said, staring at the calendar. "Two weeks until I start teaching. Tomorrow, I go in to get my schedule and my office key."

On the pale green walls above the oak wainscoting in the living room, we hung our several pieces of art: a voluptuous charcoal nude in a heavy, dark wood frame; an Eskimo print of winged, half-human creatures in flight; another nude, finely drawn lines barely suggestive of a body. The dreadful reproduction of a still life by Paul Klee—two eggs on a frying pan—we hung in the kitchen, along with a mounted print of Robert Indiana's bright blue and green LOVE poster.

Then, I pulled out a tube of posters. "Here's a map of Middle Earth."

"Great. I'll hang that in my study," said Jack, grabbing the roll of masking tape. "And how about the hippos? And the soup can? And there's the one of Lyndon Johnson holding a rifle."

"Maybe not," I said, rolling them back up before he could protest.

We were eating lunch when a *Cargill Seeds* baseball cap appeared in the kitchen window and Fred White knocked on the door. He scraped his boots on the metal boot-scraper attached to the back step, stepped into the enclosed back porch, took off his cap, and peered into the kitchen as though looking for something lost. Erica and Robin looked up from their grilled cheese sandwiches.

"I just stopped in to tell you we've got the reaper comin' in today and we'll be shuckin' oats down at the lower barn field," he said. "Just so you know."

"Thanks," said Jack. "But you don't have to check with us. The fields are yours 'til your crop is in."

"Just wanted to see how you're gettin' on, too," he said.

"Well, we're doing great," I said. "So nice to move in to a really clean place."

"Yep, had the whole family helpin' out. House and barn. One last get-together in the place." He put his cap back on his close-cropped grey head, shifted his feet, and then turned to open the door. "Well, I'll be seein' you."

Later that afternoon, hot and sweaty, I leaned against the stone wall in the basement and let the battle between excitement and exhaustion play out in the cool and quiet. Reluctant to return to the heat and confusion upstairs, I lingered, surrounded by the workings of this old house. The plumbing system: a huge pressure tank, six feet tall, beside a black cast-iron pump mounted on the floor. A hot water heater in the corner. Iron pipes for cold water; copper for hot. The electrical system: a fuse box on the wall, and thin wires running tautly along the exposed beams, from one porcelain spool to another. The heating system: a black furnace and a roomful of wood.

I remembered Fred's comment the day before: "I wish I had my winter's heat stacked in my basement." That's what I was looking at, our winter's heat: split hardwood stacked from floor to ceiling, lining both sides of a narrow room that ran the full width of the house. I thought of Dad's coal bin.

The house where I grew up, in central Pennsylvania, was heated with coal, an anachronism even then. By the 1950s and 1960s, most people heated with oil, but Dad, a man nostalgic for his own childhood and with a fondness for tinkering, loved his coal furnace. Every year, a dump truck full of coal backed into the driveway and poured a dusty black load into the chute that went from the outside wall into the coal bin in the basement. We kids stood outside and watched the river of coal coursing from the elevated truck bed onto the chute, crashing like a violent waterfall and spewing a mist of black dust on its way to the basement. Our winter's heat.

For the next few months, the furnace became a member of our family. Dad alternately stoked, "poked", and banked the fire, and fussed with the steam radiators that bubbled and hissed the heat through our home. Dad's furnace, equipped with a thermostat and a conveyor belt that delivered the fuel to the fire on command, was a miracle of modern technology compared to the furnace I was looking at now.

It was as wide as a refrigerator and twice as deep. Its bottom half was a firebox, big enough to hold several four-foot logs. Above the firebox, the plenum, an enclosed air chamber, captured the heat generated by the fire below. Huge pipes sprouted out of the top of the plenum and immediately split into several asbestos-covered arms that snaked through the basement. As the warm air rose through a maze of ducts and vents into the house, it pushed cooler air down through return air vents and back into the plenum, creating a continuous warming cycle. No fans. No thermostats. Just heat and gravity. So Fred had explained.

I stooped down to open the door to the firebox, and that's when I saw it: *Happy Thought Foundry, Guelph, Ontario.* How could we ever be cold? My delighted shriek brought Jack clamoring down the steps with Robin in his arms and Erica on his heels.

"Just look at this!" I pointed to the ornate raised letters arching gracefully along the top of the curved, cast-iron door:

Erica crouched down to look, too, "Is this our wooden furnace?" she asked, peering up from under bangs that needed to be cut. Jack and I burst out laughing.

"Wood furnace, sweetie," I said, and gave her pigtail a tug. "This is it."

"We'll burn all that wood to stay warm this winter, Erica," said Jack, as she peered into the wood room.

I smiled at him. "Our winter's heat."

"And when it's gone, we'll have to fill it up again," said Jack, holding his hand in the air as though struck by a revelation. "I guess that's another summertime job."

"Will the house burn down?" Erica asked, her eyes wide, her little brow furrowed. "Will we have to call the fire truck?"

Jack looked at me and raised his eyebrows. "She is your kid, isn't she?" He turned to Erica and said "No. We'll be very careful."

• • •

It was after eight o'clock, but the sun hadn't set yet. The kids were in bed, Jack was sorting through papers on the kitchen table.

The pile of boxes to unpack had shrunk to just a few. Time to call Mom and Dad.

Dad answered. "You're there?" he said. "All moved in? Goats and all? Let me get your mother. She's just back from a walk."

"Mae!" I heard Dad call, then I heard the kitchen screen door bang shut as Mom came in. "It's Paula! They're at the farm!"

She picked up the kitchen phone. "Well, what's it like?"

"Flat," I said. "And hilly."

"Which?" said Mom. "Hilly or flat?"

"Well, both," I said. "The fields are really flat, but there's a wonderful big hill at the back, very rocky, very wild looking. And there's a river right across the road from the house. And a barn, of course — two barns, actually. And lots of fields. And it's huge. It's 300 acres. I already told you. But half of that is the hill and the forest — or bush. They call the forest 'bush' here."

I rushed to fill in the silence from Pennsylvania. "We have a tractor, and some equipment, and two cows along with the goats, and the horse, and we have new chickens." When I stopped to catch my breath, Mom finally spoke.

"Well. It sounds like a lot of work. But I guess it's what you want." It sounded like a question. Silence on my end now.

"We're looking forward to seeing it," said Dad. "Probably in the spring. Will you be coming home for Christmas?"

Home?

"Um. No. I mean, we haven't talked about it. But I don't think so. I think we'll stay...um...home."

When the call ended, I turned to Jack who was still working at the kitchen table. "They say they're eager to see it." My voice felt flat. "But I think they figure we've lost our senses."

He looked up from his notes. "They won't think so when they get here," he said. I nodded, and he returned to his paperwork.

I wandered outside to sit on the back step. Voices drifted across the broad, deep field between the house and the storage barn — the "lower barn", as the Whites called it. The men were following the reaping machine, picking up the last of the bundles of oats and leaning them against one another, a hundred little teepees scattered across the field. I could hear their voices, but not their words.

Had we lost our senses?

Just past the lower barn, close to the road, someone turned a light on in the little white house with green trim. Past there, the river and the road bent to the right and disappeared. The trees across the river etched an irregular border along the darkening sky as the sun set behind them. On my side, several large elm trees with dying upper branches cast their faint, final shadow of the day as the sun dropped below the horizon.

The men and equipment were getting ready to leave. The reaping machine, with its paddle-like blades, disappeared into the barn; someone slammed a truck door; headlights bounced as the truck moved down the laneway and turned toward town.

The air was cooler now; I rubbed my arms, and turned away from the lower barn, looking in the other direction toward the barn close to the house. That barn, where our goats were housed for the night, loomed large in the foreground. In front of it, a collection of farm equipment—a tractor, a hay mower, a hay rake, a baler, a plow, discs, something called a harrow—ours now, tools of our new trade; on the other side of the barn, the cows and Karma in the pasture, and the schoolhouse acre with its huge willow trees. What was it like to live here twenty years ago, I wondered. I'd have been seven then, a little kid in a one-room school, like Laura. But maybe I was Ma now.

Barn swallows swooped and darted, feasting on the summer's last mosquitoes, but as the night deepened, they retired and bats emerged to take their turn at the banquet. The settling darkness erased the rest of the farm—the fields that stretched from the schoolhouse acre to the neighbour's barn, with its goats, half a mile away. Then, it was just the land, the night, the stars emerging in an impossibly dark sky.

• • •

The Echo River valley perches on the very southern tip of the Canadian (or Precambrian) Shield, which includes more than half the landmass of Canada and the earth's greatest area of exposed Precambrian rock. The river itself flows for just five miles, southwest from Echo Lake to Echo Bay, a shallow swelling in the wide St. Mary's River that drains Lake Superior into Lake Huron. That's its usual and inevitable trajectory. But from time to time, when local conditions raise the waters in Echo Bay to a level higher than Echo Lake, the river really does change its mind and flow backwards.

Over the last billion years, erosion and glaciation have reduced the giant volcanic mountains of the Precambrian era to low, rocky hills, just a few hundred feet high. As the glaciers of the last ice age shifted and eventually retreated, they scraped most of the soil from the Precambrian rocks, leaving the characteristic topography of northern Ontario: a vast rocky plateau dominated by lakes and rivers, rugged low hills, broad expanses of forest. During that slow process of glacial melt, low-lying areas captured and held deep deposits of heavy clay. Beneath the topsoil in these old lake bottoms, like the Echo River Valley, hundreds of feet of soft wet clay, the consistency of toothpaste, cover the ancient bedrock.

For thousands of years these lands provided a fertile environment for the dense forests that were home to the Anishinabe, Cree, and Sioux peoples of northern Ontario. For the last hundred and fifty years, in isolated pockets along the southern boundary of the Shield, they've provided farmland for people persistent enough to cope with heavy clay soil, poor drainage, and a short growing season.

This was the land I watched disappear into that August night in 1972. When I finally roused myself from my reverie and returned to the house, Jack was still at the table, working on becoming a professor. For the moment, *Introductory Psychology* had pre-empted *Grow It!*

• • •

The phone rang at ten o'clock the next morning — one long, two shorts. I let it ring three times to make sure; it was our first call on the party line we shared with three other neighbours. And then I picked up.

"Mrs. Dunning?"

"Yes. It's Paula." I was stretching the phone cord, trying to keep Robin from climbing from a kitchen chair onto the table.

"Well, it's your neighbour, Marg. Just down past the far end of your farm?" Her voice rose as though this were a question, but I figured she knew where she was, so I waited for what came next. "Fred's dog Ranger is here. Thought you should know."

At Fred's request, we'd adopted the old collie. He'd been avoiding us, and I hadn't missed him.

"Fred didn't think he'd want to leave the farm, so I guess he's our dog now," I said.

"Did you wanna come get him?"

Jack had already left for the Sault, for his first official day as a college professor. I grabbed Robin, hustled Erica away from the toys in the new playroom, and sat them in the back seat of the station wagon, ignoring the car seats for this short jaunt.

"Mommy, I'm not buckled. I don't feel safe."

Please, kid. Give me a break.

"You're safe, Erica," I said, backing out of the driveway and turning sharply. "We're only going a tiny ways."

"Mommy stop, stop! We're going into the river!'

69

"Erica, we are not going into the river. Now please just be quiet."
She began whimpering.

Marg was a plump, dark-haired woman in her late thirties with a friendly smile. She met us outside her two-story frame house, at the end of a driveway that ran along the edge of a deep, overgrown yard. Behind the house, several cows and a pony stood outside a barn much like ours. A hay wagon with a broken axle blocked the laneway between the house and the barn.

"Hi. I'm Paula," I said, and stuck out my hand.

She took it in a firm grasp. With her other hand, she held Ranger's collar. "My oldest daughter's Paula, too. And these are your kids?" She peeked into the car. Erica had stopped whimpering and was staring out the window. Robin was bouncing on the back seat.

"You've got yourselves quite a farm there," she said. "Fred tells us you've never farmed before."

"We've had goats for a year or so. Chickens. A horse. But this will be a lot more, we know." As the words came out, I thought I should probably work on a better line. I was obviously going to need it.

"Well, good luck to you. And you should know, my two younger girls babysit. Pam and Patsy." Paula, Pam, Patsy. A family of P's.

"Sorry about Ranger," I said. "He's pretty confused."

"Don't worry. Just thought you'd want to get him home."

I loaded the dog into the back of the car and drove him back home where he sat by the steps waiting for his owner to return.

My chat with Marg had apparently telegraphed to the neighbourhood that we were approachable. That evening, I looked out the back door to see Jack talking with two men in the barnyard — both big men wearing green work pants, button-up work shirts, and heavy boots. One had a thick dark beard. Both had a beer in hand. A beat-up Ford pickup was parked on the road. This was our second full day on the farm and as close as we'd come to a welcome party, except for the kids on moving day.

Jack came in chuckling.

"Those were the neighbours, Graham—that's Marg's husband—and George. He's the one with the goats. And the beard."

"Are they nice?"

"Nice enough. Welcomed me to the neighbourhood. Wanted to see the bus. Chatted about equipment. They both work shifts at the steel plant in town. Asked about the 'little woman' and the kids."

My mouth dropped. "Little woman?" I said, pronouncing each consonant with sharp precision.

Jack smirked. "Yeah, well…George has a manure spreader we can borrow. And I offered to lend him the goat book and some of our magazines with goat articles."

"I've got a copy of *Ms. Magazine* here, too," I said. "He might get a kick out of that."

• • •

In 1972, the business section of Echo Bay, a ten-minute drive from the farm, population 500, consisted of a gas station; a take-out pizza joint with a pin-ball machine; a small variety store specializing in cigarettes, bread, milk, and candy; a post office; the Country Place restaurant; and Buchanans General Store. Also "in the Bay" were three churches—Anglican, United, Baptist—and an elementary school.

By day three we were reaching the end of our meager food supply and I decided to check out the town. First, the post office to make sure our mail would be delivered to the right house. The postmaster, turned away from his newspaper and looked up when I opened the door. He appeared to be chewing a cigarette. "You're at the White farm?" he said, repeating what I'd just told him, through barely opened lips.

"Yeah. I guess it's the Dunning farm, now."

He grunted. "You'll need to get your name on the mailbox so's the Findlays know who y'are."

"Who are the Findlays?" I asked.

He stared at me as though I were speaking Chinese. Apparently, this was a stupid question. "They deliver the mail." He took another hungry puff on his cigarette. "They'll need to know who y'are," he repeated, just in case I hadn't got it the first time, and turned back to his newspaper.

Next stop, Buchanans General Store. I parked in one of the dozen parking spaces in front and pulled open the heavy glass door. Immediately to my left, an overweight woman of about fifty, with tightly-curled grey hair, sat on a stool behind an old-fashioned cash register. I smiled hello at her, took a grocery cart, and headed down the first aisle. As far as I could tell, I was the only customer in the store.

I picked up a head of lettuce, a bag of onions, a bag of apples, some carrots and potatoes from the meager display of produce. Opposite the produce, several shelves held bread, hamburger buns, and cookies. I'd start baking again soon but in the meantime, a loaf of white bread was the best I could do. I pushed my cart up and down the five aisles, taking stock first of the canned goods and dry groceries, then cleaning supplies, school supplies, sewing notions, greeting cards, magazines, garden tools, work clothes, and miscellaneous hardware items. This side of the store smelled like nails and rubber boots. At the back of the store, I found a cooler with dairy products, and beside them, the meat counter.

I was trying to decide between hamburger and pork chops when a tall, heavy-set man in glasses and a white apron came out of a man-sized refrigerator door carrying half a pig. He looked over at me, dropped the pig on a butcher's table, wiped his hands on his apron, and approached the counter. "Good afternoon," he said. "You must be Mrs. Dunning from the White farm, right? I'm

Garfield Buchanan. Welcome to the neighbourhood." It was the warmest welcome I'd received yet.

"Thanks," I said. "How did you know who I was?"

He chuckled. "Word gets around, you'll see. I hear you're Americans."

I sputtered. "Not really. Not anymore."

He smiled—indulgently, I thought. "What can I get for you?"

I was walking toward the check-out with both pork chops and hamburger, wrapped in brown paper with the price marked in grease pencil, when Garfield called out. "Eva! This is Mrs. Dunning from Fred White's farm. Open an account for her!"

Really? I hadn't asked for that.

Eva Buchanan didn't have her brother's charm, but she was efficiency itself. "I'll just mark it down," she said as she totaled up the items on the clattering cash register.

"I can pay," I insisted.

She shook her head. "This'll get your account started. Then, you can pay up every month." She pulled a big, flat book off the shelf beside her and opened it to a page with D written on the top and rows of little pockets neatly labeled Dean...Downy ...Doughty. She tucked my bill into an empty pocket, labeled it Dunning, and closed the book. I was in.

"Al-ex!" She called, her voice rising on the second syllable. The third Buchanan appeared, a taller, lankier, and somewhat younger man. "You want to carry these bags out for Mrs. Dunning? She's on the Fred White farm."

"Y-y-yes, b-be glad to, Mrs. Dunning. Welcome to Echo Bay."

On the way home, I saw a sign, *Fresh Bread for* Sale three houses down from ours. I knocked on the door and poked my head through when someone called out "C'mon in." Keith Nelson slouched on a vinyl kitchen chair, wearing an undershirt, smoking a cigarette, drinking coffee, and rolling more cigarettes from the pile of loose tobacco and cigarette papers on the table. Nellie had put her cigarette down to take six loaves of bread from the oven. "I sell bread on Tuesdays, cinnamon buns on Fridays," she said. I drank a cup of powerfully strong coffee with them, met all five of their children, and bought a loaf of fluffy, crusty, pure-white bread smelling only slightly of tobacco smoke.

I'd barely pulled back onto the road when I stopped again to introduce myself to Lorne and Irene Smith in the little white house on the edge of our first field, our closest neighbours. Their grandson, Jody, had been one of the older children greeting us on moving day.

Irene was cutting back rose bushes along the road. "Jody told us about you," she said. "He's our grandson, y'know. He lives with us."

"He's just eleven, but big for his age," said Lorne. "Could give you a hand on the farm next summer."

Irene went on, "I hear you've got two little ones. Bring 'em down some day. I'm grandma to a lot of little ones, not just my own."

Before I left, Lorne handed me a bag of cucumbers.

Fred White continued to come by daily, to Ranger's intense joy, retrieving a few things from the attic, fussing about the barns and sheds, harvesting late-season garden produce, and supplying us with corn and squash. When Robin was outside, he followed Fred around like a puppy. Now that he had decided to walk, he was making up for lost time. "The young lad is fine with me," Fred said, and it was clear he meant more than that. As he walked out of the kitchen one day, after depositing a cabbage on the counter, he said, "A lot of Americans have been buying up land around here, y'know. But I said to the wife yesterday, we're lucky to sell to a good Canadian family."

I squirmed, and wondered how Alex Buchanan knew more about us than Fred White did.

● ● ●

Jack and I celebrated our first week on the farm with a glass of wine on the back steps. Shastek lay beside us, alert, wagging her tail against the grass with a soft, thumping sound. She'd adjusted easily to the move.

I sat on the bottom step beside Jack, looking at the stars and listening to the silence. Deep, deep silence. The moon rose slowly above the hill.

"I start teaching in a week," said Jack.

"Hmm." I didn't much feel like talking.

He did: "Next week, maybe I'll go get that manure spreader from George. Fred says the first little field past the barn is due to be plowed up. It would be a good one to start on. If I can get the manure on it next week, I can plow it some weekend in the fall. That's what he says to do."

I leaned back against the top step, breathing in the night air. Jack put his arm around me, and though he spoke softly, I could feel the excitement in his voice. He went on.

"Then, we'll have one field to plant next spring. He says we should aim to plow and plant a fifth of the farm every year, to keep the hay crop strong. I guess you plant new hayseed at the same time as the oats, then the hay keeps coming back. That's what Fred says, anyway." He reached down to pet Shastek, whose tail thumped harder. "I have to go into the college Tuesday and Thursday next week. And then, when classes start, every day — except maybe Fridays. Two night classes, so I guess I'll just stay in town for supper those nights. You okay with that? With all the chores those days?"

"Sure," I said, rousing myself from a contented fog. "Fine. Especially if it means you'll be home Fridays."

He reached over and pulled me close; I snuggled against him, feeling the coolness of the evening on his arms and neck. Shastek had gone to sleep at our feet. Clouds were drifting on and off the moon, obscuring, and then illuminating, the dark shapes of the barn up close and the hill in the distance. I reached down, picked up my wine glass, and let the last sip linger in my mouth.

CHAPTER 6 • COLLIDING CULTURES

The first Friday in September, just one week after he started teaching at Algoma College, Jack donned a new pair of green overalls and a shiny pair of steel-toed work boots, started up the tractor we'd bought from Fred White—an International W-4, circa 1950—and drove down the road to George's farm with *Goat Husbandry* and a few copies of *Mother Earth News*. No copies of *Ms.* He came back an hour later pulling the manure spreader, a wooden wagon equipped with a chain-like mechanism for moving manure from the front to the back, where spinning metal blades broke the clumps and broadcast them off the moving wagon. Using a pitchfork, Jack filled the spreader from the manure pile behind the barn and drove it to the field Fred had instructed him to plant in the spring.

After half an hour on the field, he parked the spreader, still heaped with manure, in front of the equipment shed.

"What a piece of garbage!" he said as he stomped into the kitchen, leaving a trail of manure behind him. He ran his hands under the hot water in the kitchen sink, then picked up the dish soap, depositing greasy smudges on the bottle, and dried his imperfectly clean hands on a clean towel.

"The chains are rusted through. Two links are broken, probably more under the manure that's still in the wagon. Piece of crap. It'd be easier to spread it with a fucking wheelbarrow."

"Fuckin we'barow," said Robin, who had come running into the kitchen when he heard Jack come in. I grimaced at Jack, who shrugged in reply.

Over the next week, Jack made several trips to the farm supply store to buy replacement links, but for every new one he replaced, another old one broke. Finally on Sunday, after one last replacement, he decided to return the spreader. He'd spent hours fussing with the chains and managed to spread only three loads on the field.

"It's working now," he said as he left, "but it won't last long."

No one was home; he left the spreader in the barnyard.

On Tuesday evening, just as I was tucking Robin into bed, Shastek started barking and I heard a loud banging on the back door. I opened it to a tall, heavy-set, bearded man in grease-stained green coveralls who leaned menacingly toward me. He raised a fist in the air and shouted. "Where's your husband?"

"You're George, aren't you?" I hoped he couldn't tell I was trembling.

"Where the hell is he?" Venom and beer breath spewed from his mouth.

I didn't want to tell him I was alone, but I couldn't conjure up Jack. "He's teaching tonight."

"Teaching! Brainy professor, eh? Doesn't know shit about farming, though, does he?"

"Maybe you should come back tomorrow," I said. Erica was standing by the kitchen door in her pajamas, looking as frightened as I felt.

"Hell, no. You tell him he's busted my manure spreader, and he can bloody well fix it." He raised his fist and shook it in my general direction.

"It was already broken. He tried to fix it," I mumbled, and reached back to hold Erica's hand.

"Bullshit. He broke it. He can fix it. You tell 'im"

He turned to leave, then turned back and pulled something from inside his coveralls. I flinched as he flung his hand out. *Goat*

Husbandry and the magazines flew into the air and landed on the floor. "Fuckin' books."

By the time Jack got home from his evening class, the children were asleep and my heart rate had returned to normal. The next afternoon he drove down to George's, found no one home, and decided the story was over.

George had obviously given up on Jack, too; he never returned to insist on reparations, and Jack never offered any. We continued to wave when we passed his truck on the road; he continued to stare straight ahead with a scowl on his face. For years.

• • •

Jack was adjusting to a dual life, but so far I hadn't met anyone from the college. So, in late September, we invited one of his colleagues and his wife to dinner.

Jack spent all that day on the tractor, learning to plow on the small field near the house. Back and forth, the dry grasses curled under as the plow pulled the soil to the surface in long, unbroken ribbons, slowly turning the field a dark, moist brown. Not as dark as it would have been with manure, of course, but Jack had given up on that for this year.

While he plowed, I prepared for the evening. I dusted and polished the cherry wood dining table and the old rocking chair from Jack's mother. I shook the crumbs off the striped madras cover on the sofa, fluffed up the cushions on the swinging rattan chair, vacuumed the shag rug, and dust-mopped the wood floors. I scrubbed the bathroom and closed the bedroom doors. In the kitchen, I mopped the faded tan-and-white linoleum floor and wiped down the 1940s kitchen hutch with its enamel work surface. I covered the round, maple kitchen table, also from Jack's mother, with a fringed yellow cloth, moved its four matching plank-bottom chairs into the living room, placed them around the dining table, and set it with placemats and matching dishes. We only had three wine glasses, but otherwise, things looked pretty good.

With the children underfoot, I prepared my foolproof chicken *con arroz* from the company dinner section of the Betty Crocker *Dinner in a Dish* cookbook, tossed a salad, and baked a cake. The temperature was dropping outside, so I started a fire in the furnace. The house smelled of chicken, saffron, and faintly — charmingly, I thought — of wood smoke.

Jack stomped the mud off his boots at the back door and sniffed the air as he came into the kitchen. "Smells good. And you started a fire." He walked over to the kitchen vent and knelt down to feel the warmth on his hands. "Good idea. It's getting cold out there. I was wishing I had gloves, especially for this one." He was rubbing his left hand, trying to get the blood moving through the mutilated fingers.

He approached the kitchen sink. "Not here," I said. "The bathroom's for washing up. And try not to leave a mess behind." He sighed and headed upstairs. "Keep the bedroom doors closed," I shouted after him. "And don't dry your hands with the guest towel!"

I fed Erica and Robin early and tucked them in bed. This was to be a grown-up affair. A plate of cheese and crackers waited in the living room; Jack looked presentable in clean jeans and a sweater. I wanted to look casual and relaxed, a country woman with a sense of style. After rejecting jeans as too casual and a pant suit as too formal, I settled on a pair of tan corduroy bell-bottoms with a dark brown turtleneck, dangly earrings, my favourite string of beads-and-seeds, and a long knit vest. I pulled my hair into a ponytail at the nape of my neck and dug through my top dresser drawer for a tube of lipstick, then changed my mind and rubbed most of the lipstick off with the back of my hand.

By seven o'clock, Robin was settling into sleep, and Erica's toneless singing had become quieter. In the living room, Jack had already helped himself to the cheese and crackers, so I rearranged them on the plate, straightened the cover on the sofa once more, and looked out the window in time to see a shiny red Toyota Celica pull in behind the truck. Greg got out first, a short man with a tidy goatee, glasses, and a bit of a paunch; he was wearing a blue-and-tan striped shirt tucked into tan chinos. Kathy was an inch taller, slender, with short dark hair, and dressed in dark slacks with a yellow cashmere sweater and pearls.

"Nice car," said Jack as Greg came in the door first and handed him a bottle of French wine.

"Just off the lot. C'mon, I'll take you for a spin."

As the two men sped away, raising dust on the gravel road, Kathy came into the house. "He just loves that little car," she said. Her eyes lit up as she walked across the kitchen. "Oooh, and *I* love your kitchen hutch," she said. "It'll be so great when you get it cleaned up!"

Oh. "We picked it up in southern Ontario. We like collecting odds and ends," I said.

"Yes, I can see that." Her gaze drifted through the door into the living room. "We're into American colonial ourselves."

"Good furniture hardly makes sense with little kids." Then, feeling on the defensive, changed my tone. "Do you have kids?"

"No. Greg's not interested in having children, and I'm fine with that." She took the glass of wine I handed her — Blue Nun — took a sip, then arched her perfectly shaped eyebrows and glanced across the room at the bottle they'd brought.

"Are you working, then?" I led the way to the living room, where the kitchen chairs suddenly clashed with the dining table, which obviously took up way too much space. Why hadn't I noticed?

"Not now. I'm taking a couple of courses. I'd like to get my degree in English, maybe teach later on. You?"

"No, with the two kids and the farm, I figure I'll be busy enough. We'll be getting more animals. And I'll plant a big garden in the spring. Do you garden?" I motioned Kathy to take a seat on the trundle bed that was posing—unsuccessfully, I now realized—as a sofa. I sat down on the swinging chair.

"That's an interesting chair," Kathy said, watching it sway on its heavy chain, and helping herself to crackers and cheese. "We cultivate roses. We've planted seven different varieties."

"So maybe you'd like some manure," I said, leaning back in my chair. "We could even deliver it in our truck."

She wrinkled her nose. "No thanks. We buy it in bags. You know, that way there's no *smell*. Do you have any napkins? I'm dropping crumbs."

Jack and Greg returned from their spin, deep in conversation about intermittent windshield wipers and front-wheel drive, and joined us in the living room.

"My goodness," said Kathy, tugging at the neck of her sweater. "It is warm in here, isn't it?"

The behemoth in the basement was doing itself proud. All during dinner, heat poured out of the big living room vent. I reached over and snapped the vent door shut with a sharp clang, but heat continued to seep out around the edges. I'd already ditched the vest. Greg pulled a handkerchief out of his pocket and wiped his forehead. Jack slipped off his sweater to reveal a clean but rumpled shirt, buttoned askew. I looked over at Greg's ironed, button-down shirt and tried not to care.

"Sorry about the heat," Jack said, stifling a yawn and turning to Greg. "I think I'll check the fire again. Would you like to see the furnace?"

Greg shrugged. "Sure, I guess so." He stood up, pushed his glasses against the bridge of his nose, and exchanged glances with Kathy, whose eyebrows shot up again.

At that moment, it occurred to me that I'd never been invited to see someone's furnace. Maybe most people weren't that interested in furnaces; and perhaps a trek through our basement wouldn't improve our social standing around the college. But that was beginning to feel like a lost cause, anyway.

I tugged the turtleneck away from my neck to let the sweat evaporate.

"Don't you find it all a little…" Pause. "*Primitive*?" Kathy's voice took on a conspiratorial tone. Us against them. "Wood heat, and manure, and everything?"

"Um…I don't know. Not primitive. No. We want to live, you know, closer to nature."

"I guess it just seems strange for a college professor."

The wine, the heat, the American colonial furniture, the seven varieties of roses, and the bags of manure caught up with me. "Not so strange," I said, suddenly articulate. "We think it's a healthier way to live. Healthier for our kids. Healthier for the world. I love collecting eggs, milking goats in the mornings, burning wood in the furnace. I'll be happy to butcher our own meat, too."

"Was that *goats'* milk in my coffee?"

I grinned. "Yup."

● ● ●

I don't remember exactly when Jack built the sandbox, but it must have been soon after we arrived, because that's when we met Morley and Gloria Trotter.

Jack walked up to the two-story, yellow brick farmhouse and knocked on the wooden door with fading white paint on the bottom and a single pane of glass on top. Clothes flapped in the breeze on a line that began near the door and ended at a pole close to the riverbank. The tall, large-boned woman who answered the door was wiping her hands on a flowered apron that covered brown plaid pants and a pink t-shirt.

"Of course you can have some sand," I heard her say as I helped Erica and Robin from the car.

She stepped outside and shouted "Moor-leey!" then turned back to Jack. "You just go down the road and help yourself from the gravel pit while I get to know Paula and the kids. By the time you get back, Morley'll be back from the barn and we'll have a cuppa."

She turned to me. "We should have introduced ourselves sooner, I know. I'm Gloria. And this is Stacey." A red-headed toddler peered at us from behind her mother. "The boys are in the barn with Morley."

Gloria ushered the three of us into her kitchen, past a pile of work boots, shoes, and several jackets on hooks by the door. A chrome kitchen table filled most of the floor space. It was covered with a mixing bowl, a milk pitcher, and cookie sheets. The sweetness of fresh baking mingled with a different sweetness, the earthy smell of damp barn jackets. On one side of the room, an enamel sink hung from the wall; opposite it, an electric stove and a propane heater where a kettle steamed. The single kitchen window looked past the mouth of the river and across Echo Lake.

"Don't take off your shoes," said Gloria as I bent down to untie my sneakers. "We don't stand by ceremony here." A warm smile softened her angular face under short, permed brown hair. "I'll find the kids something to play with, and then I'll make tea."

Before I could respond, she took my children by the hand and led them into the long living room lined with sofas on both sides. She settled the three kids with a basket of toys. "There you go. Stacey, you share now."

Only Robin spoke. "Tractor," he said and began pushing a toy tractor along the worn green rug. Erica started building a farm with blocks and plastic animals. Stacey stood and watched.

"Can they have a cookie?" Gloria asked, and without waiting for an answer she lifted three huge peanut butter cookies from a cooling rack beside the stove.

"Now, I'll try and find this table."

Within minutes, the baking project had disappeared, replaced by a plate of warm peanut butter cookies and four pink-flowered teacups and saucers with matching cream and sugar.

The outside door opened and a lean man, with a tanned face and hair so short you couldn't tell its colour, came in. He was wearing baggy jeans held up by a wide leather belt, a plaid flannel shirt coming untucked in front, a down vest, and a baseball cap. He handed a pail of milk to Gloria. "I already gave some to the pigs," he said. "This is for the house if you need it."

Then he turned to me and offered a calloused hand. "You must be Paula. Nice to meet you. Where's Jack? I wanna meet this professor-farmer." His handshake was quick and firm.

"Gone to get some sand for a sandbox," Gloria answered.

Morley threw his vest and hat onto a hook and glanced out the window. "Is that him now?"

Jack came in at the same time as eleven-year-old Scott and eight-year-old Brian. Gloria introduced the boys quickly and shooed them out of the kitchen with cookies in hand.

"Pull up a chair and take a load off your feet," Morley said as he pumped Jack's hand.

Over the next hour, we learned that Morley had been born on this farm; his grandfather and father had farmed it, and his mother still lived in a little white bungalow next to the house. He raised beef cattle for sale, milked a cow, and kept pigs and chickens for the family. He also worked at a small engine repair shop in the Sault during the winter to help make ends meet. Gloria had grown up on a farm in Sylvan Valley. She shared the farm work and ran a tourist operation in the summer, issuing fishing licenses and renting out cabins, camping spots, boats, and motors, mostly to farmers from Ohio and Indiana who came to fish on Echo Lake.

"Farming's a lifestyle. If you're gonna do it right, you've gotta love it," said Morley. He took a swallow of tea and a bite of cookie, then rubbed his hand over the top of his stubbly head. He looked directly at Jack, squinting his bright blue eyes so that his entire face crinkled. "You folks have got yourselves a real fine farm, there. And Fred White was a first-rate farmer. Big shoes to fill."

Jack started to speak, but Morley beat him to it. "Just holler when you need a hand."

• • •

Gloria and I began visiting regularly, and over many cups of tea I began to understand that she and Morley were taking us under their wing—and to realize what a comforting place that was going to be when the real farming began. They had both been on farms all their lives, and they were eager to share both their knowledge and their opinions, though sometimes I had trouble telling which was which. Did milk really curdle before a thunderstorm? Should we really "worm" the children twice a year, like puppies? And what was this thing about phases of the moon?

At Gloria's invitation, I attended my first Women's Institute meeting at a tidy little bungalow with blue siding, just four houses down the road. The hostess, Helen—a thin, stern-looking woman of forty with glasses and tight brown curls—led me through the warm kitchen to the living room just as the ladies were taking seats. Irene from next door smiled a greeting. Six others sat sedately on the sofa, two armchairs, and a couple of kitchen chairs. Except for me, Gloria was the youngest. She patted the seat beside her on the sofa and moved over to make room.

A large woman on a straight-back chair was carrying on a monologue. As I sat down Gloria whispered, "That's Elsa Jones."

She'd warned me about Elsa a few days earlier: "She's very crude and, well, I've heard she entertains men, if you know what I mean."

Surely not, I thought as I looked at her.

Her silky red blouse barely buttoned across her bosom, and her dark hair, streaked with grey, hung limply to the bottom of her round face. Her tight skirt was so short that when her hefty thighs separated, you could see her underwear. Years later, when I shared this memory with a neighbour, she laughed and said, "At least she was wearing some. She didn't always, you know."

Elsa had just returned from a two-week trip to England, and that evening she spoke with a studied gentility: "Then, after you do your business, you pull a chain to flush it down. And of course, with the strange food, you do your business more often than at home." She pursed her lips primly while the others exchanged embarrassed glances and I wondered what English food could be so strange.

Gloria put a stop to Elsa's story by reaching into a large leather satchel and pulling out a hard-cover black notebook with a red spine and a red ribbon marking a page halfway through. "Well." When Gloria said "well", it sounded like "whale". I think we should start. Auntie Grace, do you want to call the meeting to order?"

"Oh, yes, I guess I should," said Grace, a short, soft-looking woman in her fifties. "I keep forgetting I'm president this year." She giggled softly, smoothed her dark wool skirt over her knees, and stood up. Everyone followed her lead. As they began to chant a prayer in unison, Gloria handed me a small blue booklet opened to "The Mary Stewart Collect."

"Keep us, O Lord, from pettiness," it began. "Let us be large in thought, word and deed. Let us be done with fault finding and leave off self-seeking…"

When the ladies sat down, Grace spoke up again. She was fidgeting with her glasses on her lap. "What's the role call this month, Gloria?"

"A recipe using a fall vegetable," Gloria said.

"Oh, yes. That's right. So, Gloria, you have the book. Do you want to read the names out?" Perhaps everyone was under Gloria's wing.

Mrs. Mert Alcock? A carrot salad. Mrs. Don Gordon? Parsnip patties. Mrs. Lorne Smith? Candied turnips. Mrs. Ronald Jones? Pumpkin loaf. Those who had no recipe paid a twenty-five cent fine. When she'd reached the end of the list, Gloria turned to me.

"This is our new neighbour, Paula Dunning. You all know, Paula and Jack bought Fred and Gertie White's farm."

The ladies nodded. "Nice to meet you, Paula...Welcome to the valley...I've seen you on the road..." As I tried to keep track of the names and faces, I realized that almost everyone here was related: Gloria's mother-in-law sat across the room; Grace was apparently Gloria's aunt; there were two Gordons, Helen and her mother-in-law; Irene and Grace were sisters—so that must mean Irene was Gloria's aunt, too.

"Well, since I'm secretary, I'll read the minutes," said Gloria, "and then we can get on with the business."

After the minutes and the treasurer's report, Gloria reminded Grace to move on to old business—there was none—and then to a single item of new business, a motion to contribute ten dollars to a scholarship fund, passed unanimously.

The meeting ended half an hour after it began with the singing of God Save the Queen. Over salmon sandwiches, pickles, date squares, and tea, the ladies shared the latest news about children and grandchildren, doctors' appointments, and plans for the upcoming Thanksgiving holiday.

"We hope you'll decide to join our chapter," said Helen as I was leaving. Her smile seemed warmer, now. "We need more young people who are committed to rural values."

• • •

Life began to take on a comfortable rhythm. I did barn chores twice a day on Jack's two long teaching days and once a day the rest of the week, although I often went along to do the milking since Jack still found that difficult with his lame hand. Erica attended nursery school in the Sault two mornings a week, riding in with Jack and committing me to two town trips a week to pick her up and do errands. In the house, I made red curtains for the bay windows, painted the kitchen wainscoting a bright blue, and wallpapered the children's bedrooms in bright patterns — houses and children playing in Erica's room, tractors and cows in Robin's. I was baking bread again and making yogurt from our own fresh milk.

As the weather turned and the goats began to give less milk, I tried my hand at milking one of the dual-purpose cows. Fred had assured us she was a gentle cow, so I first approached the huge, reddish-brown animal with confidence; but as soon as I crouched beside her and reached for her udder, she began a spastic, repetitive kick with her back leg that sent me scurrying backwards. For the first few days, Jack stood beside her, pressing his fist into a spot just above her hind leg that made it impossible for her to kick, a trick we learned from Morley. But Jack couldn't always be there. One morning, she raised her leg and, with a powerful, spring-like action, planted her hoof squarely on my cheek. "You Big, Fat, Ugly Beast!" I shouted, and reached up to feel blood oozing on my already-swelling face. And so she became B-fub.

That ended B-fub's career as a milk cow; we switched to our second dual-purpose animal, a gentler soul we named Mama Cow.

I bought a hand churn with a wooden dash at the local farm co-op store and churned butter from the cream I skimmed off the top of the milk every day, feeling like Ma as I kneaded the soft globs of butter in cold water to extract the last of the buttermilk and shaped them into blocks with a wooden butter-press we'd found in the shed.

Robin's allergy to cow's milk, if that's what it was, had disappeared.

One Friday afternoon in early November, just after Erica's fourth birthday, Jack was cleaning stalls in the barn and I was putting a second coat of off-white paint on the living room walls while Erica kept Robin at bay. Three walls white, one deep yellow. That was the plan. Jack had just built a plywood structure to fit under the bay windows and house a small family of gerbils in three aquariums, attached to one another with black plastic plumbing pipe. I hadn't decided yet how to paint that; maybe an orangey-red to match the newly-sewn curtains.

I put down my paint roller to answer a knock at the door. Two slight figures stood on the back step. She was shorter than me, not much over five feet, and wore a man's overcoat over a long woolen skirt, heavy boots, and wool socks. He was six inches taller with a sparse beard that hung several inches below his chin.

"My name's Jeff Fritzland," he said. "This is Jane. We heard you might be willing to board a cow."

Before I could respond, Jane chipped in. "We met some of Jack's students, and they told us about your farm."

"Come in. Jack's in the barn."

While I ran to get him, Jeff and Jane returned to their ancient black pick-up truck, all curved lines and rounded fenders, and unloaded their two children.

When Jack and I got back to the kitchen, the Fritzlands were making themselves comfortable. Jane took off her toque, setting free a mop of curly dark hair. Her brown eyes sparkled with enthusiasm. Jeff leaned back on a kitchen chair like a man who could be at home wherever he found himself. Erica and five-year-old Amanda had already disappeared into the playroom.

How, we asked, did they come to have a homeless cow? Over cups of tea ("herb tea, if you have any"), with baby Anaîs nursing in her mom's arms and Robin, suddenly clingy, sitting on Jack's lap, they explained.

They had moved from a commune near Ottawa so that Jane could study nursing at the community college in the Sault. Eventually, she wanted to become a midwife. Jeff stayed home with the children. They brought the cow with them, hoping to rent a farm, but ended up living in a tiny, dilapidated house on the edge of town. The cow, Guernsey-Girl, was still outside on rented pasture. With cold weather coming fast, they wanted her in a barn.

An hour after I put down my paintbrush and answered the knock on the door, Erica had a new best friend and we'd agreed to keep Guernsey-Girl for the winter. She arrived in an open U-Haul trailer the next day, a pretty little cow with short horns curving out of her honey-coloured forehead, a bovine aristocrat beside B-fub and Mama Cow.

So, we entered our first winter with three cows, two calves, a horse, and three goats in the barn, and an emerging friendship with the Fritzlands. We'd met most of our neighbours, alienated one, and found reliable mentors in the Trotters. Jack was gradually getting to know most of his colleagues at the college and from time to time we joined them at social events, using Patsy and Pam as babysitters. For those occasions, we tried to set aside our farm personas. Not so hard for Jack, who was simultaneously growing into his teaching job. Harder for me; converting fantasy to reality on the farm had become a fulltime job.

CHAPTER 7 • NOT QUITE A CHRISTMAS CARD

My mom's mother adored Christmas. She lathered her tree with fake snow and decorated it with every sparkling, blinking, and singing ornament the local Five and Dime had to offer. She bought extravagant gifts she couldn't afford. In Grammy's front yard, a life-sized plastic Santa and his reindeer, laden with their gifts, nearly collided with the three wise men, laden with theirs. And every Christmas, every one of Grammy's seven grandchilden received a stuffed animal—sometimes with a sewn-in music box, sometimes with eyes that blinked, and always with a fuzzy body that smelled of new, synthetic material. That was because Grammy worked in a toy factory. Long after I had outgrown the toys, I saw them as a sign of Grammy's status, for she would often point out that she, personally, had sewn this bunny's ear or that monkey's tail.

My dad's mother, Grammy Smith, on the other hand, celebrated the holiday with the reserve of a good Pennsylvania Dutch Lutheran. She attended church activities. She baked molasses and sugar cookies in the shape of Santas, birds, trees, and wreaths. And in honour of the season, she wore a special Christmas apron and a special Christmas pin. The gifts under her table-top Christmas tree were sensible: sweaters for me and my brothers, a wallet for Dad, a mixing bowl for Mom, and long, snake-like stockings, discarded nylons before the days of pantyhose, distorted by strangely shaped, paper-wrapped lumps. A barette with my name on it, a comb from an insurance company, a pocket calendar from the bank, cellophane-wrapped jacks from the Wheaties box, a tiny book of Bible stories, a pen advertising real estate agents, shiny hard candies, an orange, an apple, and always, in the very toe, a penny. To remind us how lucky we were.

• • •

By mid December 1972, as we approached our first Christmas on the farm, the temperature never rose above freezing and the snow reached our knees. No sooner did we shovel the driveway clear than it snowed again, the plow came down the road and dumped a new load at the end of the driveway, and we had to dig out again. I loved the stark beauty and revelled in a sense of survival in the True North. I didn't mind the driveway-shovelling and the path-breaking for chores. It all fit my evolving image of the young rural family roughing it in the wilderness, as did Jack's mother's surprise decision to spend Christmas on the farm with us.

Two weeks before she was scheduled to arrive, I was sweeping the kitchen floor while Jack marked exams at the kitchen table.

"Move your feet," I said and ran the broom under the table, gathering up bits of straw, kernels of corn, the broken wheel of a tonka truck. "I was wondering, do you think your mom will want to go along to get the tree?"

"To the bush? I don't know," said Jack, not looking up from the paper in front of him. "She's not such an outdoor person, you know."

Where was Jack the enthusiast when I needed him?

"But don't you think she'd get a kick out of it? Cutting our own tree? With the whole family? In our own forest?"

"We'll get a kick out of it. I don't know about her. But maybe." He sighed and stretched back his shoulders as he moved the paper he'd been reading onto a growing pile and picked up another from the slowly shrinking one.

I swept the last of the debris into the corner, leaned the broom against the wall, and looked at the calendar beside the phone.

"Great, then. Christmas is on a Monday. She gets here the Wednesday before. We'll go for the tree on Friday. Then we'll get the goose on Sunday." I held my breath and looked at Jack, who finally looked up from his papers.

"What goose?"

• • •

Mother's Wednesday afternoon flight was fog-bound in Toronto. Along with the rest of the passengers, she travelled nine hours by overnight bus to the Sault, where Jack picked her up early Thursday morning.

He came in the house first, carrying Mother's suitcase. "Mmm. Muffins." He sniffed the air, gave me a quick kiss, and rolled his eyes.

Mother stepped into the kitchen as though expecting an ambush. Her cheeks were flushed—from cold or excitement, I couldn't tell. She took off her burgundy knit hat, unwrapped the matching scarf, and began unbuttoning her navy-blue wool jacket. Erica and Robin, still in their pajamas, stood beside me, cautious and curious. They didn't remember this grandmother.

"Well, look at my lambies!" She leaned over and gave them each a quick hug. Erica opened her mouth to speak, but Mother had already moved on.

"Well, now. Let me see your house, Paula." She was walking slowly from the kitchen into the living room. "It's really quite . . . well. It has real possibilities, I'd say. The wainscotting will be lovely once you've refinished it. The floors could be, too. And I'm sure you're looking for a sofa. I don't suppose you've had much time for the house, what with the barn and all the animals."

I let out a long, controlled breath. Here we go. Seven days. And this had been my idea. I led her to Jack's study, which we'd converted to a guest room, and explained that the only bathroom was upstairs. Then I left her to unpack and rest.

Back in the kitchen, Jack had settled Erica and Robin at the table with muffins and juice. He handed me a cup of coffee.

"You'll need this," he said, trying not to laugh. "Mother figures she's at the North Pole." He took a sip from his cup and spoke in a conspiratorial whisper. "Apparently she struck up a conversation with 'the nicest young woman' on the bus, a university student on her way home, and explained that she was travelling to the wilderness — Sault Ste. Marie. Of course, everyone on the bus was coming here too, but she wouldn't have thought of that." Jack chuckled. "The young woman seemed 'quite normal,' so Mother felt better."

I snorted. "I wonder how the quite normal young woman felt."

"Exactly," said Jack, biting into his second muffin. "So, we're almost home and she says, 'You've always been a little unusual, Jack, but this is too much. Think of the children!'" He was mimicking his mother's exaggerated tone. I gave him a warning glance and tilted my head toward Erica, who was all ears.

"Doesn't Grandma like it here?" she asked.

"Oh, I think she will," said Jack. "She's sure glad to see you." He gave me a look that said, "Oops, we'd better be careful."

By the time Mother reappeared, the children were dressed and Jack was back from the chores. She had smoothed her light brown hair and freshened her makeup, but the newly etched lines around her eyes and mouth reminded me that she'd been through a rough few years since the divorce. I'd try to be tolerant, try to play to her sense of adventure. At sixty and newly single, she and a friend had begun travelling to places she considered exotic — Mexico, Central America, New Zealand. Surely northern Ontario wouldn't faze her. And indeed, the short rest seemed to have infused her with some enthusiasm.

She patted Robin on the top of his curly head, accepted a cup of pretend-tea from Erica, and turned to her son. "You're very brave to heat your house with just wood, Jack. It's so cold here in the north."

In fact, we were learning to master our primitive central heating system, but it erred on the side of excess as we'd learned at our fall dinner party. The only temperature control was on the furnace itself, a sliding damper on the door that determined how much air reached the fire and how hot it burned—in theory. In fact, a warped furnace door had turned the whole "heat control" issue into something of a farce. But once Jack patched the door with a bit of asbestos and we'd learned to select the sizes and types of logs to burn—poplar or spruce with lots of air to get a fire going fast and hot, maple or oak with minimum air for a slower, steadier burn—we figured we'd tamed the beast. However, Mother was in the north and determined to be cold.

I checked the thermometer. "It's seventy-four in here," I said.

"Oh, don't bother yourselves, I'll just bundle up. I brought my long-johns. Figured I'd need them here in the wilderness." She rolled up the bottom of her camel wool slacks to reveal a riotous assortment of lavender flowers decorating thermal-weave legs bordered by a brilliant purple cuff.

The next day the outdoor thermometer read five degrees Fahrenheit and a stiff wind blew from the west. Christmas tree day, according to my script. Jack dragged the molded plastic sled into the house and carefully secured a cardboard box on the front with enough room on either side for a small pair of legs. We tucked Robin into the box with Erica behind, her pudgy legs helping to hold him steady.

"Is Grandma coming? Will she help get the tree?" asked Erica.

"She's coming," I said. I tightened the scarves around both children's necks and pulled their fur-edged hoods forward. Shastek, sensing an adventure, dashed around the sled in irregular circles, barking and throwing up clouds of snow.

Mother bundled up for the excursion, tightening her scarf and tucking her slacks into the tops of fur-rimmed boots, exclaiming all the while about the cold, our bravery, and the wilderness.

We'd been shoveling snow for a month, stomping across snow-covered paths to the barn and the chicken house, building snowmen and romping with the children in the yard; we hadn't yet ventured onto the snow-covered fields. As we moved beyond the yard and began the long trek across the field toward the bush, the snow deepened, reaching almost to my knees. Every step was an effort, a lift-and-kick goose-step that introduced me to hip muscles I hadn't known about. We hadn't gone far when Mother spoke up. "I don't really think I'm up for this, Jack. I'll go back and make hot chocolate."

I wasn't sure I was, either, but as script-writer, director, and star performer, I took exception to Mother's departure. "Oh, sure you are. Don't desert us now!"

But she did, and within moments I longed to join her.

"Why isn't Grandma coming?" Erica turned in the sled, almost tipping it over. "I wanted Grandma to come along," she wailed.

"She'll be waiting for us when we get back." I tried to sound cheerful. "With hot chocolate."

Jack broke trail with the sled, followed by the dog, and I walked behind carrying the axe. I couldn't see Jack's face, only the hunch of his back and the slow lift-stomp, lift-stomp of his steps. Snow packed into my boot tops and melted down into my socks. The field stretched forever. An uninvited image of Christmas trees leaning against each other in a gas station parking lot flashed before my eyes.

Occasionally, with no warning, Robin shifted position in his cardboard box, the sled veered into the deep snow, and Erica screamed "Mommy! We're falling!" When that happened, I leaned over and righted the sled, repositioned the box, wiped the snow off the children's faces with my cold, damp mittens, and tried to keep Shastek from smothering them in sloppy kisses.

"Tismas tee tomorrow," whimpered Robin. "Cold." I leaned over to tighten his hood. Except for her shrieks of terror when the sled tipped, Erica was numbed into a sullen silence.

This had been my plan, a key scene in my Christmas pageant. One character had already left the stage. Now I began to have doubts about the main event: choosing and cutting the tree. In the years that followed, we learned to select and mark a Christmas tree before the first snowfall, but on this day, as we approached the bush, I noticed for the first time that only poplars and elms grew on the edge. The evergreens I could see from the house were much higher up the hill.

Jack dropped the sled rope and straightened his shoulders. Little icicles hung off his beard and mustache. "You and the kids wait here. I'll go up the hill a bit and look for a tree." I was too exhausted to protest. The reality of cold, wet feet and whimpering children had trumped my Laura-like image of family togetherness. Shastek followed Jack into the trees and out of sight.

We waited. I jumped up and down to warm my feet. Robin clung to my legs; Erica refused to get off the sled. We waited some more. A dog — could it be a wolf? — howled in the distance. Jack finally returned with a scrawny, lopsided balsam in tow.

I pulled the sled back across the field, retracing our steps on a partially-broken path. Jack took the lead again, this time pulling the tree behind him. A pitiful tree, I thought, a Christmas tree reject that would never have made it as far as the local gas station. For once, I kept my opinion to myself.

But that evening, looking at the scraggly tree, its coloured lights reflecting off the windows, gifts piled beneath — too many for a back-to-nature family — it really did feel like Christmas. Robin, in his blanket-sleepers, was running back and forth at full-speed between the tree and the kitchen door; Erica was picking through the packages, trying to find her name; Mother sat in the rocking chair, crocheting. Back on script.

• • •

"Alive!" Mother shrieked at the breakfast table two days later. "That's disgusting. Really, children" — she meant Jack and me, of course — "why can't you be like normal people and buy a nice turkey in the supermarket?"

But she put on her coat and boots and followed us to the car. This time there was no backing out. We drove half an hour on snow-packed back roads listening to Mother's exclamations about the absence of civilization and the folly of a live goose.

Of course, we didn't know a thing about geese, but we looked several over carefully, pretending to judge their suitability for Christmas dinner, before making a choice. I held the burlap bag open while Jack stuffed the bird in head-first, slung the loudly protesting bundle over his shoulder, and placed it in the back of the station wagon, where the honking continued, only slightly muffled by the burlap bag.

"It'll quiet down in a few minutes," Jack assured his mother as we drove away.

"Did you read that in one of your books, dear?" she asked. The goose continued to honk.

By the time we pulled into the driveway, any qualms I may have had about the bird's fate had vanished. Jack carried the wriggling bag toward the barn. I opened *Grow It!* to the section on poultry and was reading under my breath when Jack came into the kitchen holding the limp (and quiet) creature aloft.

Plucking was straightforward enough, although partway through the procedure I had second thoughts about doing it on the kitchen table. Next, I turned to the gutting instructions.

"First, slit the skin where the neck joins the body, being careful not to cut too deeply lest you slice open the crop." I paused. "This is for chickens. Are geese the same? What's the crop?" No one answered. Jack was wandering through kitchen, carrying a strangely-shaped parcel and chanting "ho, ho, ho!' Mother was in the play-room with the children, avoiding the goose-gutting procedure.

"Cut a small circle around the vent. Then cut down from the bottom of the circle toward the breast as far as the tail bone…insert your fingers and extract the intestines, gizzard, liver, kidneys, heart, and lungs…Remove the gall bladder from the liver…" Okay, then, here goes. My right hand gripped a sharp knife and hovered above the bird.

At that moment, Mother reappeared. She brushed a stray hair away from her face, along with several feathers, and spoke in practical tone I hadn't heard before. "I'll never forget the time the bridge club was coming for dinner and I brought home a fresh chicken. Never dreamed it hadn't been cleaned. I just put on some rubber gloves, stuck my hand inside, and pulled out everything that was loose. I'll never know what got left behind."

I didn't have rubber gloves.

I made one deep slice with the knife, reached my bare hand into the warm, squishy insides, moved my fingers gently from edge to edge, and pulled out everything that was loose. After several forays, I was pretty sure nothing was left behind.

Mother nodded in approval. "Now, just wrap it in cellophane, and we can pretend it came from the store."

"Like normal people?" I looked down at my bloodied hands.

"Well, that's pushing it." She was casting her eyes around the kitchen with its blood-stained table, feathers stuck to the floor, and down wafting through the air. Erica was playing with a goose foot, shrieking with delight at its clutching action when she pulled the loose tendon that dangled from the leg end. Robin was stomping feathers onto the floor with wet socks. Both cats were clamouring at the counters. Mother began to speak, and I prepared to defend myself.

"I've decided to write a story about this visit," she said. "None of my friends believes my children actually live like this."

There was nothing I could say.

• • •

That night, after mopping the kitchen floor, after Santa had done his work, after Jack was asleep, I lay awake for a long time, thinking about other Christmases. I remembered the time Dad gave Mom a cast-iron griddle, with a poem penned on ticker-tape that wound around the tree. I could still recite the silly words and see Dad's smile: "To the sweet little wife with the cute little middle, who mixes the batter and greases the griddle." Unenlightened, but somehow lovely. I would miss them tomorrow; we'd always been together for Christmas before. Then I remembered lying awake at Grammy and Pappy's house on Christmas Eve, charged with excitement, listening to the grown-ups moving around the house and wondering if I would get the 45 rpm record-player I wanted. (I did. It was beige and pink.) As I drifted off, I thought of Grammy Smith in her Christmas apron with the Christmas pin at her neck. She would have known what to do with the goose. My eyes were moist when they finally closed for the night.

After the Christmas morning flurry of stockings and gifts, after phoning my parents in Pennsylvania, I checked Irma Rombauer's *The Joy of Cooking* about how to cook a goose.

"Bring a large pot of water to a rapid boil. Protecting your hands with rubber gloves" — there we go again, rubber gloves. "Submerge the neck end of the goose in boiling water…Then submerge the tail end…refrigerate, uncovered, for 24 to 48 hours…essential for crispness." So much for crispness, then. I'd already missed that boat. I stuffed the bird with a simple bread stuffing, forgoing Rombauer's suggestions for apples, nuts, and dried fruit, and put it in to roast.

When it finally turned golden — though not crisp — and all the trimmings were ready, the five of us sat around the table for our first Christmas dinner on the farm. There was no sign, now, of feathers; I had arranged a festive table, the children were happy and scrubbed, and Jack was beaming as he, somewhat ineptly, carved the goose. Mother and I had both worn long wool skirts for the occasion; I felt both elegant and self-sufficient, a rare combination.

As I sat admiring the feast, mother shifted position in her chair and I caught just a glimpse of lavender-colored thermal-weave between her shoes and the hem of her skirt. She was, after all, still in the wild north.

• • •

The next day, I gathered all the wrapping paper together and shoved it into the furnace. Upstairs, a few minutes later, I heard a strange, whooshing sound.

"Has the wind come up?" I looked out the window; a few snowflakes drifted straight downwards. "What's that noise?"

"Dunno," said Jack. "Sounds like an engine." He opened the back door and stuck his head out. "Nothing on the road that I can see." He took a few more steps out onto the driveway. I stood at the door. The noise continued, like a loud wind.

"Something smells hot," I said. Before the words were out of my mouth, Jack was shouting.

"Fire! Fire! We have a fire in the chimney!" Outside, flames shot from the chimney, and embers dropped on the snow-covered roof. I dashed to the basement and opened the furnace door to find an inferno, fueled by scrunched up wrapping paper, the smiling Santas and festive ribbons totally consumed by flames.

"Call the fire department! Get the kids out!" shouted Jack.

I rushed up the basement steps, two at a time, nearly ripped the telephone off the kitchen wall, and frantically paged through the phone book.

The local fire chief answered. "Merry Christmas!"

"We have a fire. Dunnings'. The old White farm on Echo Lake Road."

"Right on it," he replied and hung up.

"Erica, Robin. Come here. Now." Somehow, they knew I wasn't kidding. I shoved them into jackets and boots and pushed them out the door.

Mother suddenly appeared out of nowhere in her navy jacket and scarf, carrying her purse. I'd forgotten about her. "I'll watch the children," she said, pursing her lips. "And you know, I really don't think it's wise to be heating with wood."

There were no longer flames coming from the chimney, but Jack, back inside now, was holding his hand against the wall in the kids' playroom, where the chimney passed from the basement on its way to the roof. "It's hot. Very hot."

Ten minutes later the township fire truck came into sight, sirens blaring.

"Fire truck! Fire truck!" shouted Robin, jumping up and down in the snow.

Erica wailed, "Is our house going to burn down? Where's my Giga?"

"The cat will be fine, Erica," I said. "Please be quiet and stay with Grandma."

Three local volunteers leapt out and ran toward the house, Shastek barking at their heels. Jack met them at the door. "It's a chimney fire. Under control now, I think," he explained, suddenly calm, man-to-man.

The firemen looked up at the chimney, where a wisp of black smoke rose into the cold afternoon air. Then they followed Jack to the basement and looked in the furnace. I brought up the rear. Ashy bits of burned paper smoldered on the floor of the firebox and floated upwards on the draft.

"Burned your Christmas wrapping paper, did you?" asked the tall one, not really needing or expecting a response.

They walked through the house sniffing, feeling the walls and saying, "Smells hot. Yup, sure smells hot."

"Well folks, welcome to the neighbourhood," said the Fire Chief, a stocky man with a friendly smile. "It looks like you had your first chimney fire. A little chimney fire now and then helps keep your chimney cleaned out. You enjoy the rest of the holidays, now."

Before the door had closed behind them, the phone rang.

"Paula, it's Irene. I saw the fire trucks. Everything all right there?" I assured her it was, and before I took my hand off the receiver, it rang again.

"This is Nelson. You folks have a fire? What'd you do? Burn your wrapping paper?"

That's when I heard the clicks as other members on the party line picked up their phones. Might as well fess up and reassure everyone at once.

"Yes, that's what we did. But everything's fine. Thanks for checking."

Chapter 8 • Spring Fever

It's the last day of April 2014, and I'm watching the ice from Echo Lake float downstream, dissolving as it moves forward in the steady current, the river swollen with spring runoff. There's an urgency to the current; spring is not a time to drift backwards. Some years, like this one, the ice cover breaks up and floats away, losing volume as it goes, breaking into glass-like shards that melt on contact when they bump against stumps and docks; the ice will be gone before the Echo River joins the bigger waters of the St. Mary's River. Other years it stays on the lake, three miles upstream, becoming softer and softer, heavier and heavier, until one day it sinks. Either way, says Gloria, it's always the very end of April. And so it is again this year.

I fix my eyes on an ice floe, slowly dissolving and changing shape as it moves forward on the current, and wonder how far it will go before it disappears altogether.

• • •

Fred White's doctors said staying on the farm would kill him, but I was sure—am still sure—it was leaving the farm that did it. He'd stopped coming by the house before that first Christmas. In February, he died. His memory haunted me; he'd loved this farm, and I felt somehow complicit in his death. We also lost both Shastek and Ranger that first winter. Ranger wandered away and never returned; a neighbour found his frozen body in the bush. Shastek developed a serious eye condition that required medication several times a day, a treatment that would only delay the impending blindness. It was my decision; I'd be the one to do the medicating. I didn't want to lose her; but I didn't want to be tied to a medication schedule. For a dog. I drove to the vet with Shastek licking my neck from the back seat. I remembered her as a puppy, licking the baby Erica's face in the yard of our little Dundas house with Mrs. Swackhammer lecturing me over the fence just three years before. I remembered her on the camping trip in the bus, swimming in circles around me in some unnamed lake, almost drowning me in her attempt to herd me back to shore. In the end, I set sentiment aside in favour of practicality and returned home alone, the absence of her wet tongue a dry and silent rebuke.

• • •

On an ordinary morning in mid-March, Jack left in time to drop Erica at nursery school, and Robin and I headed to the barn to do chores. His purple jacket was zipped to the neck to keep out the damp wind, the once-fluffy fur trim of his hood was tied loosely under his chin, and straw-encrusted wool mitts hung by their strings, swinging with each step. I gripped his left hand in my right hand, lifting him slightly to keep his rubber boots from sinking into the mud. With every step, a crisp, frozen skin shattered into icy shards and gave way to the muck beneath.

Even on this damp, cloudy morning, the fresh air delivered a rush of energy. I smiled to myself and chanted the chore-chant under my breath: *It's not doing the chores that makes me downhearted, it's thinking about them and getting them started.* True. Time to get them started.

First, check on the goats. Eowyn already had two kids, elfin creatures, black like their mother with soft coats and floppy, velvety ears. They danced and frolicked and answered their mother's strangely mournful bleating with warbling treble replies. Pippin, Eowyn's daughter, had failed to become pregnant during the two weeks the does had spent with a billy goat in the fall, but Gloin was due any day. I opened her stall and slipped in while Robin climbed onto the bottom rung to peer over. Her udder was swollen and hard—normal for animals approaching delivery. I lifted her stubby tail, looking for the tell-tale discharge that would tell me the birth was imminent; she tried to circle away to avoid this intrusion into her personal space. Nothing yet.

"No more baby goats today, Robin," I said as I lifted him into a "playhouse" constructed from a dozen hay bales in the middle of the thrash floor. "Stay here. I'm going up to feed the cows." This always felt irresponsible. He was, after all, only two, and from the haymow, I couldn't respond quickly to an emergency. But I couldn't take him with me, either, and if I was quick I could be back down before he escaped his little cage.

Looking down from the haymow into the cattle area behind the barn, I saw Mama Cow, with her bulging pregnant belly, and Guernsey-Girl, but no B-fub. Back on the ground, I found B-fub beside the barn, her head down and a trail of bloody mucous hanging from her tail end. She was nuzzling a calf lying in the mud. The calf pushed its upper body and straightened its front legs, but its back legs couldn't get enough purchase in the soft mud, and it collapsed again onto the ground.

Our first calf. In trouble. On my watch.

I wrapped my arms under the calf's belly and pulled it onto all fours. By taking much of its weight, I managed to slowly walk it into the barn. B-fub followed, mooing anxiously, a sucking sound erupting from around each hoof as she lifted it from the muck. I put both mother and calf into an empty stall, gave B-fub hay and water, and held Robin up so he could see.

"He's trying to stand, see?" It was a bull calf. "And his mommy is helping him." She was trying. She butted the calf gently, but he was too weak to stand. He must have exhausted himself trying to get up in the mud. I went into the stall and tried to lift him to the udder, but he turned his head away and refused to suck. His rough, damp tongue curled around my fingers in his mouth; he began to suck hungrily, and with surprising power, but when I tried to transfer that sucking action to his mother's teat, he fell limply to the ground.

I couldn't call Jack; he'd be teaching all morning. I had to leave in a few hours to pick Erica up from nursery school. How long could this wait?

"Let's go see Gloria," I said to Robin.

The mud in Trotters' laneway was almost as deep as in our barnyard. I could hear it spatter against the bottom of the car as I kept the wheels turning in the ruts. I wondered, was spring always like this?

Gloria, dressed in barn overalls, was bent over a sheet of paper on the kitchen table. She waved me in. The enamel sink was full of dishes. Heat radiated from the oil heater beside the stove, melting the frost that still formed a rim around the single-pane window.

"The kettle's already on. Let's get your boots off, Robin, and you can play in the front room with Stacey. Isn't this mud something?"

She bent over and started unbundling Robin, shaking her head when I said, "We really can't stay."

"Just for a cup of tea, surely you can." She took the simmering kettle off the top of the propane heater, put two teabags in a brown teapot, and poured boiling water over them. I told her about the calf while she took teacups from the cupboard and put milk and sugar on the table.

"What have you tried?"

"I got him sucking my fingers, like the book says, and then tried to move him to the udder. But he just collapsed. He's too weak to stand on his own. He just goes limp. I'm afraid he'll die."

She shook her head. "Okay. I'll come help you in a few minutes. But first, take a look at this." The letter was on school board letterhead, and began "Dear Parents." I couldn't read much farther before Gloria started talking, but I could see the words "sex education" and I was pretty sure I knew what was coming.

"It's just not right," she said. "They shouldn't be teaching that at school. It just gives them ideas."

Dangerous ground, here. I added a spoonful of sugar and blew gently on the hot tea before taking a sip.

"They have the ideas anyway," I said. "Lots of parents don't talk to their kids. If they don't learn about it in school, they'll learn about it from their friends. And then they'll think they know, but what will they know, really?"

Gloria drew her lips together and shook her head. "Well." *Whale.* "That depends on the kind of friends they have. Let the kids spend some time on the farm. That'll teach 'em the facts of life."

I wanted to say that most kids didn't live on farms, lots of them never set foot on a farm, and — just possibly — what you learned in the barn wasn't what young people needed to know. But Gloria knew what she thought, and she wasn't likely to change her mind.

"They should be teaching them good, old-fashioned morals. Then there'd be no need for the other. Why does a fourteen-year-old need to learn about contraceptives anyway?"

I swirled the last inch of tea around in my cup. I wouldn't be changing my mind, either. And this wasn't why I was here.

"About the calf, Gloria?"

We bundled the two children into their coats and boots, Gloria pulled on her black rubber barn boots, and we headed out to the cars.

In the barn, I straddled the back of the calf, holding him on his feet, while Gloria knelt beside B-fub. She put the three middle fingers of her left hand in the calf's mouth and moved them gently until he was sucking vigorously, using her right hand to gradually led the calf's mouth toward his mother's stiff teat. She swiftly transferred the sucking mouth from fingers to teat, but the calf turned his head away, just as he had for me. After two more tries, he finally grasped the teat and took several strong sucks before dropping back to the ground.

I lifted him up again, and Gloria went through the process once more. This time the calf butted his head into his mother's udder. "A good sign," said Gloria. After several seconds of sucking, he pulled his milky mouth away from his mother, then butted her again and took all his own weight on his legs.

"We've got 'im now," said Gloria.

As we left the barn, I started to thank her.

"No thanks needed, Paula. That's what neighbours are for." She smiled. "You'll be a farmer yet."

• • •

When I was growing up in central Pennsylvania, we didn't know any farmers. Our back yard in the small town of Lemont abutted a mountain-side expanse of grass and weeds, where we flew kites, played Frisbee, and took walks to an old family cemetery at the top of the hill. "Forrest Evie's field" we called it, after the farmer who owned it and whose family was buried in the cemetery; but I don't remember any farming happening there.

We weren't totally isolated from the world of agriculture, though. Every September, Mom drove into the country and brought home bushels of fruit and vegetables to can and freeze. The local dairy delivered milk to our back door in glass bottles featuring a cartoon picture of a cow whose swollen udder was surrounded by angry red lines. Under this poor cow were the words, "If you folks don't return all empties, I'll bust!" — providing an elementary lesson in the supply side of dairy farming. And Dad had a small vegetable garden in the back yard where he grew onions, lettuce, carrots, and beans; whenever I sang "This is My Father's World" in Sunday school, I envisaged Dad in the garden

110

with a hoe, wearing his funny straw hat. *This is my Father's world, and to my listening ears, all nature sings and 'round me rings the music of the spheres.*

In my high school, the Future Farmers of America, a cohort of boys (all boys) wearing dungarees and flannel shirts, barely touched the edge of my consciousness. I didn't know who they were, what they did, or if they were actually destined to till the land.

At eighteen, in my emerging view of the world, farming was either an occupation for those who could do no better, or a wholesome, largely imaginary, escape from modernity to the virtues of rural simplicity. At twenty-eight I was farming, and when the ice finally melted in the spring of 1973, I was already entangled in the web of contradictions that reality weaves around stereotypes and fantasies: Gloria was smart in ways I would never be; there was nothing simple about rural simplicity; and Laura didn't know it all.

• • •

April in northern Ontario is the ugliest month of the year. After the snow but before the green, when rhubarb, chives, and the occasional crocus poking out of barely-thawed clumps of mud are the only signs of colour in a damp, brown and grey landscape. By May, the swallows have returned, the hill has turned limey-green, and the dandelions are blooming in the yard. The honeysuckle bushes are drenched in pink blossoms, the lilacs are budding out, trout lilies open their freckled faces to the sun, and the peepers sing their evening song.

I eyed my new, blue rototiller longingly, but we had to wait another week, at least. Even though the ridges on the plowed field crumbled at the touch, the soil in the furrows still clung to the bottoms of our boots.

111

Morley warned us, "You drive the tractor on that field now, you'll be stuck and I'll have to come up and pull you out. Might look dry on the surface, but don't you believe it. We don't plant here 'til Victoria Day weekend." End of May. "That goes for the gardens, too," he added, looking at me.

And then it rained for two days.

The Saturday before the Victoria Day holiday, our chore list included mowing the lawn, putting up the screen windows, and cleaning the chicken house. We decided to go to a farm auction instead, to look for a manure spreader.

When we arrived, the bidding was already under way. A crowd of a hundred or so stood in an open area, near a barn surrounded by furniture, boxes of hardware, kitchen utensils, and farm implements. Several small children were playing tag, darting among the bidders. Groups of friends sat on the grass and visited. To one side, women in polyester pants and colourful blouses sold ham-and-cheese or egg salad sandwiches, brownies, cookies, coffee, and lemonade from long tables covered with flowered oilcloth.

Charlie the auctioneer, a short, compact man of fifty dressed in a plaid, button-up shirt tucked into ironed blue jeans, with a string tie at his neck, cast his spell over the crowd.

"And what-am-I-bid-for-this-fine-wheelbarrow? Do I hear thirty dollars? Thirty dollars?" Someone in the crowd called out a bid. "Ten dollars, I-hear-ten-dollars, just ten. Do I hear fifteen? Just fifteen dollars for this wheelbarrow. Get-your-potatoes-to-the-cellar-in-record-time, I have ten." Then he spun to his left where someone had shouted out a number. "Twelve-fifty. I have twelve-fifty. Do I hear fifteen?" Patiently he milked the crowd. And finally, "Sold! For twenty dollars."

Charlie took a sip of water, pulled a handkerchief from his pocket to wipe his brow, and started again. "This here's a fine pig trough. Your little porkers'll thank you for this first-class dinner plate. Do I hear fifteen dollars?"

112

I watched the performance and let the kids wander where they wanted. Erica stayed close at hand. Robin was running after several older children, not quite able to catch up. On a whim, I bid on, and got, a table-top cream separator and a dozen elegant, fine-stemmed wine glasses. Erica bid on a set of water colours; nobody bid against her: fifty cents. I captured Robin long enough to let him bid on a beach ball, which he got for a quarter.

Jack wandered toward the barn to size up the farm implements. I saw him walk past a baler, a set of discs, a seed drill. We had all of those. No manure spreader. He began talking with a very tall man with a short blond beard; a second man approached them, a little shorter, wearing a ball cap and sporting a longer, dark beard. I took Robin's hand and walked over to join them, with Erica close behind.

"Hi," said the tall man. "I'm Bill. This is Gerry. You must be Paula. Seems we're almost neighbours." He glanced toward the crowd where two women, each one carrying an infant, were heading our way with three small children in tow. "Here come Sheila and Carol."

Sheila reached us first and handed the baby to Bill. She was slight with long, reddish-blonde hair pulled into a ponytail — much like my own — at the nape of her neck, and a cheerful, freckled face. She wore horned-rimmed glasses and a cotton madras blouse over jeans. Carol's baby was snug against her chest in a soft corduroy pack that hung over her shoulders. Her brown hair hung below her ears in two ponytails, accentuating twinkling eyes behind cats-eye glasses. She gave me a wide, open-mouthed smile.

"This one's ours," said Carol nodding to a two-year old girl who had rushed to stand close to Gerry. "The other two are Bill and Sheila's." A two-year-old blond boy and a thin, somewhat older girl with dark bangs that almost covered her eyes looked shyly toward us.

Robin started running at Sheila's two, throwing the beach ball at their heads. They turned away and clung to their parents, so he started running at Erica, who swatted at him. Robin wailed, and I looked pleadingly at Jack, who pulled him back while we continued to chat.

Both families lived on farms in Sylvan Valley. Bill and Sheila had been on their farm for several years; they had a herd of beef cattle, one milk cow, a flock of chickens, and a horse. Bill taught math at a high school in the Sault. Sheila and Carol, who had been friends growing up in southern Ontario, had both taught high school English until their first children arrived. Gerry had recently completed his Ph.D. in geophysics in Vancouver, but couldn't find work in his field, so he and Carol had decided to buy a farm and settle into rural life. He was working as a jail guard to make ends meet. They had goats in the barn, chickens in the henhouse, and a big garden.

"We'll be heading home soon," said Sheila. "Why don't you come back to the house with us? Carol and Gerry are coming, too."

Their white bungalow sat in a low spot in front of a fenced barnyard, with a huge willow tree in the side yard and a vegetable garden, plowed but not yet planted, in front. A dozen cows with their calves grazed in an adjacent field. When we pulled into the driveway, the three children were stomping through mud puddles in rubber boots. Erica shyly joined them, hesitant to get her shoes wet. Robin jumped in a puddle with his sneakers, laughing and splashing higher and farther than anyone else. At two, he was bigger than the three-year-olds. I turned my back on him and hoped for the best.

Inside, the house was in a state of partial completion with varnished plywood floors, doorless bedrooms, mismatched kitchen cupboards, and floor-to-ceiling bookshelves crammed to overflowing. Bill and Gerry sat at a large dining room table with mugs of tea. Sheila and Carol were leaning against the kitchen counter, keeping one eye on the kids outside. They handed me a cup of tea and gestured to a cookie sheet covered with chocolate-chip cookies.

"Dig in before the kids get here," said Sheila. "And welcome to the valley. We'll have to introduce you to the rest of the valley folks real soon." She listed half a dozen families she figured we should know and I felt lighter than I'd felt for months. Indeed, there was a path that ran between the old-time farmers and the world of manure-in-a-bag, and we were not the only ones treading it.

CHAPTER 9 • THINKING LIKE A COW, FARMING BY THE BOOK

I thought I'd met most of the neighbours, but I didn't recognize the soft-spoken man in his fifties who doffed his baseball cap and greeted me with a handshake. "I'm Earl Martin—on the farm down past Gamble's corner. I hear you folks might have some pasture to rent out."

Earl was buying a truckload of cattle from Alberta. Local farmers often bought steers from western ranches, pastured them for the summer, and shipped them to feedlots for finishing in the fall, a perfect use of the region's marginal farmland. But Earl didn't have enough pasture for the full load. Would we be interested in having some of his cattle graze our land for a rental fee?

Why not? Our one horse, three cows, two calves, and three goats couldn't possibly eat enough to keep down the pastureland which, we'd discovered, included ten acres of grazing land partway up the hill with a stream running down one side and clumps of birch, poplar, pine, and spruce scattered throughout: The Rocky Pasture.

A few days later, a transport truck backed into the barnyard. Robin rushed to the door. "Truck. Big truck." Jack and I met the truck in the barnyard. Erica's job was to keep Robin on the house side of the fence.

The smell of diesel fuel and the sound of bawling cattle filled the air. Jack stood off to one side, I stood off to the other as fourteen reddish-brown, year-old steers stampeded down the ramp. They hit the ground with back heels kicking up and heads butting one another, pushing and stumbling in all directions. I tried to di-

116

rect them away from the road while Jack managed the gate. But these animals were not B-fub and Mama Cow, who lumbered docilely from pasture to barn and back again. Before Jack could close the gate behind the departing truck, the steers careened out onto the road, I heard Erica scream and turned toward the yard just in time to see Robin squeezing through the gate into the barnyard. Erica was tugging at his arm and shouting "Mommy! Mommy! I can't hold him." Well, no. He was nearly as big, easily as strong, and twice as determined as she was.

Jack needed help rounding up the escaped animals, who were now running along the road. I had no idea where they'd run next and couldn't risk having them stampede the children. Jack tore around frantically, trying to get them into a tight group. I dashed to the gate, picked up Robin, carried him to the back door, and said to Erica. "Take him in. Don't come outside until I'm back. You're going to have to be in charge of Robin." She was four; he was two.

By the time I got back to the cattle, they had discovered the narrow stretch of grass between the road and the river and had settled down to graze. Some of them stood with their front feet in the river, drinking. Maybe this wouldn't be so hard.

I trotted down the driveway to the road, which placed me on one side of the cattle with Jack on the other side, two hundred yards away, and the gate between us. If we both walked toward them from opposite directions, they would have to go through. Yes. This was working. As I neared them from one direction and Jack from the other, they began shifting and moving slowly. But suddenly, as Jack got closer, they panicked and took off in my direction. Terrified, I leapt aside.

"What the hell!" Jack yelled at me. "Why'd you let them go?"

"Why'd you spook them?" I shouted back.

Now we would have to get to the other side of them and move them back again. The kids were alone in the house. If I checked on the kids, the cows would go farther afield. If I didn't... My heart pounded. Just get it done.

We both ran as fast as we could, but not fast enough. The steers charged past the driveway and turned into the yard, poking holes and throwing clumps of sod off their feet, and then back onto the road, farther and farther from the barnyard. I tried to keep running, but every breath tore at my lungs.

A car was coming down the road, moving toward the cattle. Now what would they do? The car stopped and a man got out. Morley. He moved slowly from side to side in front of the cows, facing them down until the ones closest to him turned around, prompting the others to do the same, and within a moment all fourteen were heading in the right direction.

"Paula! Get out of the way!" He shouted, but somehow his voice was calm. I was standing off to one side; I didn't think I was in the way. But I backed off further. Then Morley began a slow chant, "Move along, move along now, hey boss, hey boss, keep moving." He was walking in a wide arc behind them. Raising his voice briefly, he called out, "You want them in the barnyard?"

"Yes," shouted Jack from the other side of the herd. His voice was not calm.

"Paula, walk along beside them, to the front of the herd. Keep your arms out. *Don't run.* Jack, you walk past the gate and stand in the middle of the road." He spoke to us in the same sing-song voice, and continued chanting to the steers. "Move along, now, move along."

And they did. The steers were walking along the road in a compact group. Occasionally, the lead animals began to turn toward the open fields but saw me and kept to the road. When they were almost at the barnyard gate, Morley shifted his arc slightly to the left, they turned slightly to the right, saw Jack on the road in front of them, and funneled through the gate into the barnyard.

"Amazing," said Jack. "How did you do that?"

118

"You just have to think like a cow," said Morley.

• • •

Two weeks later, Jack and I were stumbling through the bush, sweating, swearing, and out of breath. Knee-high maple saplings and tall grasses, wet from a morning downpour, brushed against our legs; our water-logged jeans dripped around our ankles, deadweights. Tree limbs slapped our faces and scratched our arms. Mosquitoes landed on and munched whatever exposed skin they could find. Black flies swarmed around our heads.

"Follow this fence line to the left, I'll go right," said Jack. "If they broke out along this stretch, it'll be easy enough to see."

I waved my arms around my head. "Damn bugs. I can't stand it."

Jack ignored my whining and continued talking. "If we haven't found them at that point, we'll have to go back through the rocky pasture and check the fence on the other side."

Jack had to be miserable, too. But he kept focused on the search. All I wanted was to be gone from here. One more hour, then I could go back to the house. The babysitter had to be home by five. Thank god, and to hell with the cows.

As if he were reading my mind, Jack said, "We have to find them, one way or another."

I shook my head, not in disagreement but in disbelief. What was I doing here, on a hot late May day in the forest of northern Ontario, fighting flying bloodsuckers and looking for a herd of lost cows?

The short answer: Earl's steers, along with our two cows and their calves, had been grazing in the rocky pasture. Only a couple of strands of barbed wire ran from tree to tree to separate the pasture from the bush, which stretched for miles. Not good enough. We hadn't seen them for three days, and we were worried.

The long answer…well, I was beginning to wonder, myself. I'd try to remember to check with Laura.

But there we were. Groping along in the bush, looking for hoof-prints in the mud, breaks in the flimsy barbed wire, cow-pies in the undergrowth. Nothing. We'd already checked with the nearest farms.

"Graham? It's Paula Dunning here. You haven't seen sign of a bunch of Herefords—cows and calves—have you? They've wandered off on us."

And a few minutes later.

"Hi Nelson. We're missing some cows. Have you seen any around?"

"No, but I think your goats were on the road this morning." No doubt, I thought. They're always out. But at least they're ours.

I didn't phone George. He still wasn't speaking to us.

How would we tell Earl we'd lost his steers? Or would someone else tell him? And what would we do? Was there a law about this? Would we have to pay him the value of the animals? The transgression assumed Biblical proportions: Thou shalt not lose thy neighbour's cows. In the end, we never told him. After five days of wandering in the bush, the steers and cows showed up on a field near the house with mud up to their haunches, burrs stuck to their tails, and no sign of repentance.

Jack did confess to Morley on the day he helped move the Trotters' cattle "over the mountain" from the Trotters' home farm to their second property on the other side of the valley. Every spring they drove their herd over the hill, through dense bush, to the pasture on the other side. After a few hours walking through the bush with Morley, helping to keep his forty animals moving in the right direction, Jack came home exhausted, sunburned, bug-bitten—and wiser. He threw his cap on the table, opened a beer, and leaned against the kitchen counter.

"It's not so hard, really. You have to learn to steer from behind, almost like you're the rudder and they're the boat." He was moving his free hand back and forth. "And you have to learn about their peripheral vision. They really spook easy. Morley said he wished we'd talked to him before taking Earl's cows. Those western steers are always hard to keep in, like a herd of teenagers without any parents around to discipline them, he says. Figures we'll have trouble all summer."

• • •

Finally, it was time to plant. Jack disked the field until it was flat and even, harrowed it into a fine seedbed, and planted a combination of oats and hay. "That's what folks do here," he said knowingly. The oats would come up first, a "cover crop" for the slower-germinating hayseeds.

While Jack planted the field, I tackled the vegetable garden. With our new rototiller, I worked up the White's old garden in the schoolhouse acre, a quarter mile from the house. The soil was rich and friable from years of gardening. I planted onions, lettuce, spinach, peas, beans, cabbage, broccoli, cauliflower, corn, squash, and — because Fred had — turnips. In the old schoolhouse foundation, Jack and I together prepared a bed for asparagus, hauling in sand from Morley's pit to mix with the heavy clay soil. The strawberries were doing fine on their own, already in blossom and setting tiny berries.

The tractor hummed back and forth on the nearby field, raising a fine cloud of dust. The hill, adorned in a mosaic of greens, presided over the late May day. The fresh yellowy-green leaves of the willow trees waved in the sunlight above me, casting black, dancing shadows on the brown earth. I breathed in the smell of spring, sat back on my haunches with a seed packet in hand, and basked in the miracle of here and now.

For the first few days, Erica and Robin skipped, danced, and ran the quarter mile from the house to the garden, helped put the seeds in the ground, and played under the big willow tree. But the euphoria didn't last. Within a week, Erica sulked when I insisted she come along, and I spent more time dragging Robin off the road than working in the garden. By the middle of June, I was grabbing an hour in the garden every now and then when Jack could take a turn with the kids.

The oats were coming up bluey-green, the grasses rippled in the breeze, and we turned our attention to haying. Even with Earl's cows munching down some of the grass, we had more than eighty acres to cut and bale. We'd both read the chapters in *Grow It!* on how to cut, rake, bale and store hay, and we were checking the fields regularly, watching for the exact moment to begin the process.

"When harvesting a combination of legumes and grasses, the time to do your cutting is when the legumes are ready...Red and alsike clover are best cut when in half-bloom..." There you had it. Our fields were mostly a combination of timothy grass and clover.

The haying equipment—mower, rake, baler, hay wagons, elevator—were lined up in the barnyard, ready to go. Morley came over one afternoon to help Jack locate all the grease nipples on the tractor and each piece of equipment and to warn him that the equipment had to be greased every day. Really. *Every day.* He showed him how to replace broken blades on the mower and put new rolls of twine into the baler. "Any problems, just holler," he said.

"I think we'll be fine," said Jack.

Every day, we walked through the field closest to the house, pushed aside the taller timothy, which now dwarfed the children as well as the clover, and crouched low to check on the density of pink and white clover flowers. Erica tagged along, practicing her counting. Jack showed her how to pull the timothy stalks carefully out of their sleeves so she could chew the sweet, white ends. I held tightly to Robin's hand so we wouldn't lose him in the tall grass, and he picked the buttercups that were sprinkled among the grass and clover.

The third week of June, Jack came bounding into the house. "It's ready! I'll cut tomorrow!" He spent the rest of that day fussing with the equipment and re-reading the book. The next morning he began cutting the small field, close to the house. That left me with the barn chores and the children—a fair trade, I thought. I was beginning to sense the emergence of a balance sheet.

Back in the kitchen after chores, I poured the morning's milk through a cheesecloth strainer into the broad, stainless steel bowl of the cream separator I'd bought at the auction. With its many cone-shaped, nesting cups with holes in the side that had to be arranged exactly right—"just so" as Grammy Smith would have said—it used centrifugal force to separate the cream from the milk. Cows' milk separates on its own; goats milk doesn't. I tried to imagine what was happening inside as I cranked the handle—at first slowly, then more and more rapidly, but always with the resistance of a bicycle in high gear—and watched the skimmed milk pour out one spout into a pitcher and the thick, white cream pour out the other into a bowl. My mechanical imagination failed me every time. Magic encased in metal.

The day was already hot, and it was only 9:30. I joined the kids to watch the tractor and mower moving across the field. The six-foot-long cutter-bar stretched out behind the tractor's right back tire. As its dozens of triangular teeth moved back and forth, the grass fell behind it in broad, flat windrows.

Robin crouched by the edge of the field, transfixed. He had already established himself as the vehicle expert in the family, delighting in identifying by sound what was coming down the road—a car, a school bus, a tractor, or a boat on the river—long before it came into sight. Now he watched the tractor and mower

123

making their rounds and called out excitedly each time they approached. "Here it comes! It's cutting! It's cutting!" Jack lifted his wide-brimmed, tan felt hat, waved, and grinned as he passed, looking alternately ahead and over his right shoulder to make sure he was on course and the equipment was working well.

Erica ventured farther from the house. She charged back and forth across the cut grass scaring up little clouds of butterflies and grasshoppers, followed by our new white puppy, Strider, an unlikely husky-poodle cross. And she had a job to do. Proudly, she carried a jug of juice and some cookies to Jack, who had stopped the tractor far enough from the house to make her trek worthwhile.

Jack came in for lunch jubilant, his cheeks already sunburned above his beard, bits of chaff clinging to his forehead and eyebrows. "It's looking really good. I'm more than half done. I think we'll have a fine crop." He took a bite of chicken sandwich and a gulp of milk.

"I'm surprised nobody else is out cutting," he said as he chewed. "The clover is just perfect. I suppose they're waiting for the hay to grow taller. But," he continued with a voice of authority born of careful research, "quality is more important than quantity in this business!"

I nodded, taking another bite of my own sandwich.

"Gloria said something about the full moon—the weather changing or something. Old wives tales, probably. Robin, stop making faces at Erica and eat your lunch!"

"The old ways aren't always best," said Jack. "It says right in the book that a lot of farmers wait too long."

The afternoon passed more slowly. In the thicker parts of the field, the mower's little triangular teeth kept clogging with grass and snapping off the cutter bar. Each break meant a delay while Jack attached a new blade with tiny rivets. At three o'clock, when all but a few rounds were cut, I heard the tractor stop and looked out the kitchen window to see Jack walking slowly across the field with something in his arms. I met him halfway; it was Strider.

"I didn't see him," said Jack, breathing heavily and looking close to tears. "He didn't see the mower, ran right in front of it. He's in pretty bad shape." Strider's front right leg dripped blood and hung limply from his body as Jack passed him over to me. "Can you get him to the vet? Erica can stay with me."

The afternoon had suddenly turned ominous. I thought of Erica's earlier, carefree dashes between the house and the tractor. Jack hadn't seen the dog. Had he always seen her? Had she always seen the mower blade? It rode low to the ground, invisible but deadly in the tall grass. And Robin—so hard to keep in sight. I glanced behind me; he was running into the field now.

"It's okay. I'll take both kids with me. You finish up here."

The vet set the broken leg, stitched up the gash, and sent us home with the dog's leg in a cast wrapped in a plastic bag. It took a month for the leg to heal. Longer than that for my nightmares to stop.

• • •

The next day, we watched the grass cure on the field, gradually turning from a dark, moist green to the paler shade of fresh, drying hay.

Morley stopped by. "I see you've got hay down," he said, tipping his hat and wiping his brow. "Early birds."

Jack started explaining about the clover half in bloom and the protein content of the hay, but Morley interrupted him. "I don't know much about your book, and I don't know where that guy lives. But here, we generally wait until July when the weather changes. You just make sure it's dry before you bale it."

"Oh, yeah, we know about that," said Jack. When he went into the house, I saw him checking the book again.

"Hay freshly cut is about 75 percent water. Curing brings the moisture level down to around 20 percent...The usual practice is to let the hay dry where it lies. Then it is raked into long windrows where it continues to dry, but more slowly...Hay stored too wet will ignite by spontaneous combustion, and you'll lose not only your crop, but barn and livestock as well."

On the second day, the cut hay was dry and crinkly, but still a bit moist underneath. Time to rake, and my turn on the tractor.

I drove around the field, bouncing over the uneven ground, the long tines of the hay rake rotating behind me, picking up the wide rows of flat grass, fluffing them into fragrant windrows, and exposing their damp undersides to the sun. Dozens of gulls followed, swooping down to capture the insects that flew up from the freshly turned hay, then rising again to glide on the air currents created by the tractor. Despite the throbbing of the engine and the occasional clang from the rake, I lapsed into a reverie that bordered on the hypnotic.

As the tractor, the gulls, and I moved together on our maiden passage across that field, I thought of Bill Barkley, the man who had cleared this land only half a century ago. According to local folklore, he had cut trees by night, farmed by day, and drowned himself in the river when he felt his work was done. Even in the first month of my first summer on the farm, I couldn't imagine feeling that all the work was done. The facts tell a different story. We learned much later from some of his descendants that Mr. Barkley suffered from a fainting disorder; one of his seven children was always assigned to stay with him. On the day of his drowning, the assigned child had left Barkley's side when he was working beside the river; he fainted, fell in, and drowned.

And I thought of Fred White. When we signed the final papers in the lawyer's office, he warned us: "I worked that land for thirty years; if you don't keep on top of it, it'll grow back to bush." He must have had his doubts about us, but he never let on. Now he, too, was gone. I wondered what he'd be thinking now. Were we getting it right?

Over the next two days, Jack and I walked over the cut field every few hours, kicking at the drying windrows, picking up handfuls of the slowly curing grass and bending it in half to determine if it had achieved the exact level of dryness it needed before baling.

"What do you think?" asked Jack, handing me the latest clump, still warm from the sun.

I didn't know. I looked once again at the book: "Pick up a handful and make a bundle of it so the stems are parallel. Wring out the hay as you would a wet cloth, then bend it into a U. If your bundle is rather wilted-looking and breaks too easily…it's still too wet. If it's pliable, like a piece of rope…it's just right. If it's crisp like celery…it's too dry."

I guess so," I said without conviction. How easily is too easily? How pliable is rope? How crisp is celery? I didn't want the responsibility of a wrong decision. I turned back to the written page for comfort. The next paragraph began, "You'll get the feel of hay by talking with your neighbor farmers and checking out their crops."

"Maybe you should ask Morley?"

"Damnit, I'd like to do something on my own! I think it's ready. I'm hooking up the baler." Good. It was his decision, then.

At four o'clock that afternoon I stood, exhausted, on the flat hay wagon, picking up the 50-pound bales by the strings as they came out of the baler and passing them to Jack, who stacked them four or five tiers high. The strings dug painfully into my fingers, but there was no stopping the hay's relentless journey from field to baler to wagon. It was the second wagonload of the day. Jody, the young teen from next door, was driving the tractor. Robin sat on the bottom tier, watching the bales come shooting out, chanting "One…two…five…" Erica played on the field, far away from the moving equipment, or rode on the wagon, jumping from place to place as her seat became the spot for the next bale of hay. Strider, with his plastic-wrapped leg, watched from the yard. Except for the breeze created by the slowly moving tractor, the air hung heavy and humid under a hot sun.

The baler scooped the windrows of hay off the field and fed them through a square chamber, where moving arms packed the dry grass into a tight bale, passed it through a twine feeder and knotter, and ejected the finished bale out the other end. More magic encased in metal.

Once the load on the wagon reached five tiers—about 100 bales—we made our way back to the barn. There, Jody and I unloaded the bales from the wagon, one by one, onto a motorized elevator that carried them to an opening near the top of the barn and dropped them into the haymow, where Jack stacked them tightly against one another, the heaviest, hottest job of all. Then back to the field for another load. My hands ached, and chaff clung to every sweaty surface of my body, working its way into my socks, down the neck of my t-shirt, and under the waistband of my jeans. Lurching along on the wagon, stacking our last load as the sun inched lower in the sky, I felt dampness on the edge of a bale.

"Jack!" He looked down from the top of the load, could barely hear me over the noise of the tractor. I shouted louder. "I think it's wet."

He shook his head in annoyance. Things were moving along, almost done.

"You can keep baling if you want, but I'm taking a bale down to Morley."

Jack shrugged, and his eyebrows came together in a frown. He didn't want to rely on Morley for this. He didn't want to be wrong.

I found Morley along the road, crouched beside a fencepost, tightening a strand of barbed wire. When I slowed down, he stood up, pushed his cap back off his forehead, and waved.

"Can you take a look at this hay for me?" I asked.

He ambled over to the back of the truck and stuck his bare arm deep into the bale.

"What are you doing with that stuff, Paula?" He was suddenly animated, nearly shouting. "Not putting it in the barn, I hope."

I nodded, biting my lower lip in embarrassment.

"Well, get it out! You're going to burn your barn down!"

And so, we unloaded the hay that was on the wagon, left it lying where it fell on the field, and drove the empty wagon to the barn. We threw the neatly stacked bales out of the haymow, back onto the wagon, drove them back to the field, and leaned them up against each other, two by two—little teepees announcing to the world that our textbook methods weren't paying off very well. By the time we were finished, heavy clouds darkened the evening sky.

The next day it rained.

Somehow, we limped through the rest of that first summer. Jack taught a morning class at the college and arrived home by early afternoon to face a day on the hayfield. I did most of the chores, cooked meals, helped on the field, kept the children safe from moving equipment, and struggled to keep up with the garden, which had moved clearly onto my side of the ledger.

By the end of June, I had thirty bags of strawberries in the freezer and a shelf full of strawberry jam. By early July, when the peas were ready to pick, the garden was overgrown with weeds, but the peas were plentiful; I put twenty-one bags in the freezer. But the beans ripened in the middle of haying, and I missed most of them. The tomatoes and broccoli were fighting the weeds; the carrots had already lost the battle.

I tried to feel the intimacy of growing and putting down my own food, the satisfaction of self-sufficiency. That's why I was here. "Enjoy the fruits of your labors. The world will be a better place for them" said *Grow It*. The words "frazzled" and "overwhelmed" appeared nowhere in the index.

I complained to Gloria about the garden one day when I was at her house to borrow a tube of grease for the tractor. We didn't have much time to visit these days. Her own garden was lush with produce. She was pouring pickling solution into quart-sized jars packed with green beans and dill. The sharp smell of hot vinegar stung my nostrils. "I don't know how you do it," I said.

"A little bit every day," she said. "I don't think I could manage your garden either." Her back was to me as she lifted jar lids out of a pan of boiling water with a pair of tongs and carefully positioned them atop the jars. She took another minute to screw the tops on, then wiped her hands on a towel and turned around.

"Fred did the vegetable garden on your farm, not Gertie. So it didn't matter how far it was from the house. Just because he used that acre for a garden doesn't mean you have to. Why don't you turn some of the field by the house into a garden?"

I thought of the strawberry patch, the asparagus we'd just planted, the soil that had worked up so nicely in the spring. Then I pictured walking out the back door into the garden to pick beans for supper or to weed the tomatoes while the kids played in the sandbox or napped or rode tricycles in the yard. Gloria was right. As usual.

• • •

By the second week in August, the barns were full of hay, the oats in the small field were looking good, and Jack turned his attention to his still-pending Ph.D. He made arrangements to spend the last week of August back at McMaster in Hamilton, putting the final touches on his thesis. He phoned me from a friend's house several days after he arrived. "Not looking so good," he said. "Jenkins is giving me a hard time." Jenkins, Jack's advisor, had never approved of Jack's decision to take a job — especially at a second-rate institution — before having his Ph.D. in hand. His own reputation was at stake; he wanted his grad students placed in prestigious institutions, and he'd had high hopes for Jack.

The next time he called, I could hear the anger in his voice. "He wants me to spend all next summer here to finish up. I won't do it." There was a pause. "Who would take care of the farm?"

Jack came home at the end of the week with a waning commitment to his Ph.D. and a purebred Nubian billy-goat in the back of the car. Still into fantasy, we named him Bombadil.

Chapter 10 • Rural Sisterhood

I stood back and looked at the painting above the sofa, a landscape of rocks, trees and water. Safe. Very safe. Much better than the Rubenesque nude that had hung there just moments before. She was now tucked behind the closet door where none of the ladies could see her. Next, my eyes fell on the children's gerbils in their elaborate series of glass cages under the bay window. A distinctly rodent smell emanated from that side of the room. Where could they go?

It was my turn to host the Women's Institute. Since my first introduction to the WI a year ago, I'd learned that the local group was a chapter of the Federated Women's Institutes of Ontario. Although the parent group had a mandate to promote and advocate rural community interests and values, the ladies of Echo River made short work of organizational formalities. It was really all about the visiting, the tea, the sandwiches, and the date squares.

Not that these ladies set aside their values. Not at all. Except for Elsa Jones, who continued to embarrass the other members with her off-colour jokes and references to bodily functions, they proudly represented the rural values of cleanliness, order, and propriety. The gerbils were in violation of the first; the nude of the third.

I disconnected the plastic tubes that let the gerbils run from one cage to another, trapped the confused family of rodents in one small compartment, carried them upstairs to Robin's bedroom, and closed the door. Back in the living room, I removed the other two cages, scrubbed the floor with Pinesol, and moved a couple of chairs from the kitchen table to fill the empty spot under the windows. Then I stood back to gauge the effect. Not bad, really. Tidy.

Clean on the surface. No fuel for neighbourhood gossip. I'd have all afternoon to clean up the kitchen and prepare the sandwiches.

I left the gerbils and the nude to make my quick trip to town to pick up Robin from nursery school. Two days a week, he left early with Jack. After Erica climbed on the big yellow school bus at the end of the driveway, on her way to kindergarten, those two mornings were my own.

Robin and I arrived home just in time to watch Erica slide down from the high front seat of a bright red tow truck with a snowplow on the front, landing hard with both feet on the driveway. She waved to the driver. "See you later, alligator!" she screamed. "After while, crocodile!" he called back, and waved as he backed out of the driveway. Erica was the only kindergarten student on our road; the school board didn't want to run a bus three miles along the river and back for one child, so they contracted with the owner of the local service station to drive her home at noon.

She galloped toward us, waving a small brown rectangle in the air. "I counted to one hundred today! I won a chocolate bar!"

"Good for you," I said, pleased and dubious at the same time: should five-year-olds be rewarded with chocolate bars for counting to a hundred? There were lots of things happening in kindergarten I was dubious about. Erica's teacher, petite and proper Miss Allen, whose tweed skirts always touched her knees, was an evangelical Christian who didn't hesitate to share her beliefs with the class, a practice still tolerated in northern Ontario in 1974. Erica was bringing home colouring book pages with illustrations from Bible stories, neatly coloured in. She didn't pay much attention to the stories, but she was proud of her colouring skill.

"I'm good at staying in the lines. Miss Allen says."

Staying in the lines, standing in lines, toeing the line. Erica was a school-system kid. I looked from her to her little brother, who was doing his best to open the barnyard gate.

•••

At seven thirty, ten women, aged 28 to 75, stood erect beside their chairs in my living room, chanting in unison: "Keep us, O Lord, from pettiness; let us be large in thought, in word, in deed..." I chanted along, wondering whether it was pettiness that made my eyes keep returning to Elsa's lavishly coloured polyester blouse stretched tautly over her large bosom, the bottom buttons gaping open over the top of her short orange skirt.

We moved quickly from the prayer to the roll call, this time a school memory. Many of the ladies had gone to school in the old schoolhouse on our property. They were enjoying this exchange of memories from several decades ago when Gloria called my name: "Mrs. Jack Dunning."

I did have a school memory in mind. But first, I had already decided; this time I would take a stand. "I'm here, but I'd rather be recorded as Paula Dunning."

The room fell silent.

"Well," said the older Mrs. Gordon, one of the founding members who rarely spoke, "We've been doing it this way since we first began. I can't see changing it now,"

Her daughter-in-law, Helen, nodded her tight curls in agreement.

Mrs. Trotter, Morley's mother, never minced words: "I've been Mrs. Cecil Trotter for forty years, and I'll be Mrs. Cecil Trotter until I die. I'm certainly not changing *my* name." She slapped her hand on the arm of her chair.

Gloria looked at me quizzically and said nothing. I couldn't tell what she was thinking.

"I just thought...well, it's actually not my name. It's Jack's."

My next-door neighbour, Irene—Mrs. Lorne Smith—had a twinkle in her eye. "I don't see that it matters how Paula wants her name recorded," she said. "They don't all have to be the same." There was a prickly silence, then heads nodded reluctantly. And so it was. But I decided not to mention my discomfort with "God Save The Queen" when Canada had a perfectly fine anthem of its own. And I never did share my memory from second grade, which involved a red corduroy jumper and pretending I was Sergeant Preston of the Royal Canadian Mounted Police.

We moved on to "Pennies for Friendship", each member depositing a small handful of pennies into a jar for charity, and then made quick work of the usual motions to approve the minutes (unanimous) and the financial report ($34.12 in the bank; unanimous), accept the correspondence (unanimous), business arising (none), new business (none), and adjournment (unanimous).

Gloria came into the kitchen to help me serve the salmon sandwiches and pickles.

"I didn't want to make a fuss," I said to her as we placed the sandwich plate on a tray along with a mismatched stack of small plates and paper napkins. "We all use first names in the meeting, all except Morley's mother and the older Mrs. Gordon."

Gloria gave me a serious — was it reproachful? — look. "Well, the ladies don't like change," she said as she took the plate of salmon sandwiches into the living room. Yes, it would be better not to mention "God Save the Queen" just yet.

• • •

As our second winter on the farm closed in on us, we were juggling several identities. The college community played a big role in Jack's life, of course, but a much smaller role in mine. We occasionally attended college events together, and we developed a few friendships among Jack's colleagues, but we had established ourselves as outliers and didn't become part of the faculty social network.

After our first season of farming, most of the families in our own little valley accepted us as somewhat quirky neighbours who were serious about learning to farm. Except for Gloria and Morley, they didn't become close friends, but they became friendly neighbours who shared information, advice, and occasional cups of coffee, sent their kids to play with ours, waved from their cars or stopped to chat on the road, and sometimes called to tell us our cows were out. I felt I'd arrived when the Women's Institute bought into some of my own fantasies of rural life, agreeing to sponsor a Christmas sleigh ride and a summertime community picnic.

At the same time, we were beginning to realize that young people with a variety of non-traditional agendas were scattered across the sparsely populated and rugged area east of Sault Ste. Marie.

Some, like Jeff and Jane with their cow, proudly displayed their counter-culture credentials. They wore flowing skirts and tiny rimless glasses, chose to live on the edge of poverty, and named their children Cloud or Sky or Ché. I envied these purists their apparent clarity of purpose. They were, I thought, truer to their convictions than I was. Surely Jane would not have rearranged the art on her walls for the Women's Institute.

Closer to my own comfort zone were the friends I was making in Sylvan Valley, broader and more populous than the Echo River Valley and home to a core of young "newcomers". These families combined professional lives with farming and a commitment to rural life. They mingled with the community, joined committees, organized Brownies, and built close friendships with some of the younger local families. The result was a far deeper sense of community than we found in our own Echo River Valley, where Jack and I continued to be likeable oddities.

Of course, the local old-timers lumped all the newcomers as an amorphous group—the Sylvan Valley Crowd—whose imagined lifestyles raised eyebrows and provoked intense speculation. Bearded men, goat's milk, folk music, shared farming, shared vehicles, and who knew what else? Sheila's groceries got charged to my account at Buchanans; Jack almost paid Gerry and Carol's property taxes by mistake; the mail lady delivered Carol's Christmas packages to Elda, her next-door neighbour. We only made matters worse by borrowing each others' vehicles, picking each others' children up from school, and riding to town with each others' husbands (usually in a muddy Japanese pickup truck).

It had been a decade since Jack pronounced me a conservative based on the downward slant of my handwriting. I still wasn't ready to accept that designation, but by now I knew I wasn't really a radical. And, appearances aside, neither were most of the people I was getting to know best. Most were, in fact, pretty conventional young families with jobs, children, mortgages, a conflicted relationship with consumerism, and a quirky desire to experience a sense of self-sufficiency on the land.

• • •

Before cold weather set in, Jeff and Jane found a house to rent in the country, several miles east of Echo Bay in the even smaller village of Bar River. The floors sloped, the roof leaked, and the small porch slouched against the back door. In the winter, they wrapped the whole house in a layer of plastic sheeting to keep out the drafts. But they had a barn for Guernsey-Girl, some land for pasture and a garden, and they felt at home.

One January day, Jane invited Sheila and me to help hang wallpaper in her kitchen. She couldn't live with the peeling paint any longer. This burst of house-pride surprised me, but I was happy to help.

Sheila and I arrived together, adding our five children to Jane's two. Erica, Amanda, and Sheila's oldest, Jan, ran upstairs to

Amanda's room. We shooed Robin and Sheila's boys into the living room while baby Anaîs sat in a bouncy chair watching the action in the kitchen.

I gasped in surprise at the horizontal parade of sailing ships Jane had chosen. She laughed. "I know, it's not really me. But it was on sale at K-mart, and it's not really my house either."

I filled the waxed cardboard water tray while Sheila climbed onto a kitchen chair and held the paper to the ceiling.

"Wait," said Jane. "I've got a plumb line here."

Sheila and I exchanged glances, then burst out laughing.

"Jane," said Sheila. "The house isn't square. What are you gonna line it up with?"

But Jane insisted. As ships sailed higher and higher on the wall behind the counter and the children shrieked in the next room, Jane filled us in on her plan. She was taking courses in community nursing and women's issues. She wanted to combine them and lead a weekly discussion session on women's health for rural women. Did we think our friends would be interested?

"Look at this," said Sheila, staring at the wallpaper. "It's gone up half a ship in just one strip of paper. It would be better to line it up with the counter top."

"No, this is fine. Do you think they'd be interested?"

By the time we'd covered the cracked plaster above the sink and pasted a stray sail into the triangle of wall that was left on both ends, we all agreed the room was brighter, Jane conceded the plumb line had probably been a mistake, and we'd made a list of women for Jane's discussion group.

• • •

I had attended a few Women's Lib meetings during my grad school years, but by the early 1970s, while I paid lip service to feminism, I wasn't battling gender stereotypes; I was embracing them.

138

And by distancing myself from the vanguard of second wave feminism, I became entangled in its central contradiction.

In one ear, I heard voices telling me that women's lives and experiences were to be celebrated, their domestic and child-rearing skills, honed over generations, to be honoured. In the other ear, louder, more insistent voices exhorted me to free myself from the chains of the patriarchy and break into the world of higher learning, commerce, politics — the world of men. They hammered their message into my subconscious: women's work was drudgery and women at home with children — women like me — were slaves to the patriarchy, unknowing co-conspirators in our own imprisonment. The quieter voices resonated with my heart; the louder voices battered my self-esteem.

Jane was resisting the louder voices, too, but she was not a slave to anything, and she protected her self-esteem with an armour of conviction. She arrived at Carol's house for the first discussion group in her standard attire, a cotton skirt just reaching the tops of mismatched knee socks, with an over-sized brown cardigan hanging loosely over a peasant blouse. She radiated more energy than seemed possible for her tiny frame. She carried flip charts, a copy of *Our Bodies, Ourselves,* and a plate of small, dense-looking brown muffins. She started speaking as she set up her easel and flip-charts at one end of the room. "My idea is to have a different topic each week, something that relates to female health and anatomy." We exchanged glances; this felt more like a class than a discussion group.

"I thought we'd start with bladders," said Jane.

As it turns out, there's a lot to know about the role of the bladder in female health. Jane began with the basics. "In women, the bladder is below the uterus and in front of the vagina." She pointed to her first diagram. "It's pretty tight in there, which means that women have a lower bladder capacity than men." She flipped to a cut-away diagram of a male whose bladder did, indeed, have more room to expand. "It also means women are more prone to bladder problems than men."

"A great topic," said Carol. "Anybody else here ever wet their pants when they laugh?" Carol crossed her legs to emphasize her problem and burst out laughing. "Everybody knows where the bathroom is, right?" We all laughed with her, and I hoped Jane would lighten up.

She didn't. Serious business. "So, Carol has a weak bladder. That can be an inherited condition, or it can be brought on by pregnancy." She held up a balloon half filled with water and a pear pretending to be a uterus. "We've all experienced the pressure on the bladder from the expanding uterus during pregnancy. Sometimes the muscles and ligaments involved in bladder control weaken during pregnancy."

And so it went. We learned about bladder infections, aging bladders, and bladder repair surgery. We learned how to do pelvic floor exercises, and perked up a bit when Jane assured us they would improve our sex lives as well as our bladder control.

When there was nothing more to know about bladders, Jane announced, "I've brought muffins. They're coarse-ground wheat with extra wheat germ. And they're sweetened with molasses. Very healthy." She pushed the chipped china plate with a dozen muffins toward us while Carol hurried to the kitchen to make tea.

"And I have butter tarts," said Bonnie. Ah, yes. Bonnie's butter tarts. Perfect little 2-inch pastry cups, filled with a sweet, gooey, butter-and-brown-sugar mixture.

"We are what we eat," I thought, eyeing the butter tarts, thinking of Adele Davis, and realizing that my relationship with natural food was becoming increasingly fickle.

"I'll start with one of your muffins, Jane," said Elda, "and then have a butter tart for dessert." Elda was the gentlest, most innately kind member of the group.

"Good idea," said Sheila. "We'll have healthy and then sweet."

"Is that herbal tea?" asked Jane, as Carol came in with a teapot and mugs.

"No. Just regular tea."

"Well, I have mint tea bags here if anyone else would prefer that. Better for you." She reached into her sweater pocket pulled out a couple of crumpled tea bags.

And so we continued with Bladders — as, unbeknownst to Jane, we quickly dubbed these sessions — week after week, topic after topic, from one house to another, using *Our Bodies, Ourselves* as a guide. Pregnancy, always an interesting topic when it's your own, but as for the technicalities, we'd all been there, done that. Natural childbirth. Breast feeding, hardly controversial among this group of women who all milked cows or goats and knew how mammaries worked. Some alien process called menstrual extraction, by which we could learn to extract menstrual fluids all at once to avoid having periods, a concept that Jane illustrated with diagrams of tubes and suction devices and the rest of us dismissed immediately. Menopause, which ranked somewhere near funeral planning for a group of women who hadn't yet celebrated their thirtieth birthdays. Sometimes Jane's intensity was infectious, but more often than not I was counting the minutes until the butter tarts appeared. And the muffins.

Meanwhile, my own body was playing tricks with me. The hormones I thought I'd sedated with our decision to adopt Robin were waking up. I began to yearn for another baby, the fluttering and kicking of an unborn child, the nestling of a small body against mine, the tug of a tiny mouth on my breast. I was still young enough to be surprised when biology trumped principles.

I'd been keeping this new yearning to myself, but one night on the way home from Bladders, I decided it was time to broach the subject with Jack. He was on the phone when I got home.

"Yes, we'd certainly consider that. How old is he now?....We really could use help…A good worker? Wonderful….Oh, probably six weeks or so. We can't pay him a lot. It's not actually legal for us to hire Americans, but we'll pay him a bit."

"My cousin Terry's wife," he said when he hung up. "You remember her from our wedding?"

I didn't.

"They remember you."

"Right, Jack. I was the bride...harder to forget." Impatient. I had a different agenda.

Terry and Joan lived just outside New York City. They had three boys. They wanted the oldest, Art, to have a work experience and thought being a farm hand would be good for him. And for us.

"They say he's eager and strong. Look how much help Morley's kids are, and they're even younger. How can we pass this up?" He paused. "How was Bladders?"

"Okay. You know, I've been thinking." This timing was all wrong, but I'd decided to speak. "I'd like to have another baby. Sometime. Fairly soon."

"I think we're good the way we are," he said, as I'd known he would. He reached for me with a grin. "Of course, we can always work at it."

I pulled away. "I'm serious. I'd really like another baby."

"Well, then. Let's think about it seriously." In his professor voice, he launched into a monologue about bedroom space, bigger cars, university educations.

"Go ahead, lecture me," I said.

He shook his head. "We have one girl, one boy. Good kids. What more could you want?"

"To be pregnant," I said.

• • •

In early March, the Bladders group was sitting around Bonnie's spacious kitchen table, drinking tea from flowered china cups and enjoying the aroma of butter tarts fresh from the oven, when Jane arrived with a movie projector and screen.

I knew this week's topic was abortion. It was a topic that made me uncomfortable.

Uncomfortable because, unlike the vocal pro-choice advocates, I couldn't ignore the potential humanity of a fetus. Uncomfortable because I knew restricting access to abortion caused misery and death to women, and sometimes to children, whose humanity was unquestionable, here and now. Uncomfortable because I was the mother of both a biological daughter and an adopted son, the result of an unwanted pregnancy, a rambunctious, curly-haired, bright-eyed boy who might otherwise have been an abortion. Uncomfortable because abortion presents a prototypical dilemma: an issue that offers no solace on either side. Or so I thought. Jane's movie that night begged to differ.

The film introduced us to a series of women who had had abortions. They looked into the camera and told us how that decision had changed their lives, in every case for the better. A woman with three young children could care for them better without the burden of a fourth. A young teen could go back to school and finish growing up without the responsibilities and stigma of motherhood. A woman who felt herself unready for parenthood could now make life choices that suited her. And so it went. A liberating decision for all. No regrets, no second thoughts. "Orgasmic," one woman said, facing the camera, referring to her three abortions. I squirmed.

Suddenly Sheila, sitting beside me, pushed her chair back and left the room. I heard her pull on her boots and open the door. The movie carried on, but for the moment, no one was listening.

"I'll see if she's okay," I said. At the door, I called out. "Sheila? What's up?"

"I just have to go home," she said.

"Wait. I'll come with you." She must be sick, I thought, and it was a fifteen-minute walk to her house.

When I caught up, zipping my jacket as I ran along the snowy road, she was close to tears. "I'm sorry. I don't want to make a fuss. But I have a lot of trouble with abortion."

"Yeah, me too."

"Well, I had a baby."

We were walking along the snow-covered road between Bonnie's house and Sheila's. Our boots were squeaking in the cold. My eyes adjusted to the darkness and took in the stars, the rocky hillside to my right, the fields and Bonnie's barn to my left.

"We've all had babies," I said.

"I mean I had a baby — a little girl — that I gave up. Before I met Bill. I thought about an abortion. I couldn't do it. It's okay with me if some people can. But orgasmic? I just couldn't listen to any more of that — those shallow, insipid women singing the praises of abortion as if it were a new hairdo. Let them do it, but have some respect for the seriousness of it."

I tried to take this in. "How awful for you. I can't imagine." And I really couldn't. I'd tried before, when I thought of Robin's birth mother.

"It was the hardest thing I've ever done."

I couldn't speak. She continued.

"Hardly anybody knows. Carol. My sister. Bill. Now you. Not my parents. Please don't say anything. I know she was adopted into a good home. I gave her a locket. I don't know anything else. Every year, I can hardly get through her birthday."

I caught my breath in a wave of recognition.

"I always think of Robin's birth mother on his birthday, how she must feel." I paused. "Maybe her mom thinks of you."

The tears I felt welling up in my eyes were for Sheila, and for Robin's birth mother, whoever and wherever she was. But they were also tears of happiness. Sheila trusted me with her confidence, with the depth of her pain, with a full measure of friendship.

I pictured the women in Jane's movie. Their right? Yes, of course. Their right, their choice. I would defend that; we destroy human lives for less. But surely not so easy. Surely not *orgasmic*.

• • •

Bladders was winding down. The season for evenings of laughter and butter tarts was almost over; soon we'd be back on the fields and in the gardens.

The first week of April, we converged on Jane's house, which was still wrapped in its plastic shell for the winter. I crossed the bare wood floor with a braid rug in the centre and settled into the worn, brown sofa beside Sheila. We had a clear view of the sailing ships ascending on the kitchen wall.

"I still think we should have made them level with the counter," Sheila whispered.

In addition to the usual group, Jane had invited a couple of neighbours to join us for the evening. When we'd all settled into chairs or sprawled on the floor, we went around the circle with introductions. Alice was a quiet, heavy-set woman a few years older than the rest of us, her short dark hair beginning to grey at the temples. She greeted each of us with a whispered "Nice to meet you." Joyce, who already knew Elda and Bonnie, nodded a friendly hello.

The evening's topic was breast cancer — its symptoms, treatments, survival statistics — and how to detect it. Jane described the different types of cancer, radiation therapy, chemotherapy, and passed around her copy of *Our Bodies, Ourselves* with drawings of women after radical and simple mastectomies. Then she moved on to detection.

145

"Now, if you all want to take off your blouses, and bras if you're wearing one, I'll give you a demonstration of self-examination, and you can practice," she said, pulling off her sweater to reveal her own small breasts, dark nipples puckered in the chill of the barely heated room.

I looked around. Though none of us reached the high standard set by Jane, we saw ourselves as liberal, relatively uninhibited women. We could at least pretend to take this in stride. I didn't mind exposing my breasts, as long as everyone else did. Joyce shrugged and began to unbutton her blouse. But Alice barely knew Jane and didn't know the rest of us at all. Clearly her expectation, when she headed out for the evening, had not included stripping from the waist up. Bonnie didn't look happy either. An uncomfortable squirm made its way around the room.

Sheila finally spoke up. "Not everyone is comfortable with this, Jane. Maybe we could just stay covered up if we want to."

"Well, we're all women after all," said Jane. "But of course, everyone can do what they like. When we're done with self-examination, though, we're going to learn to examine each other."

"Over my dead body," I heard Alice mutter—the most she'd said since she arrived—as she tentatively slipped her hand under her blouse. The rest of us unhooked our bras and hunched our shirts up far enough to follow Jane's instructions on how to search for abnormal lumps and bumps. As we moved the fingers of our right hands clockwise around our left breasts, I suddenly imagined this scene from an onlooker's eyes: eight women lying on their backs feeling their own breasts while Jane stood bare-breasted before them, feeling hers. Then I fast-forwarded as my imaginary voyeur moved on to the next scene, when—at Jane's command—we began feeling each others' breasts. Then I imagined my Women's Institute neighbours at this event. A snort of laughter escaped my lips and ignited the tension in the room. All pretense of submission to Jane's lesson evaporated. Like a roomful of teenagers, we laughed until we cried.

"I think we've had enough of this," said Carol, who never hesitated to take charge. She was still gasping to control her laughter — and perhaps her bladder. "Jane, how about I put on the kettle for tea?"

Jane reached for her sweater. "I guess so," she said, pulling it down over her head and shaking her hair free. "I'm really a little surprised that this group is still so hung up about their own bodies. But let's call it off early. I've made some oatmeal cookies."

"And I have butter tarts," said Bonnie.

• • •

Bladders was not *about* women's liberation. And yet, as I page through an old copy of *Our Bodies, Ourselves,* I realize that our weekly discussions about the intricacies of hormone cycles and sexual response fell squarely into the context of the feminism of the 1970s. It's hard to remember now how radical the book was then. Its frank discussions and detailed illustrations were a primer for women just beginning to gain the right to control their own bodies as a precondition to controlling their own lives. The pill had just, finally, given them an independent and reliable method of birth control, and women's sexuality was bursting into the public arena with a frankness and a vigour that startled the timid and shocked the reserved. A few brave lesbians were emerging from the closet. But abortion was illegal in most jurisdictions; childbirth was still a largely medicalized procedure; new mothers fought for the right to put babies to their breasts before nurses bottle-fed them sugar-water; and male doctors trivialized issues relating to women's bodies. When Bonnie's doctor recommended a hysterectomy and she wasn't convinced, he compared her uterus to a baby

147

buggy in the attic—no longer of any use. "I could say the same of his aging balls," Bonnie said. To us, not to him.

Forty years later, *Our Bodies, Ourselves* is a mainstream publication in its ninth edition, sporting a pink cover. In those four decades, the women's movement has claimed a thousand personal and political triumphs, but the contradictions that plagued me in the 1970s have not been resolved. The conflicting voices that vied for my soul still compete to seduce young women, pulling them toward and away from both home and careers. Toward and away from the constraints and the joys of childrearing. Toward and away from the traditions of their grandmothers, the accomplishments of their mothers, the expectations of their peers, and the secret dreams of their private selves.

I still hear the voices, too, but faintly now. In the end, of course, my heart carried the day and my self-esteem limped along, never fully satisfied that I met the criteria for a truly liberated woman, until at some point, more later than sooner, I looked over my shoulder and noticed that the fork in the road was too far back to see clearly and the paths not taken were tangled with brambles, no longer inviting.

Our Wednesday night explorations of mammary glands, birth control, and our own sexual natures were far from the cutting edge of feminism. To assign much real influence to these sessions would be stretching the truth. In fact, Jane's earnestness notwithstanding, they were more about friendship, laughter, and food than the weighty issues of the women's movement. But Jane did give voice to the softer side of feminism, and by celebrating the role of the female body as a source of strength and traditional power, she helped clear the path I had chosen through the maze that was—and still is—womanhood.

• • •

Jane finished her studies and moved back to the commune with her family, and her cow, a year after Bladders ended. We stayed in touch for a few years, but I soon lost track of her. I wonder what effect the years have had on her—if her dark curls have turned white; if she still charges a room with energy; if she still wears an armour of conviction. I hope so.

CHAPTER 11 • A REAL FARM WIFE

In March, in northeastern Ontario, snow still covers the ground, sometimes knee-deep, and the mercury continues to drop below freezing overnight. But by mid-month, mid-day, the sun is gaining strength. Snow softens and slides off roofs; icicles drip off the corners of houses; rims of earth appear around the trunks of trees. In the warmth of the afternoons, sap begins its annual vertical journey from roots where it's been stored for the winter to branches, limbs, and leaf nodes; when the temperature drops at night, the sap changes its mind and retreats, only to rise again in the next day's warmth.

The Whites had left behind a stack of metal sap buckets, a bag of spiles, a four-foot by two-foot, six-inch deep evaporating pan, and a stack of firewood among the maples near the top of the hill. In the spring of 1974, our second on the farm, we decided to harvest our own sweetener. I read the chapter on Sugaring Off in *The Little House in the Big Woods* to the kids. I searched *Grow It* for advice on maple syrup and found nothing. Jack talked to Morley and found out what to do.

"Can we make taffy in the snow?" Erica asked, wide-eyed. "Just like Laura?"

"We can," I promised.

"And will we have a party, too? Like Laura?"

"Grandma and Grandpa will be here. That will be a party."

On the second Sunday morning in March, Jack donned his green coveralls, high, insulated rubber boots, and the blue barn jacket with the stuffing poking through small rips on the chest and sleeves. He dragged a long wooden toboggan from the shed, another left-behind gift from the Whites, and strapped the pan and pails onto it, along with a hand drill, a large plastic garbage can containing kindling, an ax, a saucepan, tea, hot chocolate, hot dogs, and buns. I bundled the kids in their warm jackets, snow pants, and snow boots. It was a long haul for short legs, so I pulled the empty purple plastic sled behind me, knowing it would be loaded soon enough.

We followed the same route across the field as we'd followed for the Christmas tree, but this bright spring morning melted away the memory of that frigid trek. I squinted into the sun rising over the hill and reflecting off the frozen crust, a shiny, pebbly surface formed by the same warming and re-freezing that sent the sap on its upward journey. We walked easily on the surface, Jack in the lead, our boots barely breaking the crust and dropping just an inch onto the firm snow-pack below.

As we left the open field and entered the bush, following an old logging road up the steep hill, both kids climbed onto the sled. "Will we have a picnic in the snow?" asked Erica.

"Yup. We'll build a fire and make hot chocolate and eat our lunch there." My arms strained, pulling their weight behind me.

"I want to light the fire," said Robin. "I can. Daddy said." He leaned over to grab a handful of snow, tipped the sled, and stood up laughing at Erica who had toppled onto her face.

"It's not funny, Robin," she said, close to tears. "Mom, make him stop."

I sighed. Here we go. "Robin, don't. You're both going to be wet and cold."

"I'm not cold." No, he never was.

"Come on, kids. Climb back on. Daddy's getting way ahead of us."

He was. By the time the kids and I reached the sugar bush, Jack had already dug the rusted fire grate out of the snow and built a small fire. I was about to grumble about being left so far behind, when Robin let out a shriek.

"Daddy said I could start the fire! He said so! He did!" He was stomping his feet and kicking at the snow, which was landing on Erica's snow pants.

"Mom! Make him stop!" Her voice rose in a shrill whine.

"Erica, just move away."

"But he's kicking snow on me."

"So. Get out of his way. Please."

Robin was now throwing snow onto the fire. I grabbed him by the armpits and plunked him down on a stump.

"Enough. Do you hear me, Robin? Enough. Sit right here until you can settle down." He kicked snow at me and blew a raspberry, which I pretended not to hear.

"Help me find some more firewood, Erica, and then we can make hot chocolate." She stuck her tongue out at Robin before following me, and I tried to decide which child's behaviour annoyed me more.

That day, Jack tapped twenty-seven trees, the kids and I gathered a great stack of small wood for starting fires, we all had a taste of the cold sweetness that began dripping into the pails, and we made a plan. I would hike up to the maple bush early in the morning for the next few days, before Jack left for work, and empty sap into the big, forty-gallon metal garbage can, where it could keep, out of the sun, for up to a week. Next weekend we'd begin the process of boiling down. Mom and Dad were arriving on Friday; they'd be here for the boiling down. Perfect. A Currier & Ives moment.

On the trip back to the house in the warmth of the afternoon, our boots sank deeper into the melting snow. "Tough going," said Jack who was pulling the sled with both kids. "But you'll have a path for tomorrow."

Early the next morning I left the still-sleeping kids with Jack and climbed the hill. The snow crunched underfoot again, the air was clear, the bush silent, and the sun still hidden by the hill in front of me. In the pre-dawn, the bush was shadowless, utterly still. A few rabbit tracks careened across the trail, now pock-marked with our boot prints and sled tracks. I breathed deep as the thrill of solitude filled my body, along with the cold, moist spring air.

In the maple bush, I sat quietly on a log and stared through the bare trees as dawn gradually lit the valley. Below me, in the fore-ground, acres of field dwarfed the house and barn. I could see the wisp of smoke rising from the chimney. On the dark band of river, white clumps of ice broke away from the edge and floated down-stream, melting as they went. The sun rising over the top of the hill behind me was casting light and shadows on the fields. I sat for a long time, my breath slow and even, my mind as still as the forest, smelling the remains of yesterday's fire, hearing the occasional squawk of a raven or thump-thump of a partridge scurrying though the underbrush.

Eventually, I roused myself and began trudging from one tree to another, following Jack's boot prints from the day before. At each tree, I broke the skim of ice on the top of the half-full sap pail and emptied the thin liquid, ever-so-slightly tinged amber, into a larger bucket, which I then emptied into the big garbage can. Now and then I tipped a pail to my lips and took a sip of the icy-cold sap.

For the next few days—after I got back to the house, put Erica on the school bus, and did the chores—I scrubbed and polished in preparation for Mom and Dad's arrival. I waxed and buffed the hardwood floors; rubbed orange oil into the oak wainscoting in the living room until it glowed; took all the toys off the shelves in the kids' rooms and the tiny playroom, scrubbed them, and organized blocks, dinky cars, books, stuffed animals, and puzzle pieces; scraped the honey and ketchup drippings off the pantry shelves.

On Friday, I put clean sheets on our bed for Mom and Dad and dragged a foam pad from the basement to the playroom, where Jack and I would camp out. I lined up rubber barn boots in a straight row, biggest to littlest, along the wall of the small, enclosed back porch, which served as entryway, mudroom, and route to the basement. The smell of bread cooling on the counter overwhelmed the lingering odours of orange oil and Mr. Clean.

Erica arrived home at noon. "Are they here yet?" Ten minutes later, "When will they get here?" And again, ten minutes later.

Two hours and a hundred responses later, Mom and Dad pulled into the driveway in their tan Chevy Nova. In a flurry of welcome hugs and kisses, suitcases, and special candy treats for the kids, Erica pulled Mom aside and said, in a conspiratorial whisper, "Grandma Mae. Mommy cleaned the whole house just for you. She even cleaned the *stove*! And the *fridge*!"

Mom looked at me with a twinkle in her eye. "Yes," she said. "Moms do that for Grandmas." She bent down to Erica and whispered, "But it's supposed to be a secret."

Robin was showing Grandpa Warren how he could pedal his tricycle off the driveway and bash into the foot of melting snow that still covered the yard, spraying slush onto his face and over his shoulders.

"You've got yourself a handful there, haven't you gal?" he said. He nodded toward Robin, then hugged me, tickling my cheek with his mustache.

The next morning, before Mom was up, Dad came with me to the barn. We weren't milking, since both the milk cow and the goats were due to give birth within the month. Dad helped me water and distribute hay to the yearlings, then crossed the yard to the chicken house with me to collect the morning's eggs. When we got back, Jack was zipping his jacket and pulling a toque over his ears.

"I'm off," he said. "Come up whenever you're ready. No rush. Erica's up and your mom's awake. I'd take Erica with me, but I don't think she'd leave your mom's side."

By the time we finished a leisurely breakfast designed to impress—farm-fresh scrambled eggs and homemade bread, toasted

154

and spread with homemade jam — it was nearly mid-morning. Erica held Mom's hand all the way across the field, hopping from one foot to another to stay on the path. In the five warm days since our first trip, the snow had softened and settled; whenever we veered off the path, we dropped in frigid, soggy snow halfway to our knees, revealing a tangled network of stubble beneath our footprints. I walked a little behind with Dad, pulling the sled, while Robin walked and rode by turns. As usual, Dad was wearing his leather shoes inside galoshes, with metal clasps holding them snug against his pant-legs. Under his trench coat, he wore a heavy sweater and on his head, a black Russian faux-fur hat.

"Well, gal," he said. "I can see the farm is agreeing with you. You seem settled and happy." Before I could answer, he added, "A real farm wife — maybe that's your calling." Was that disappointment in his voice? Had I let him down? Was this a calling? Was it enough? But the day was too fine, the memory of my quiet mornings on the hill too fresh, to leave room for angst.

"For now anyway," I said. He smiled and clapped my back.

By the time we reached the maple bush, the fire was roaring and Jack had filled the evaporating pan with cold sap. Dad sat on a log with Robin, two boys playing with sticks and fire, while the rest of us collected the morning's sap. Soon, there was nothing to do but watch the first tiny bubbles and wisps of steam become a rolling boil, sending clouds of sweet-smelling moisture into the cold air. By the end of the day, the forty-gallon garbage can of sap would boil down to a single gallon of syrup.

At lunchtime, Dad sharpened hot-dog sticks for everyone with his pocket knife. We were making maple syrup from our own trees and eating Schneider hot dogs on Wonderbread buns. I buried the irony and slathered my hot dog with ketchup.

By midafternoon, the wind had come up, the sky was clouding over, and the thrill of sitting by the fire doing very little had begun to fade. Erica sat snuggled against Mom. Even Robin's enthusiasm for the fire was waning. "Looks like snow," said Jack. "And the kids are exhausted. What say anyone who wants to goes home and I'll stay with this until I can fit it in a pail. We can finish it off at home."

By the time we reached the house, a wet, sleety snow was blowing horizontally from the west, and we couldn't see across the field. An hour later Jack slammed the back door behind him and stood in the kitchen, snow melting from his boots, soaked to the skin, a plastic pail in one hand.

"God damn snow covered the path. Couldn't see an inch in front of me, and fell through every second step. Nearly spilled this a hundred times." He handed me the pail. "It's fucking terrible out there." Mom and Dad exchanged glances. For once, Erica didn't scold and Robin didn't imitate.

After supper, I poured the two-gallon pail of sap into the big canning kettle and put it on the stove. As it simmered and I stirred, careful not to burn the syrup in this final stage, the sweet fumes rose and filled the kitchen. An hour later, I declared it done. This was the moment Erica had been waiting for.

"Put your boots on and go get some clean snow," I said, handing her a pie pan.

"Just like Laura!" she shouted. She even looked like a Garth Williams drawing in her red flannel nightie with the ruffle on the bottom almost touching the tops of her heavy snow boots.

"Just like Laura," I said. But it wasn't. When we poured the hot maple syrup onto the fresh snow, instead of forming a taffy-like candy as it had for Laura, it melted into a soupy brown slush.

"But it worked for Laura," Erica cried as she pushed the sweet slush away. We repeated the process for Robin, with the same results.

"The snow's probably too soft," said Dad.

"Or maybe the syrup's not thick enough yet," said Jack.

"Here," said Mom, "Give me a taste." She dipped the end of a spoon into the slush. "Mmmm, good. Like maple ice cream."

Erica smiled.

I tucked the kids, smelling like smoke and sweetness, into their beds and headed back to the kitchen. Giving the syrup a final stir, I glanced up and noticed a glossy sheen to the paint on the wall above the stove. I reached up and touched it with my finger. Sticky. I looked at the ceiling. Same sheen. The countertops. The table and chairs. The window sills. The salt and pepper shakers. A film of syrup coated the entire kitchen.

I filled four Mason jars with the steaming syrup, all that remained of the forty gallons of sap, the treks across the field, the tapping and collecting, the quiet moments of contemplation, the stumbling walks through snow, the squabbling children, the hot dog roasts — and the scrubbing job ahead of me.

Pancakes for breakfast. Whole wheat.

• • •

That summer, Morley and Gloria began mentoring us in earnest. After watching from a distance our first summer, as we struggled to farm by the book, they'd decided we were first, serious about farming and second, clueless.

On a sunny May morning: "That back field behind your far barn is coming up solid yellow. If you let the mustard take over, you'll lose your crop. If you don't want to spray, I'd get the family out there fast and pull the stuff." We spent hours walking up and down the field pulling and making piles of the delicate yellow flowers that quickly lost their esthetic appeal.

On a rainy June day: "Have you castrated the bull calves yet? I've just done mine. Get 'em into the barn and I'll bring the pinchers down, show you how it's done."

Looking at our new Charolais bull, Charles, a magnificent tawny creature: "He's a big one. I hope he doesn't throw calves too big for your cows."

One spring day Gloria and I drove together to the local farm co-op and came home with boxes of chirping chicks on the back seat—two dozen chicks for each of us and six turkeys for me. This year, we'd have eggs to sell, chicken for the freezer, and our own turkey for Thanksgiving dinner. I set the chicks up on the sun porch in a small area, enclosed with bales of hay and warmed by a heat lamp. As soon as they were big enough, I moved them in with the hens, where they settled in as junior members of the flock. They pecked around the yard during the day and returned to the chicken house at night where we closed the door against predators—mink, weasels, and neighbourhood dogs.

Within a few weeks, the turkeys rebelled. When night fell, they refused to go into the chicken house, insisting on camping out. At first, they flew to low tree branches and fences, where they tucked their heads under their wings and slept until daybreak. By the time they reached the size of full-grown chickens, they decided the railing of our newly-built deck would be the best place to spend the night. Just before dusk, they congregated at the steps. One by one, they flapped their wings just enough to lift their rapidly growing bodies onto the railing until they sat in a row just outside the back door—the only door anyone ever used—tail end toward the house.

"We don't raise turkeys anymore," said Morley looking at the mess they'd left on the deck one morning. "Too stupid."

• • •

The first week in July, young Art Wing, the "eager and strong" son of Jack's cousin, arrived from New York City. As the passengers emerged from the small prop plane at Sault Ste. Marie's tiny airport, I watched for a strapping teenager to come bounding down the steps. As the last passenger came through the door, I looked around anxiously, then noticed a slight, uncomfortable-looking boy—a child, really—with light brown hair and glasses, dressed in stiff new jeans and a polo shirt buttoned to the neck, and carrying a cardboard box. Surely not. I moved toward him.

"Art?"

"Yes. Arthur Kyle Wing III, actually. But people call me Art. Are you Paula? My mom said to give you this." He thrust the box toward me. "It's a popcorn popper. For the family. I have a suitcase too. It's checked."

"Thanks … and nice to meet you, Art." I hoped I was hiding my astonishment.

As we drove home, I learned that Art liked to read, watch late-night television, and do magic tricks, and that he didn't like soup and annoying small children. He hoped ours weren't. So did I. He was excited about spending the summer in a foreign country, but eager to demonstrate his own roots.

"There's not much Dutch colonial architecture here," he said as we drove through Sault Ste. Marie.

I shook my head. "There weren't any Dutch who settled here, Art."

"It's very common in New York."

I nodded. "Yes. That's where they settled. Not here." Dutch colonial architecture? What kind of thirteen-year-old was this?

"What's this body of water?" he asked as we drove east along Highway 17 toward Echo Bay.

"The St. Mary's river. It connects Lake Huron to Lake Superior."

"It's not as big as the Hudson River."

"No." I suppressed a chuckle and glanced over at Art, who was adjusting his glasses on his nose as he turned to look at me.

"Dad says you live on the river."

"Yes, but not this river. The Echo River — much smaller. We're almost there," I said, slowing down as we drove through the village of Echo Bay. "That's where Erica goes to school."

"It's not a very big school."

"It's not a very big town," I said. God, give me patience.

"How big is your house?" Apparently size mattered.

"Not real big, Art. I've turned our front sun porch into a bedroom for you, so you'll have a room to yourself." A room that still smelled faintly of chickens on a hot day, but I left that detail out.

"You know I don't like soup?"

When we pulled into the driveway, Jack and the children came out to meet us. Erica and Robin were thrilled to have a "big brother" for the summer. Jack greeted Art with a handshake, but his eyes widened as they met mine over the boy's head. Quite far over the boy's head.

Later, while Art was settling into his room, arranging his books and clothes and his collection of magic tricks, Jack and I stood on the deck, looking at the hayfields rippling in the breeze, almost ready to cut according to Morley. I doubted Art was up to the job. Jack was upbeat.

"With teenagers, you just have to give them responsibility and they'll take it." He was doing the psychology prof thing again.

The next morning — after Jack and Art had hooked a wagon loaded with fence posts and wire onto the tractor and driven to the back fence line, and I'd milked the goats, put them out to pasture, and cleaned the turkey poop off the deck — Gloria stopped by on her way to the Sault.

"Jack's right," she said. "He'll probably shape up. 'Course, we've never had a city kid on the farm. And *New York* City. That's *really* city."

"Yeah. He thinks he's on another planet. One without Dutch Colonial architecture."

• • •

"Good night, Art," we said as we turned in after his first full day on the farm. It was ten o'clock; Erica and Robin were already asleep, and we were tired. "Don't stay up too late. We have a busy day tomorrow," said Jack.

Art was lying on the sofa, staring at the tiny black-and-white television. "I'm just going to watch TV for a while," he said.

"How'd it go today?" I asked Jack as we closed our bedroom door and enjoyed the first moment of privacy we'd had all day. He and Art had mended fences in the morning and gotten a start on shoveling what remained of the winter's manure out of the barn in the afternoon.

Jack hesitated. "I think he'll be okay." He was pulling off his t-shirt, which smelled of sweat and manure and left behind the sharp lines of a farmer's tan on his pale skin.

"He isn't that strong, and he'd rather talk than work. But when Jody showed up this afternoon, he put on a little more steam." We'd hired Jody to help out for the summer too, so Art would be seeing a lot of him. Maybe a little competition would be a good thing.

During Art's first week, we learned just how many things we couldn't offer. Bagels and deli sandwiches. Haagen Dazs ice cream. A magic shop. A dishwasher. Cable TV. And what we could offer—fresh garden produce, fresh milk, home-churned butter, and the "satisfaction" of hard work—didn't particularly impress this boy from the Big Apple. Neither did our children.

"Robin was in my room again, playing with my magic stuff."

"I'm sorry, Art. I'll try to keep him out. But he's just three and doesn't always do as he's told. You need to keep the stuff that matters in a drawer." I was pulling dry clothes off the line, folding and sorting them into baskets as I went.

He wasn't finished. "When I was three, I'm sure I wasn't like that. I could already read. And I wasn't allowed to mess stuff up. I really don't like little kids much."

"Well, Art, he lives here. You'll have to manage." I hung the clothespin bag back on the line and handed Art the basket with his clothes.

"And Erica just follows me around. I'm getting tired of that." He took the basket, but didn't move.

I sighed. "She likes you, Art. She thinks you're a wonderful big brother."

"Well, I'm not really her brother."

He didn't much like cleaning the barn. He found the goats cute, but didn't want to learn to milk. Mowing the lawn was a lot harder than at home. "This isn't even grass. It's just weeds. And why is it so big?"

But driving the tractor — that was another matter.

At thirteen, most farm kids in rural Northern Ontario are driving, if not the family car on back roads, at least a tractor. As soon as the Trotter children were heavy enough to engage the brake and clutch, around eight, Morley taught them to steer and attached blocks to the pedals so their short legs could reach. Reckless, I thought. But I soon realized that, not only is tractor-driving the easiest job on the field, the tractor seat is the safest place, away from the moving equipment. Reckless or not, putting children behind the wheel frees stronger arms for the heavy work.

Jack started Art on the tractor right away, first letting him drive it around in the barnyard while Jack balanced on the drawbar behind him, then hitching up a hay wagon and letting him drive it across the field.

"He may not be strong, but he's a pretty good driver," said Jack. "I think I'll start him off on the hay rake tomorrow." Haying was already underway. Only Jack could drive the mower; it was a fussy piece of equipment that required constant attention and frequent repairs. But anyone could rake; just drive up and down the field, no need for judgment and mistakes were of little consequence.

The next afternoon, Erica and I were flattening peanut butter cookies with a fork when I heard the truck in the driveway. Jack opened the back door, stomped into the kitchen in his work boots, leaving clods of mud behind, took a glass from the cupboard, and ran cold water in the sink. "I need your help. On the field." He gulped down the water and explained.

He had ridden around the field twice with Art to make sure he knew what to do, then left him alone and came back to the barnyard to get the other tractor hooked up to the baler. We'd acquired a second tractor, a faded International 504, only a little newer than Fred White's W-4 but with a lot more power. It meant two field operations could be taking place at one time, a huge increase in efficiency.

"I heard the W-4 stop," said Jack. "I don't know what the hell happened, but the rake and the tractor are both in the ditch."

"Is he okay?"

"He's fine," said Jack. "Shook up."

I put Robin in the truck, told Erica to stay in the yard, and drove to the field where Art was slouched against the tractor tire on the edge of the ditch.

"I couldn't help it," he said. "There must be something wrong with the steering."

"There wasn't anything wrong with it an hour ago," said Jack, who was hooking a heavy chain onto the front of the W-4 and the back of the 504. I crawled onto the smaller tractor, tensing against the precarious angle, and steered while Jack hauled it back onto the road.

"You know, I think I'm really too tired to work this afternoon," said Art.

"Why would that be?" I asked. He did look tired. "What time did you go to bed last night?"

"The late movie didn't end until two," he said.

Jack and I gasped. We'd gone to bed at ten-thirty, slept until seven, and wakened Art at eight.

"Do you do that every night?" I asked.

"Yeah. Most nights."

"Well, you're not risking your life and our equipment by driving a tractor on five hours' sleep," said Jack. "But there's still manure in the barn to be cleaned out. You can't hurt yourself doing that."

"I think I really just need to rest," said Art.

"I don't," said Jack. "I think you really just need to work. And I'll be working with you to keep things moving." He sounded like a father, not a boss.

Art glowered at him, like a son, not an employee.

Jack turned to me. "Do you mind raking? I'll just be in the barn. The kids can stay with me or play in the yard."

He knew I wouldn't mind. I loved tractor work—long hours alone with nothing to do but steer the tractor, enjoy the view, let my mind wander, and watch the hay fluff into windrows behind the rake; or the grass turn to dark soil behind the plows; or heavy clumps of clay break into a fine seedbed behind the disks.

I phoned Sheila that evening. She'd invited teenagers to stay with her many times. "Well, sure, Paula," she said. "He's thirteen. What did you expect? A little adult?"

That evening, we sent an exhausted Art to bed at ten o'clock.

• • •

I know now, of course, that avoiding work is a skill common to most thirteen-year-olds. When I was about that age, my dad decided to tackle the challenge by creating a little pegboard, sort of like a cribbage board, painted black with a list of chores along the left hand side and two columns — "to-do" and "done" — along the right, with holes drilled in each column. He painted little pegs in three colours, one colour for each child. I was green. My brother, Rod, three years younger, was blue. My two-year-old brother, Selden, was red and got to move his pegs around just for fun; by the time he was old enough to have chores, the pegboard was long gone. But for a few months, on Saturday mornings, Rod and I awoke to find our pegs beside our assigned weekend tasks. I remember the board and the pegs and moving my pegs to the "done" column, but I don't remember doing much work. I'm sure that what I did was under duress, and I'm also sure it wasn't very hard: sweeping down the steps, dusting the living room furniture, mowing the small front lawn, pulling a few weeds in the garden.

Dad was a putterer. He repaired the toaster with parts from the collection of old toasters on his workbench, planted a small garden, and fiddled with his coal furnace. These were pleasurable distractions from the real work of his life, which took place almost entirely between his ears and was invisible to his children, save for the tapping of the keys and the dinging of the carriage return on the old Underwood typewriter in his study.

Mom's work was in full view, when we were home to see it. She cooked, cleaned, shopped, sewed — though she leaned more heavily toward cooking and sewing than cleaning, which left sweeping down the steps and dusting the living room prime candidates for our little peg board. When I was in my teens, she took a couple of Russian language classes, acquired a Russian typewriter, and began typing manuscripts for the university's Slavic Languages Department. So, on many evenings, we heard the dinging of two carriage returns. A busy household, but not one where anyone broke a sweat, at work or play. We lived on a mountainside, but the first time I climbed to the top was at the age of thirty-five, with my own children.

The few childhood encounters with physical labour that I remember ended badly. I remember Dad insisting that I help him hoe the garden. I was probably ten. I stood on the edge of his little plot, slamming the hoe onto chunks of recently-spaded earth and protesting so loudly that Dad gave up in disgust, choosing to do it alone in the quiet of his own company rather than listen to my complaints. Some years later, when I was in my teens, my Sunday school class spent a weekend retreat working at a tree farm, digging drainage ditches down the side of a steep gravel driveway. I remember the mosquitoes, the heat, the near-tears hopelessness of stabbing that spade into hard ground, encountering roots and rocks that wouldn't budge—and the guilty sense at the end of the day that I'd done less than anyone.

In my home, I learned to tackle ideas, struggle with confusion, suffer the discomfort of unpopular opinions. But nothing in my childhood prepared me to endure physical discomfort, to push myself beyond the point of physical exhaustion—and then to keep going until the job was done.

Jack's family didn't climb mountains or dig ditches, either. But Jack, the enthusiast, always managed to stick with the job, whatever it was, long after it stopped being fun. Jack, the psychology professor, says that's because he comes from a long line of entrepreneurs who passed on a "can-do" attitude—a sense of control over their environment—that generates its own energy and commitment to task.

On the farm, I worked long days, spent hours on the tractor, took my turn on the hay wagon, shoveled manure, and stacked firewood; but when physical exhaustion or discomfort set in— when it stopped being fun—I looked for escape routes. The simplest was the persistent call of traditional women's work. Given the choice between backbreaking physical labour and the puttering, repetitive demands of house, barn, and garden, I always chose the latter. Sometimes in the aftermath of a difficult job, though rarely in the midst of it, I regretted that the scales had tipped as far as they had, but I didn't dwell on it. There was always more work than time to do it, however you divvied it up.

• • •

It was almost lunchtime on a muggy July day. We had no hay to bale, and Jack had declared a holiday. He was in the equipment shed greasing the mower and Art was still lounging about in his pajamas when Gloria called. "Are your guys on the hayfield to-day?"

"Nope. Nothing down today." I tucked the phone under my chin, stretched the cord, and reached for a towel. I was just getting around to the breakfast dishes.

"That's what I thought or I'd never have called. Morley's in a bind here. He doesn't want me to call you. But it looks like rain's moving in. He's got that whole big field down and only the kids to help."

"No rest today, Art!" I shouted. "Morley needs a hand."

Ten minutes later, Art burst into the kitchen, ready to go. Where did this sudden burst of enthusiasm come from?

"Morley's neat," he said. "Even if he is Canadian."

I looked at him and raised my eyebrows.

"He calls me a stupid American city-kid. So I call him a dumb Canadian farmer."

"If we called you stupid, would you work harder here?" I asked.

He looked back at me like I was — well — a dumb Canadian. "I'll call Jody," he said.

Jack and Art hitched the baler and a wagon to the 504. When Jody arrived on his bike, they drove the two miles to Trotters where they'd spend the afternoon baling, loading wagons, and fill-ing Morley's haymow. They'd be hot, sweaty, itchy, exhausted, and working harder than they wanted to work. They'd also be laughing, teasing, and leaning against bales of hay drinking iced water — the only thing to drink on the hayfield, according to Morley; no sugary drinks allowed — and eating Gloria's date cookies (plenty of sugar).

I looked at the pile of laundry, the sink full of dishes, the pail of unwashed eggs, the overgrown grass in the yard, the weed-infested garden, the goats already fussing at the fence. Erica was shrieking at Robin, who had dared to set foot in her room. A cat jumped on the counter and began licking the puddle around the milking pail.

No hayfield camaraderie for me today.

The afternoon dragged, hot and muggy. I tidied the kitchen and decided to ignore the laundry; it wouldn't dry anyway. I mowed the side yard, and let the kids rake the grass in into piles, then spread it around again in damp clumps. I didn't care. I ran screaming at the goats when they escaped yet again and headed for the vegetable garden. I thought about supper. Jack, Art, and Jody would come back late and ravenous. I took a package of hamburger out of the freezer; chili would be easy. Maybe corn bread — no, toast. Too hot to bake. I yelled at Robin, swatted his behind for tracking grass through the house and then wallowed in guilt for my poor mothering.

The heat and humidity rose all afternoon. I couldn't imagine being on the hay wagon, and I was annoyed because I wasn't part of the action. Dark clouds were moving in. At five-thirty, Gloria called.

"Come on down whenever you're ready. They're finishing up on the field, thanks to your guys. Supper'll be on when they come in."

"You don't have to feed them," I said, looking at the hamburger dripping red juice onto the countertop.

168

"Well," she said. "I guess I do. And you and the kids, too. The table's set."

We were there by the time the men came in — Jack and our two helpers, Morley and his boys, and one of Gloria's nephews. They all lined up at the kitchen sink to wash their hands and gulp down glasses of water. I'd spent many hours at Gloria's kitchen table drinking tea and visiting, but this was the first time I'd sat down to a meal in the dining room. As we filled our plates with chicken, stuffing, mashed potatoes, gravy, beans from the garden, a lettuce salad, pickled beets, coleslaw, fresh-baked rolls, and cold glasses of milk, I tried not to compare this feast to the chili and toast I would have dished up. The joshing and teasing among the guys continued right through the still-warm apple and cherry pies — not too hot to bake here, apparently — and the mugs of tea that followed.

"What'd ya think of that last load?" said Art, rolling his shoulders back and looking at Morley.

"Looked kinda tippy driving toward the barn," said Jack, who'd spent the afternoon stacking bales in the haymow.

"Naw," said Jody. "Solid as a rock. 'Course, I had to give the stupid American some help at the end."

"It was good enough..." began Morley.

"...for the girls we go with!" the boys and Jack joined in, and they laughed together at one of Morley's favourite expressions.

The sun was still high in the sky at seven o'clock. It disappeared behind dark clouds for a moment's respite, then reappeared as hot as ever. A slight breeze off Echo Lake barely moved the chintz curtains at the Trotter's kitchen window. "You boys go down for a swim before the lightning starts," said Morley. "Scott, you can lend Art and Jody swimsuits"

"Can I swim too?" asked Erica. "I'm hot."

"A quick dip," I said. "Then we'll help Gloria clean up."

Gloria and I watched the younger kids splash along the edge of the river where it widened to meet the lake. The air was a bit cooler here, and we relaxed on the grass, swatting at the mosquitoes that discovered us within minutes. The boys swung from a rope attached to an overhanging tree, dropping with a shriek and a splash into the middle of the river. Several old aluminum rowboats, orange on the bottom and blue on the top with the words "Trotters' Rentals" stenciled in black, rocked in their wake.

"Do you cook like that every day?" I asked, straightening up as Robin leapt off the end of a dock, then relaxing again when he landed in water only waist-deep.

"Well, yes. The men have to eat."

"What about lunch?" I asked. *Please say sandwiches, maybe some soup.*

"Depends on the day, but I always make a dinner with meat and vegetables. Morley likes two full meals a day. We had pork chops this noon."

Half an hour later, the boys were still shouting from the river, Jack and Morley were rehashing the day, and the younger kids were playing in the living room. I washed dishes while Gloria dried. It wasn't quite eight o'clock. Today, the work had ended early because of the weather. On a normal haying day, at both our houses, the field work would just be coming to an end.

The darkening sky suddenly lit up, followed ten seconds later by thunder. Gloria stuck her head out the back door and shouted. "Boys. Out of the water. Now."

"And we'll be on our way," said Jack.

"Will I see you tomorrow?" I asked Gloria at the door.

"Not likely," she said. "I've got two cabins to clean in the morning and a load of work clothes to wash. Morley'll want to cut hay in the morning if it's not raining, so I'll be doing barn chores while he's on the field. Then after dinner, I have to go to the Sault for tractor parts and get back in time to fix supper. The garden should be weeded. And the grass needs mowing." She laughed. "No rest for the weary."

"I thought it was the wicked," I said. "No rest for the wicked."

"If the shoe fits," said Gloria with a chuckle.

Morley was pulling his boots on and calling to Scott. "We'd better be moving, son. Those animals have waited long enough."

"We've still got chores, too," I said. "Fair enough for me to do them, I guess."

Nobody argued.

In mid-August, when Art's six weeks had come to an end and all the hay was harvested and in the barn, we invited the Trotters for supper. I cooked a meal to rival Gloria's—pot roast with potatoes and carrots, coleslaw, pickles, fresh bread, and raspberry upside down cake. When Morley clapped Art on the back and wished him a safe trip home, Art responded, "See you next year, all you dumb Canadians!"

"Next year? I don't know about that," I said to Jack later.

"Actually, Paula, he's come a long way. And we really can't do it alone."

• • •

The words "farm wife" make me cringe now as much as they did then. Gloria was a farm wife, but surely I wasn't, a liberated woman of twenty-something. And yet, I have chosen to use that designation in these pages precisely because it still makes me squirm, nearly four decades later.

The term reeks of male dominance. "The farmer takes a wife, the farmer takes a wife, heigh-ho the-derry-o, the farmer takes a wife." If I was a farm wife, why wasn't Jack a farm husband?

At the same time, though, the term provides a short-hand way of acknowledging the traditional division of labour that had come to dominate our lives, a decision made deliberately, in recognition of our personal strengths and preferences. And, by continuing to trigger that cringe so many years later, it also mirrors those moments when I felt diminished by my acquiescence to tradition. The term and its underlying assumptions express the self-denigration that often haunted me as I tried to reconcile my real life with my various imagined ones.

• • •

Our second summer had gone more smoothly than the first. The new garden had yielded vegetables enough to feed us through the winter, and the corn was still to come. We'd managed to get the hay crop in without major mishaps. The oats would be ready to harvest in a few weeks. All the cows were bred. So were the goats.

Erica would be going to school full-time in a couple of weeks; Robin was registered for nursery school again in the Sault; Jack was turning his attention to his third year of teaching.

I was just back from an afternoon in town with both kids in tow. Jack was sitting at the kitchen table working on his course outlines. He looked up and smiled. "How's your afternoon been?"

"Why can't you do that at your desk?" I asked, shoving his papers aside to make room for bags of groceries.

His smile faded. He was about to tell me, for the umpteenth time, that he preferred the light in the kitchen, and I was preparing my usual reply about the kitchen being my workspace and how would he like potato peelings on his desk, when the phone rang. I dropped a bag of flour on the counter and answered.

"That was Trudy. The cows are in their garden again. She's fuming mad."

"Shit," said Jack, pushing his chair away from the table and heading for the door. "It's going to take both of us."

"Daddy said shit!" said Erica, just coming in from the car.

"Erica, you'll have to keep an eye on Robin," I said. *Again.* "You can watch from the yard if you want to, but stay away from the

172

gates. We'll be moving the cows into the barnyard. And don't cross the road!"

"I want to help," said Robin.

"Not this time, Robin," I said as Jack and I raced out of the house. "Please. Stay with Erica. Stay in the yard."

We ran the quarter mile down the road where we could see Trudy waving her arms to chase the cows out of her perfectly maintained, weedless garden. As we approached, she turned her attention to us.

"If you can't keep your damn cows in, you should get rid of them. I won't stand for this. You people don't know what you're doing and the whole neighbourhood is paying for it."

She had a point.

Jack circled around behind the cows to get them moving, and I stood off to the side to steer them back toward home. I prayed that Erica could keep Robin from running out on the road toward us. Both kids had developed a healthy respect for the river, and traffic was almost non-existent; but at the moment, a herd of cows was moving toward them en masse.

Jack walked behind the cows. I walked between them and the river, keeping them together. As we approached the gate, I moved slowly forward until I was in front of them at just the point where they needed to make an abrupt left turn into the barnyard. Even in the urgency of the moment, I marveled at this graceful dance we'd perfected, knowing where to stand and how fast to move to keep the cattle in a single group and maneuver them through a narrow gate. *So there, Trudy. We do so know what we're doing. We're thinking like cows.*

When the last one was in and the gate closed behind them, we stopped and looked at each other. Who would go back and talk to Trudy? I waited for Jack to offer.

"I really have to get back to work," he said.

"Nice for you," I muttered.

Trudy stood on the road in front of her house, arms akimbo, watching me. Waiting. I walked down the road as though approaching my own execution, knowing I'd get no mercy at her hands. When I was close enough to make eye contact, I tried to appear both friendly and contrite.

"Trudy, we're terribly sorry. We'll replace your rose bushes, of course."

"That's the least you can do," she said. Her voice was loud and harsh. "I just planted them this spring. I still have the tags. I want exactly the same."

"No problem," I said, though it would turn out to be quite a problem. The selection in September wasn't the same as it had been in June.

Trudy wasn't finished with me. "Come over here and look at the vegetable garden." I didn't really want to; I knew what I'd see. Ripe tomatoes oozed juice and seeds where hoofs had sunk through them into the damp soil; bent and broken corn stalks lay tangled between the rows; a half-ripe pumpkin was split in pieces.

"I'm so sorry," I said again.

"You're sorry, and we're left to clean up the mess." She could offer a degree in righteous indignation, I thought. With a minor in spitefulness.

"We'll come down and put things in order as well as we can," I offered.

"Thanks anyway. I'll do it myself." She turned her back and began picking through the fallen cornstalks for ripe ears.

I walked home, cursing cows, fences, grumpy neighbours, farming in general, and Jack in particular—for what, exactly, I wasn't sure. For not fixing all the fences; for wanting to have twenty cows instead of five; for the fact that Trudy was right; for making me feel like a pariah in the neighbourhood. Mostly, for having a pile of papers to take him into another world.

174

"She'll get over it," he said when I got back to the house, fuming.

I doubted it.

"Where d'you suppose they got out?" he asked "Can you drive down the road and check while I finish up these outlines? I have to have them for the Dean tomorrow."

"What's the point? They'll just break out somewhere else, won't they?" I was close to tears. "Nice to have that paper work, isn't it? Try not to forget you have kids somewhere in the house. And get your stuff off the table so we can eat when I get back."

As soon as I'd slammed the door behind me I heard Erica ask, "What's the matter with Mommy?"

• • •

A week later, I stood on the top of the bluff behind Sheila's house, a small pail of blueberries beside me, struggling to keep my eyes open. Erica and Robin were playing tag with Sheila's two older children, stopping now and then to pick and eat the berries that grew thick on the sparse soil covering the rocky hilltop; her youngest, barely toddling, was playing on the ground near us. It was only two o'clock, but I was exhausted, and I was pretty sure I knew why.

"My period's two weeks late," I said to Sheila. "This never happens."

She grinned.

I grinned back. My hormones had won out over Jack's rational arguments.

"When are you due?" asked Sheila.

"April, I figure. I haven't been to the doctor, but it's pretty obvious. I'm so tired I can hardly walk from the living room to the kitchen, and my boobs hurt. Not sick, though. I wasn't with Erica, so here's hoping."

"Who knows?"

"So far, just Gloria and you. Jack, of course. And my mom. She's pretty excited. We'll tell the kids soon."

We waited until just before Jack's first teaching day in September to gather Erica and Robin together in the living room for a family meeting.

"You're going to have a baby brother or sister," Jack said to them, beaming. He'd more than adjusted to the idea. "The baby is growing now inside mommy's tummy. It's very, very tiny now, but it will grow bigger and bigger, and after the winter's over, after the snow goes, we'll have a new baby in the family."

Robin was propping an orange plastic race track on the edge of the sofa and sliding a Tonka car down the chute, apparently oblivious to the conversation.

"Will it come out like kittens? And goats?" asked Erica.

We nodded. That seemed to be enough for now.

"Can I hold it?" she continued.

"Me too!" said Robin. "I want to play cars." So, he was listening.

"You'll both be able to hold it. But it won't be big enough to play cars for a long time, Robin," I said.

"I grew in mommy's tummy, too, didn't I?" said Erica, puffing up a bit. "I grew right there! Right in mommy's tummy." She was jumping up and down with excitement and poking playfully at my stomach. "But Robin didn't, did he? He didn't, did he?"

"Erica, stop it!" I said. I looked at her sharply. She stopped poking me, but that wasn't my point.

"Yes, you did," I said, "and Robin grew in someone else's tummy. But he's our boy, and we're so lucky that he is."

I looked helplessly at Jack. This had been one of his objections. As the only adopted child, would Robin feel less a part of the family? At three-and-a-half he already exhibited a troublesome combination of defiance and fragility. And to complicate things further, he was the size of most five-year-olds. What if this new

176

baby made it even harder for him? I looked into Robin's dark blue eyes, rumpled his brown curls, and pulled him close. He smelled of sunshine and little-boy sweat. His long, tanned arms wrapped briefly around my legs.

Oh, you beautiful child. What am I doing to you?

Jack was still talking. "You kids will have to be especially helpful now because having a baby growing inside makes Mommy very tired. She's going to need your help in the barn when I'm not here. Robin, you're big enough to help with the watering. And Erica, you can help with the hay."

"Will I have to go to the haymow alone?" She looked worried.

"No pumpkin. I'll still do that," I said. "But you can help carry it to the animals."

"I'm not scared of the mow," said Robin.

"We know that," I said. "But you can't go up the ladder alone. Not 'til you're bigger."

"I am bigger."

CHAPTER 12 • NEW LIFE GROWING

As soon as I knew I was pregnant, I began preparing for a natural birth. I read the sections on pregnancy and birth in *Our Bodies, Ourselves* — "It is of course best to be as awake and aware as possible during labor" — and bought a copy of *Thank You, Dr. Lamaze*. I wanted to make up for the fact that I'd given in to drugs after the first few contractions with Erica. I'd gone through twenty-four hours of labour, gasping in pain when contractions ripped me from a drug-induced, semi-conscious state. In the end, Erica was tugged into the world with forceps.

"I really want to do it right this time, but I don't want to go into the Sault for the Lamaze classes," I said to Carol as she handed me a dog-eared manual of natural childbirth.

"This isn't Lamaze," she said. "It's what they used in Vancouver when I was pregnant with Alana. Exercises and breathing stuff. You sing a song while you're in labour."

"Seriously? What did you sing?

"Three Jolly Coachmen. Know it?" Carol cleared her throat and burst into song. "Here's to the maid who steals one kiss and stays to steal another." I joined in. "Here's to the maid who steals one kiss and stays to steal another. She's a boon to all mankind, she's a boon to all mankind, she's a boon to all mankind." Our voices rose together, "For she'll soon be a mother!" We both laughed and I put my hand to my still-flat belly.

During the first couple of months, when my centre of balance was still normal, I began by practicing squatting, one of the first prescribed exercises. Keep your back erect and your feet flat on the ground; this is a natural position for giving birth, and an important skill to master, strengthening your legs and your pelvic muscles. I squatted while weeding the strawberries. I squatted while scrubbing the floor. I squatted while milking the goats. My body leaned forward as I balanced on my toes. I could keep my back straight, but whenever I flattened my feet on the ground, I fell onto my back. If this was so natural, why couldn't I do it?

Sheila laughed at me. "The baby's going to come whether your feet are flat or not. Anyway, they're not going to let you deliver the baby on your feet. You'll be flat on your back with your feet in stirrups." My earnest preparations didn't make sense to her because her babies popped out like kittens. "What's the fuss? It's a few hours of hard work."

"Not my experience," I said, embarrassed by my anxiety.

By the fourth month, I gave up on squatting, and focused on singing. Choose a song, said the book. A song you won't forget. And during contractions, sing the song, taking only shallow breaths. I could do that. I chose a favourite song from my childhood: *A capital ship for an ocean trip was the Walloping Window Blind.* When I struck up the tune, I was transported to the back seat of the old maroon Packard station wagon, my brothers on either side of me, Mom and Dad in the front seat, all of us belting out the tune. *No wind that blew dismayed her crew nor troubled the captain's mind.*

I sent a letter to my high school friend, Carolyn, telling her about my pregnancy. "Dear Paula," she replied. "So, there's to be yet another child. I trust this will be the last…Carl and I are taking a ski trip over Christmas, then back to work. I'm teaching two graduate level courses next semester…"

The road not taken. Mine was a one-way street.

Then blow ye winds heigh-ho, A-roving I will go. I'll stay no more on England's shore, so let the music play-ay-ay.

• • •

We bought a couple of piglets that fall, named them Pork and Beans, and set them up in the last empty stall in the barn—cute, pink squirmers and squeakers with upturned snouts and curly tails.

"Pigs are smarter than cows," said Morley. "Cows'll lie in their own manure; they don't care. Not pigs."

I guess that's evidence of pigs' intelligence, but I was learning to bite my tongue when people assigned an IQ to animals. Smart pigs, dull cows, stupid sheep. Two years on the farm, and I'd already been outsmarted by all of them. It was particularly humbling, though, to have my intellectual prowess challenged by a turkey, reputedly the stupidest of them all.

It was a long time ago, and there are all sorts of people now defending the rights and reputation of animals—even turkeys—so before writing this, I thought I should check on the current wisdom about the "wisdom" of turkeys. A University of Nebraska website, prepared for 4-H clubs, assures me, with apparent political correctness, that turkeys "are not stupid, they are different." The source goes on to explain that turkey breeders need to be vigilant because young turkeys will drown en masse trying to drink from a half-full bucket of water, and that they have been known to starve to death in the presence of food because they prefer to eat the sawdust litter. Which begs the question: where is the line between "different" and "stupid"?

In search of balance, I also read a report from the University of Oregon's Extension Service entitled "OSU Scientist Debunks Dumb Turkey Myth." Poultry Scientist Tom Savage, who has spent a lot of time with turkeys ("the winged kind") is quoted saying, "I've always viewed turkeys as smart animals with personality and character, and keen awareness of their surroundings...The dumb tag simply doesn't fit." That makes me feel a little better.

On a September evening in 1974, we arrived home from a family trip to town to see four of our five turkeys—one of the original

180

six had already provided a midnight snack for a weasel — perched, as usual, on the deck railing. They were huge, now, promising to be thirty-pound roasters. Little mounds of poop had already begun to form behind them on the deck. But where was the fifth?

We were just beginning to search when Jody and a friend rode into the driveway on their bikes.

"One of your turkeys is across the river," said Jody.

"Impossible," Jack said. I had just unbuckled the kids and was loading up with bags of groceries.

"Yeah, really." Jody and his friend joined Jack at the edge of the river. I put the groceries on the ground and walked across the road with Erica and Robin at my heels. The six of us stood on the bank staring at a lone turkey settling down for the night on the branch of a tree overhanging the river.

Turkeys don't really fly. They flap their wings and rise a bit off the ground, but these big birds bred for meat are too heavy to soar. I'm quite sure they don't swim, either. Somehow, though, we had a turkey on the other side of a river, twenty yards away. We spent some time standing on the bank and watching the bird, willing it to fly home. It wasn't working.

There was no road on the other side of the river; we were looking at dense bush. "I don't know how we'll get it," said Jack.

"You could swim over for it. It's a warm night."

"So could you."

"I couldn't swim back with it."

"Neither could I." Stalemate.

"Jody?" I asked.

"No way. Not me." Jody said. His friend guffawed.

"C'mon Jody. Let's get movin'." The two teenagers swung their legs over their BMX bikes and pedaled down the road, leaning forward, bums far above the bikes' banana-seats.

After a few moments of silence, Jack sighed. "I guess I'll have to get it with the canoe."

181

Together, we carried the canoe from the barnyard to the river. As Jack scrambled out on the opposite riverbank, the kids and I stood on our side and watched. The turkey flapped its wings in protest, stuck its neck out, and ran into the bush, making guttural clucking noises.

Robin shrieked in delight. "Run, Daddy. Get it!"

A passing car slowed down. The driver rolled down his window. "You folks need a hand?"

"Nope, thanks. Just trying to catch a turkey," I said. He looked across the river just in time to see Jack stoop down and disappear into the underbrush.

"Well, good luck," said the guy in the car. He shook his head and drove on.

The kids and I could hear Jack crashing through the bush, but he didn't reappear for several minutes. When he did, his ball cap was askew, his jeans muddied, his beard decorated with twigs and leaves, but he held the turkey, flapping and loudly protesting, under his arm. He climbed awkwardly back into the canoe and paddled back one-handed. When he let the turkey loose, it dashed across the road and joined its cohort on the porch railing. By morning, its pile of poop was only slightly smaller than the others.

• • •

Mom and Dad spent Thanksgiving with us that year, only six months after their spring visit during maple syrup time.

Canadian Thanksgiving falls on the second Monday in October. It's impossible to avoid the spillover from the United States, so shops display cardboard pilgrim hats among the pumpkins, but the Canadian holiday actually pre-dates the Pilgrims. In 1578, in Newfoundland, explorer Martin Frobisher held a formal celebration, which became an annual event, to give thanks for safe return from a long (though unsuccessful) journey in search of the North-west Passage. Later, French Canadians added a harvest feast to the fall calendar. A celebration of safe haven and good harvests. Home and abundance.

This was their third visit to the farm, the second in half a year, and I didn't try so hard to make an impression, didn't have the energy. The early months of pregnancy were an extended sleepwalk; I wasn't sick, and I did everything I had to do, but I rarely felt truly awake. I tried to filter out what I couldn't (or wouldn't) deal with—the messy basement, the muddy barnyard cluttered with equipment, the stack of firewood that refused to line up with the geometric precision of the neighbours'—and train my sights on the manageable. Some days, that didn't extend beyond the kitchen sink.

Before Mom and Dad arrived, unwilling to give up my own bed this time, I managed to convert Jack's study into a temporary guest room. I bought a new tablecloth in fall colours, and planned a holiday meal that would feature as much of our own farm produce as possible. We made sure the turkeys were dead and in the freezer; for a small fee, a neighbour added ours to her turkey-butchering assembly line—chop, dip, pluck, gut—five turkeys in an hour, no feathers in the kitchen.

Mom got out of the car first, and Erica ran up to claim the first hug. Robin hung back, suddenly shy. Dad stood up and stretched his shoulders back, then gave me a quick kiss, and rubbed his five-o'clock shadow on my face. I smelled the faint, familiar odor of witch hazel. Then he patted my tummy. "Another little Dunning on the way. So, how are you doing, gal?"

"I'm fine. We're fine. Tired."

I turned away just in time to hear Erica say to Mom, "Wanna hear a joke?"

"Sure," said Mom.

"Okay." Erica took a deep breath. "How did the turkey cross the river?" She jumped from one foot to the other, bursting to tell.

Mom shook her head. "I don't know. How?"

"We don't know either," said Erica, doubled over with laughter, her blond hair falling across her face and swinging back and forth as she artificially prolonged the hilarity with forced, rasping inhalations. Mom looked at me, and I laughed too.

"It's an in-joke."

Mom started walking toward the house. "The hill is lovely, Paula," she said, as though I'd arranged it for her benefit. It was lovely. Past the peak of fall colour, but still a patchwork of muted reds, rusty browns, and fading yellows, all interspersed with patches of dark evergreen.

I glanced up to admire it with her, but my eyes didn't reach as far as the hill. They landed closer to home, on the unlovely sight of twenty cows and calves wandering across the field toward the road. The whole herd had broken through the fence. And Jack wouldn't be home for another hour.

I screamed. "I've got to get the cows!"

Mom and Dad looked alarmed as I rushed past them and ran as fast as I could to head the cattle off before they reached the road. Out of breath but still running, I circled around behind, then slowed down to get all but a couple of stragglers moving back toward the house and the barnyard. The stragglers would follow. I could move more slowly now, catch my breath.

"Hey boss, move along, move along, hey boss."

Mom and Dad were moving in my direction. I shouted, "Get back! Someone open the big gate!"

Dad loped over to the gate between the yard and the barnyard, opened it, and stood beside it, a slight, dapper man with his trim salt-and-pepper mustache, seersucker jacket, and leather shoes, staring down a herd of cattle.

"Move!" I shouted as the cows approached. "Dad, get out of the way!"

He shifted a bit, but too little, too late. The cows had seen him, and instead of going through the gate, they veered away from it and ran out the driveway onto the road, thundering past Mom, the car, and the kids.

"Damnit, Dad!" I screamed as I panted by, my breath coming in painful gasps. "Just get out of the way! Erica, go open the gate to the road."

Erica rushed through the barnyard while I kept running until I got behind them again and moved them down the road toward the gate. Erica stood just far enough away from the oncoming cows to turn them through the gate without spooking them.

"Good job, Erica!" I said, doubled over and heaving, blood pounding in my head.

Dad slowly closed the gate to the yard and walked back to the house, picking up the suitcases from the car on his way. His shoulders stooped slightly; I'd never noticed that before. Maybe it was just the suitcases.

I walked back, still breathing heavily and clutching my side. Mom met me at the door. "Dad was only trying to help, Paula."

Tears flooded my eyes. "I know. I'm sorry. But he was standing right where they had to go. He freaked them out. You have to know how cows think."

Mom looked at me strangely. "And don't forget you're pregnant, Paula. You shouldn't be running like that."

How could I forget? And what, exactly, was my choice? "I'm fine. And I'll talk to Dad."

I wasn't fine. Not because I was pregnant, but because I'd shouted at my dad, who, in all my life, had never shouted at me.

The rest of their visit went smoothly. Mom played with the children as always, baked shoo-fly pies, a Pennsylvania Dutch favourite, and tackled the pile of mending and ironing that I'd neglected. "Mommy said you'd do that," Erica told her. Dad and I walked along the river together and talked about farming and raising children and Jack's work. Not about chasing cows. One afternoon, Dad found some washers on Jack's workbench and repaired a leaky faucet. The day before Thanksgiving, Jack and I took the kids across the river in the canoe to pick high-bush cranberries from the bushes that hung heavy with fruit over the water's edge. Mom and I checked Euell Gibbons, *Stalking The Healthful Herbs*, for a recipe.

Following his instructions, we cooked the berries with an orange to blunt their unpleasant odour, mashed them through a colander to remove the seeds, and re-cooked them with gobs of sugar and a package of pectin. The tart red sauce completed a Thanksgiving dinner that featured a stunning array of our own produce — the turkey, of course, and potatoes, corn, coleslaw, carrots, peas, pickled beets, squash. I basked in a sense of accomplishment. It was a real harvest feast.

"Will you carve, Dad?" I asked as Jack carried the turkey platter to the long cherry-wood dining table that now filled the space in front of the bay windows where the gerbils had lived during their short lives.

"Sure, gal. It's an honour," he said. While he was slicing thick slabs of white meat and piling them on a serving platter, Erica asked, "Is this the turkey that crossed the river?" We all laughed, and Jack told the story.

A thankful family time. Home, abundance, and new life growing.

But through it all, the persistent echo: "*Damnit, Dad, get out of the way!*" His defeated look. His slow walk to the house. I knew sometimes I disappointed my dad; now, it seemed I could also hurt him. It was a power I didn't want.

• • •

186

We now had more than twenty cattle — ten cows and calves, including the herd matriarchs, B-fub and Mama Cow, and the cows we'd bought the summer before with their calves. Charles the bull had done his job; the cows would all give birth in the spring. We had that in common, I thought, as I watched my own belly begin to swell.

In late October, we weaned the calves by moving them into the barn. They had been on pasture with their mothers all summer. For the next four or five days, the mothers stood outside the barn and bellowed for their calves, who were inside bawling for their mothers. Bedlam. Eventually everyone gave up, the mothers returned to the pasture to enjoy the last of the year's grazing, and barn chores began again in earnest. The calves would spend the rest of the fall and winter inside, and at the end of next summer all but the few heifers we decided to keep would be butchered. I was learning that farming demanded a stripping away of sentimentality without rupturing the caring that underlies it.

We had only two yearlings that fall, Mama Cow's heifer, who was now bred to calve in the spring, and B-fub's steer, the calf Gloria had helped me save a year and a half earlier. We'd known his fate from the outset and named him T-Bone as a reminder. He had become a big, lumbering creature. His meaty name suited him. I can't say I had a great affection for him, but I'd cared for him and watched him grow.

I shouldn't have been surprised when Jack the enthusiast announced he would be doing the dirty work himself. He would borrow a rifle from Morley, he said, slaughter T-Bone and eviscerate him in the barnyard, then take the carcass to a local butcher to be cut and wrapped.

"Do we have to?" I begged.

Jack was adamant. "If we're going to do this, we're going to do it all. It's not easy for me, either, but it's part of the process."

He was right. I hadn't objected to slaughtering the goose, chickens, turkeys. The difference was only a matter of scale, and a perception of shared consciousness with animals that could look you in the eye.

"You shouldn't have to help," he assured me.

The day before the butchering was to take place, Morley stopped by to deliver the rifle and give Jack some last-minute tips.

"You're not doing this alone, are you?" he asked Jack.

"Paula will be here if I need help."

I waited until Morley was gone. "I thought you said I wouldn't have to help."

Jack rolled his eyes and let an exasperated breath whistle through his teeth. "You probably won't. Just be around if I need an extra hand. Is that too much to ask?"

I knew how these things worked. Halfway through a job, I couldn't refuse to help. But I thought I'd made it clear enough I wasn't in on this one.

"Can't you get someone else?"

"Oh, for god's sake. It's not such a big deal. I probably won't need you anyway."

Tears filled my eyes and overflowed onto my cheeks. Maybe it was hormones. Or maybe—just maybe—I was married to an idiot.

The next morning, after the school bus had scooped Erica up from the end of the driveway and Robin was still in his sleepers, Morley showed up at the door.

"Good morning," I said. "What's up? Do you want coffee?"

"Sure, thanks. Where's Jack?"

"Upstairs. Down in a minute."

He pulled a chair up to the table and took off his cap. I poured him a cup of coffee, got the jug of milk from the fridge, and sat down across from him with my own cup of now-cold coffee.

"I'm here to help with the slaughtering," Morley said, pouring milk until his cup almost overflowed.

A moment of silence, tears close to the surface again. I waited for them to subside. Then, "It's okay, Morley. I can help." What else could I say? "Gloria helps you slaughter, doesn't she?"

He nodded. "But not when she's expecting, she doesn't. It's heavy work. And you shouldn't be anywhere near. It could upset you and harm the baby. This isn't something to mess with."

"Harm the baby?" I scoffed, but Morley was serious. He wasn't going to argue with me, but I wasn't going to leave the house until the deed was done. He was here to make sure of that.

Robin came padding into the kitchen from the playroom, the rubber feet of his blanket-sleepers flapping on the hardwood floor, dragging a long-necked stuffed animal by a string around its neck. "Hi Morley," he said with a grin. "I have a g'raff."

"Besides," said Morley. "Who's gonna look after Robin?"

I pushed a dirty cereal bowl aside and leaned my elbows on the table. "Well, I thought maybe I'd just need to help for a minute or two now and then."

Morley stared at me and shook his head. "Has Jack been reading that damn book again?"

Jack and Morley worked together all that chilly October morning. Definitely not a one-man job. I did look out once to see a carcass hanging by its back legs from the tractor's raised hydraulic bucket, both men working at removing the skin. I'm not sure how Jack ever thought he could do it alone, and he never did it again. For all his insistence on "doing it right", he didn't have the stomach for it either. When he finally came back in, blood-spattered and cold, he found me sitting on the sofa reading a story to Robin. I looked up.

"Morley was right," he said. "I'm glad you weren't there."

Maybe not a total idiot after all.

• • •

189

I was still doing the morning chores by myself after Jack left with Robin for nursery school and Erica got on the school bus, but the kids came along for evening chores on Jack's late teaching days. They took their new responsibility seriously, helping to get ready for a new baby. We always fed the pigs first just to quiet them down. The squealing began the moment we opened the door and didn't stop until I'd dumped chopped grain into their trough. Another point for pigs on the intelligence scale.

Then I set up the hose and turned on the water. Robin moved from stall to stall, letting water run into the flat plastic watering pails while the animals drank. I left Erica in charge of Robin while he watered and I climbed into the mow to throw bales of hay onto the thrash floor. From there, I carried the hay into the stable where Erica and I broke the bales into wafers and distributed them to the yearlings and the goats.

"No problem doing anything you're used to," the doctor said. I guessed that included climbing ladders and hefting the fifty-pound bales.

One cold evening, as I was finishing up in the haymow, I heard Erica shouting "Robin! Robin no! I'm telling Mommy!" I braced myself for the usual squabble: spilled water, a stolen mitten. Then, sobbing, "Mommy. Robin's on the ladder!"

Across the thrash floor, on the ladder leading to the opposite mow, Robin moved steadily upwards, rung by rung, almost at the peak of the barn, more than forty feet from the ground.

"Mommy!" Erica was in tears. "I tried to stop him. I did."

"It's not your fault, Erica. He'll be fine." *Please.*

I climbed down from my side, speaking to Robin softly through the pounding of my heart. "Please come down now, Robin," I said, trying to make it sound like his choice. "Very carefully. You're very high."

He turned to look down at me, causing a moment of even greater panic as he shifted his balance. His grin showed only joy, no fear. Then he began to reverse his climb, right rubber boot down one rung, right mittened hand down one rung. Why now, of all times, had he left his mittens on? Left rubber boot joining the right, then both hands together. One rung down. Then another. And another. The baby, sensing my anxiety, began a drumbeat in my belly, as rapid as my heart.

"Erica's scared of the ladder," said Robin when, after forever, he dropped off the bottom rung. "I wasn't scared."

"*I* was scared, Robin," I said. "You are not old enough to climb the ladder alone. Do you understand?" I held him close, then turned to Erica. She was sobbing quietly beside the stable door. "Erica, it's not your fault, and he's okay."

But, I reminded myself, for the umpteenth time, she wasn't old enough to be responsible for her younger brother, who was nearly as big and twice as persistent as she was. I took a calculated, and perhaps irresponsible, risk every time I asked her to.

How do you measure reasonable risk? It's tempting to say, now, that we got it right. After all, everyone survived. Everyone in our household, that is. Not everyone who took similar risks. We let children ride in the back of our pickup truck until one of Erica's classmates, in grade four, was thrown from the back of a truck and killed on the way home from the beach. We let them ride down the road on the front of the hay wagon until we heard about a child who fell off and was run over by the wheels; after that, they had to sit on the back of the wagon. We considered the bale elevator one of the less dangerous pieces of equipment until the chain mechanism of an elevator on a neighbouring farm trapped a child, carrying him to the top and crushing him to death as it pressed his body against the edge of the barn on its downward journey. Some of these lapses in judgment resulted from our own ignorance and lack of experience. But not all.

I knew that children left alone can come to terrible harm, and that a five-year-old is not old enough to look after her little brother.

And yet, I left them alone in the yard when I chased cows; alone in the stable when I climbed into the haymow; alone in the house when I ran out to the barn to check on a sick cow or a frozen water supply. A wave of anxiety and guilt swept through me when I left, and a flood of relief when I returned to find them safe, yet again. Each time I told myself this had to stop. It didn't stop, but the children grew older, and the risk receded. Those risks. But others emerged. Ten-year-olds drove tractors. Erica spent hours alone in the bush with her horse and galloped bareback down the gravel road. Robin swung from ropes in the barn, climbed to the top of the tallest trees, drove the motorboat to Trotters, did wheelies on a three-wheeler. Everyone danced on moving hay wagons, kicking loose chaff off the front of the wagon; the hay-wagon shuffle was a family tradition that helped make the hard work fun. All the kids built forts and imaginary dwellings in the hay mows. Work and play. Risks all around.

In 2007 Canadian social worker, Michael Ungar, published a book entitled *Too Safe for Their Own Good* in which he argues that risk is essential to growth, that our natural urge to protect our children can go — has gone — too far. Kids will only learn their own limits and a sense of their own competence by being allowed to test themselves, by going to the edge where it's not so comfortable, where it is, in fact, risky. Of course, he doesn't encourage foolish risk-taking, and looking back to those early years, when we were overwhelmed with trying to balance too many unfamiliar tasks with responsible parenting, I know we were sometimes foolish, and only dumb luck prevented tragedy.

If I had it to do again, I'd have a better idea of where the serious threats lie. I'd probably strike a different, more cautious balance. But I hope I wouldn't see danger at the top of every ladder, behind every tree, at every bend in the river, in the smile of every passing stranger. There's a risk in that, too.

When the calendar changed from 1974 to 1975, Jack and I had been in Canada for almost seven years and landed immigrants for five, finally eligible for citizenship. About the same time, we made our first political protest.

The Ontario Ministry of Transportation was planning to upgrade and re-route the Trans-Canada Highway. We were eager to become enfranchised because a member of the local township council was pressing for a route that would run through the agricultural backcountry. We wanted to help vote him out.

We went to a few meetings to protest the proposed route, attended mostly by the Sylvan Valley crowd; the proposed route would cut their valley in half. I wrote a letter to the editor of the *Sault Star*, denouncing the proposal. One morning we awoke to find a sign in our lawn: 4-LANE HIWAY HERE. YANKEES GO HOME, with an arrow pointing roughly south. It seemed one of our neighbours was a cousin of the counselor in question. Apparently we needed our citizenship credentials to back up our right to protest as well as our right to vote.

We studied the citizenship booklet, made sure we could name all ten provinces and their capitals, committed key historical facts to memory, boned up on the finer details of parliamentary democracy, memorized the words to *O Canada*, and passed the test.

The citizenship ceremony itself was appropriately solemn. Twenty people gathered in an upstairs room of the old stone courthouse on Queen Street in Sault Ste. Marie. One family of Asians sat together, dressed to the nines, young children squirming, clearly in awe. Our children didn't need to be here; they'd been born in Canada and were already citizens. Most of the others in the room were couples of American or European origin. Flags and a photo of the Queen festooned the front of the room where a federal judge presided. He welcomed us and reminded us of our good fortune in becoming citizens of Canada. He then called us, one by one, to the front of the room to swear an oath of allegiance with one hand on a Bible and the other raised to the heavens, a rite as divorced from my reality as the oath itself, which didn't speak to my own growing love of this sprawling and hopeful country: *I swear that I will be faithful and bear true allegiance to Her Majesty Queen Elizabeth the Second, Queen of Canada, Her Heirs and Successors, and that I will faithfully observe the laws of Canada and fulfill my duties as a Canadian citizen.*

Jack had the courage of his convictions to refuse the Bible and "affirm" rather than swear. I just followed the script, emotionless. But after the last oath had been sworn, and we were all singing *O Canada*, my eyes teared up. I had pledged allegiance to a Queen and a body of legislation; Canada is, after all, a constitutional monarchy, a member of the British Commonwealth. But, in fact, I had made a commitment to this place, where I had staked a claim, where I had begun to build a life. I sang out through my tightened throat: "With glowing hearts we see thee rise, the true north strong and free."

We did vote in the next municipal election, but the counselor got in anyway. Many years, information sessions, and public meetings later, when the Ontario Ministry of Transportation finalized the Trans-Canada Highway's new four-lane route, it bypassed our Sylvan Valley friends and cut straight through the edge of our own Echo River Valley. No one protested. The other people in our valley didn't seem to care; our friends in Sylvan Valley — well, they didn't care much, either.

• • •

The winter and the pregnancy dragged on. Jack started throwing enough bales of hay from the mow to last for several days so I didn't have to make the climb.

I arranged with Gloria to be on call when I went into labour, and with my mom to fly up and hold down the fort while I was in the hospital and help out for my first week at home. My Sylvan Valley friends passed on baby clothes, a bouncy-seat, a Snugli pack, a buggy, a stroller. We bought a used crib, a new crib mattress, and several dozen diapers. All set.

In mid-February, I suffered a bout of flu and lay swollen and helpless on the sofa for three days while Erica brought me drinks of juice and Robin hovered nearby, observing my pregnant belly and returning his unborn sibling's visible kicks with little pokes of his own, each time waking me from a fevered stupor. I recovered from the flu, ravenous after several days of starving myself, worried that I'd deprived the baby of nourishment. Then, in early March, the wife of one of Jack's colleagues—a woman I barely knew, who was also due to give birth in April—learned that her baby had died in utero. She had to endure an induced labour and delivery, knowing her child would be dead. I became obsessed with this horror, grieved as though it were my own fate, and for the remainder of the pregnancy panicked if twenty minutes passed without a reassuring kick.

Gloria phoned on one particularly dreary afternoon in early March. "I'd like to have a shower for you. Of course, I'll invite the ladies from the neighbourhood, but what about your other friends? Can you give me a list?"

"That'll make an awfully big group. Are you sure?"

She was sure. So on a Friday evening two weeks later, twelve women sat in Gloria's living room on two plaid sofas, three over-stuffed chairs draped with crocheted afghans, and several chrome kitchen chairs.

To my left sat the ladies from my neighbourhood dressed in dark polyester slacks and print blouses. To my right sat my Sylvan Valley friends, who had dressed up their jeans for the occasion with embroidered blouses and wooden beads. I occupied a seat of

195

honour in one of the comfortable chairs and opened gifts, one by one, from a plastic laundry basket: an assortment of receiving blankets and sleepers in gender-neutral colours from the neighbourhood and bright purples and reds from Sylvan Valley, some with rattles attached, soothers, hand-knit booties and hats, powders and creams for the baby's bottom.

With each gift came a card, which I read aloud, as instructed by Gloria, maintaining a steady voice through saccharine verses and jaunty prose until I came to one extolling the pleasures of both little girls and little boys. When the little boy on the blue side of the card lost his kite by "getting it up in a tree," someone from the Sylvan Valley side of the room snickered. That's all it took. The six of us dissolved into a fit of giggles that would have done a slumber party of fourteen-year-olds proud. As we struggled to regain our composure, the neighbourhood ladies looked puzzled, and for a moment their lips drew tight against their teeth.

Over cream cheese and olive sandwiches on white bread—cut into squares with the crusts removed—and an assortment of sweets, both sides of the room tried to keep a conversation going.

"Do you want a boy or a girl?" asked Helen.

"I'll be happy with either, and the sooner the better," I answered, balancing a bowl of impossibly green jello topped with dream whip on my bulging belly, where the baby's occasional kick set it jiggling.

Carol turned to the older Mrs. Trotter. "How long have you lived on this farm, Mrs. Trotter?"

I waited for the answer. I knew Morley had been born here. His mother answered, "I moved here in 1935 from Paris, Ontario. Thought I'd come to the end of the earth."

Gloria was now scurrying around the room, handing out little pink and blue index cards and stubby yellow pencils.

"And how many children do you have, Elda?" Irene asked. Before Elda could answer, Gloria announced the beginning of the first game.

"Now, all the ladies with blue cards list as many nursery rhymes about boys as you can think of. And all the ladies with pink cards list rhymes about girls. The rhymes with boys *and* girls don't count." She looked at me: "Unless you're having twins, Paula." Everyone chuckled obediently. "You have five minutes. One...two...three...go!"

The neighbourhood ladies bent over their cards at once. The Sylvan Valley ladies exchanged glances, struggling to retain their composure. I stared intently at the pink card in front of me and wrote: "Mary Had a Little Lamb; Mary, Mary, Quite Contrary..."

Irene won that game for the girls, Mrs. Trotter for the boys. They each received an embroidered tea-towel. And here came a quart jar filled with plastic-topped safety pins. "Now, who can guess how many diaper pins are in this jar?" asked Gloria.

By nine o'clock, the games were finished, the conversation had completely stalled, and I was drooping in my chair. I looked pleadingly at Sheila, who nodded and undertook a mass rescue. "I know it's early, but I'm driving, and it's starting to snow. I'm afraid it's time for the Sylvan Valley crowd to head out."

In the hubbub of boots, jackets, and scarves at the kitchen door, the two sides of the room mingled briefly, exchanging goodbyes and thank-you's and "how nice to meet you's" as they headed for their cars. I stayed long enough to thank Gloria for hosting this gathering and to be reassured, once again, that she would drop everything to look after Erica and Robin when I went into labour.

• • •

In the early morning hours of April 15th, my mother's fiftieth birthday, I felt the first contractions. I waited for two more, then woke Jack. Together we timed the contractions while I sang. *The man at the wheel was made to feel contempt for the wildest blow-oh-oh.* After half an hour, Jack said, "I'm convinced."

At three o'clock, I phoned Gloria. *Though it often appeared when the gale had cleared that he'd been in his bunk below...*

During the half hour drive to the hospital, the contractions came more and more swiftly. Maybe it really would be easier this time! They were only a few minutes apart when the nurses settled me into a labour room. I alternated between pacing and lying down while Jack kept count of the intervals. Three minutes. *Then blow ye winds high-ho, a-whaling I will go...*Two minutes. *I'll stay no more on England's shore, so let the music play-ay-ay.*

"Just three centimeters dilated," said the doctor on call. "We'll phone Dr. McNabb when you're at four."

Two minutes. Two minutes. *I'm off on the morning train, we'll cross the raging main...* Three minutes. Four minutes. Four minutes. Five minutes.

"This is going backwards," I said as Jack handed me a glass of water and wiped my forehead with a damp cloth. Maybe I should change songs."

Six minutes. The nurses shook their heads.

"Uterine exhaustion," said the doctor. "We'll start a drip to get it going again." Someone poked a needle in my arm and hooked it up to a plastic bag on a pole.

Five minutes. Four minutes. Three minutes. By 11:00, I was four centimeters. *I'm off to my love with a boxing glove ten thousand miles away.*

"They're calling Dr. McNabb now," said the nurse on duty. "You sure you don't want anything for pain?"

"No, nothing," I said through clenched teeth, determined to do this one by the book, intravenous drip notwithstanding. *The Bosun's mate was very sedate, yet fond of amusement too.*

Sometime after noon, my legs in stirrups and Jack by my side — and with the aid of a suction device that had replaced forceps in the six years since Erica's birth — our eight pound, ten-ounce son, Galen, was vacuumed into the world.

He was, of course, a beautiful baby. Although the suction contraption had temporarily deformed his head, the hormones rushing through my body blinded me to this imperfection. By the time I noticed, it was well on its way back to a normal shape. Even without the aid of hormones, Jack was flying as high as I was. When Erica was born, he had waited in another room and saw her only after she was cleaned up and wrapped in a blanket. Together, we had picked Robin up in the hospital at ten days of age. This time, Jack was by my side throughout the birth and held the still-wet baby in his arms even before I put him to my breast.

"It was wonderful," Jack said with a silly grin, to anyone who would listen.

• • •

I spent the usual five days in the hospital recovering from the birth. At least we now had the option of "rooming in" so I had the baby with me rather than in a nursery down the hall as Erica had been. I could hold him, gaze on him, and nurse him on demand, his tiny, sweet-smelling body pressed against mine.

Between nursings and visitors, I read, I paced, I did the tummy exercises the post-partum nurses gave me, and on the third day, I became obsessed with the thought that I was apparently unable to give birth without drips, forceps, vacuum devices. A century ago, I would not have survived Erica's birth; perhaps not this one, either, a moot point, since I'd have already been dead. Whenever I looked down at Galen, sleeping in the plastic hospital bassinet, or put him to my breast, tears filled my eyes, tears of joy, love, awe, but also of a sense of doom and my own mortality. I was a probable victim of natural selection, saved only by modern medicine. I remembered my aunt, who had suffered severe post-partum depression, tried to harm her own babies, been hospitalized for weeks. Is this how she felt? Was I en route to a mental hospital, months of insanity, electric shock therapy, missing this child's babyhood? The baby fussed, my nipples were sore, the nurses told me not to keep him on the breast so long, he fussed more.

When Jack arrived that day after his classes, I wept. I couldn't explain. He couldn't understand. He left an hour later shaking his head. That night, I awoke to thunder, lightning, and a fullness in my breasts. I picked up the baby, who was crying again, winced as he grabbed onto my tender nipple and began to suck, weakly at first, but with increasing enthusiasm. After three days of meager drinks of colostrum, the milk had come in. I'd been side-swiped by hormones again.

I was sane now, and desperate to get home. "The kids are fine," Mom assured me. "But Robin's a handful. Sometimes I think he might benefit from a swift swat on the backside, but I know you wouldn't approve."

"I don't approve, but I've tried it anyway. It doesn't make any difference."

At last, at last, we brought tiny Galen home, less safe than today's car-seated infants, but wrapped in blankets and snug in his mommy's arms, which—statistics notwithstanding—seems the right place for a baby to be for a homecoming.

Fuzzy black-and-white polaroid photos document the moment: both children holding their baby brother, Robin grinning from ear to ear, Erica looking proud and serious. They both talked at once, filling me in on the five days since I'd left: the overcooked oatmeal Gloria made them eat that first morning, Robin's soaker in the big puddle behind the house, the new kittens in the barn—had I really been gone so long? Then Erica brought me an orange school notebook entitled *GRADE ONE DAILY NEWS, Erica Dunning.* It was opened to Wednesday, April 16. I read the carefully printed entry:

It is raining today. The snow is melting. Nancy's Grandmother saw a bear at the dump. Jamie is going to the dentist today. Erica has a new baby brother. His name is Galen.

CHAPTER 13 • THE PAIN OF LOSS

I think of the decade after Galen's birth as the "middle farming years", when the routines were well established and the learning curve had levelled out. In my memory, the years between the mid 1970s and the mid 1980s blend into one another: one field plowed, another fenced; calves born, weaned, shipped; late spring frosts wiping out rows of corn, early fall frosts zapping tomatoes before they could ripen; children passing milestones and growing into adolescents; and in the midst of the growing and the learning, almost as a footnote, all of us becoming inured to the inevitability of animal deaths.

When I was fourteen, we had a black cat named Kim, named after a Japanese print that hung above the sofa in our living room. Kim found a home with us the way many kittens find homes; she seduced my eleven-year-old brother with her irresistible cuteness at a friend's house, where a new litter was seeking a home. In time, of course, Kim herself gave birth to a litter. Our whole family — Mom, Dad, my two younger brothers, and I — watched the birthing with appropriate awe, though at fourteen I pretended nonchalance.

For two weeks, the little creatures mewled and suckled on a bed of blankets in the basement to protect them from the other family pet, Frisky, a cocker spaniel who had outlived his name. "Close the basement door!" echoed through the house until, one day, no one noticed. My brother found them, or rather the mangled and bloody evidence of them. To my big-sister chagrin and to his credit, he wept. Kim was his cat more than anyone's, the kittens too. The dog was just a dog, doing what dogs do. Dad kept saying, "If they'd been rats, we'd be praising him." To my knowledge, there had never been a rat in our basement. Kim, distraught, wandered through the basement crying, searching. In our various ways, the family mourned these tiny creatures whose eyes had never opened to the world.

On the farm, we tried to prepare ourselves for the inevitability of loss. We read, and heeded most of the time, warnings not to become attached to animals destined for slaughter. That's why we named our first calf T-bone; we named the second one Hamburger, but he died of natural causes before we could make him into a sandwich. Our first two pigs were Pork and Beans, the second two Male and Chauvinist. Later, we stopped naming them altogether. But still we grieved for tiny newborn corpses lying frozen beside their distraught, hormonally-charged mothers, and for aging beef cows sent to slaughter at the end of their productive lives.

Those years also saw the final and inevitable erosion of our homestead fantasy as we accepted the demands of a full-scale, working farm. I grieved for that loss too.

• • •

It was a May morning in 1975. Galen had kept me awake much of the night, and all I wanted was sleep. Jack's teaching term had finished at the end of April, and he was now in full summer mode. He'd milked the goats so I could stay in bed a little longer and was already on the tractor, preparing a twenty-acre field for seeding. On call for a hungry baby, I wasn't much help on the fields. I cast a weary glance at the kitchen counter, cluttered with the dirty milk pail, a grimy bucket filled with eggs, cereal bowls, coffee cups, and toast crusts. Robin was chasing Erica around the house with a rubber spider, and she was, as always, rising to the bait.

"Mommy, make him stop!"

"Not doing anything," said Robin. Then turned and waved the spider at Erica. "Eeee. Spider get you, Ca-Ca!"

"Would you two stop it! Now! Robin. Put that thing down and go outside to play. Erica. Find something to do." With the baby in the crook of my arm, I went to the back door and opened it for Robin. "Out," I said, as though speaking to a dog. "Stay in the yard."

He turned to Erica, made a face, wiggled the spider at her one last time, then threw it at her and went out the door. She shrieked.

I glanced up to see all four goats—Eowyn, Gloin, Pippin, and the billy goat, Bombardil—standing on hind legs, devouring the only apple tree on the farm.

"What next?" I shouted. "I can't take this anymore!" The baby started screaming, and Erica ran upstairs to her room. Running from me. I had to call her back.

"I have to deal with the goats," I said, trying to sound calm. "I'm putting Galen in his crib. You can try to keep him happy. Don't try to pick him up. I'll be as quick as I can."

Still sulky but pleased to be babysitting, she tickled Galen's tummy and dangled a brightly coloured plastic keychain over his scrunched-up eyes. He continued to scream. I slammed the door behind me and ran toward the apple tree. Robin followed.

The goats scampered in all directions, tails in the air, long Nubian ears flaring out like wings, udders flopping against hind legs. I finally got them through the gate and onto the pasture, but I knew there'd be a repeat performance before the day was over. And I wasn't up to it.

Back in the house and out of breath, I lifted the still-crying Galen into my arms and held him close as his screams settled, my breath slowed, and he nuzzled at my breast. I ran my fingers over the fine blond hair, still damp from the effort of crying, and said "Sorry, little one. I'm here now." I hitched up my t-shirt, settled into the rattan swinging-chair that hung in the corner of the living room, and slowly swung back and forth, trying to settle my thoughts as I relaxed into the comfort of nursing.

Jack had been saying for months that it was foolish to keep the goats when we had a herd of cattle — duplication of work, waste of barn space, fencing hassles — but I'd resisted. The goats were the last vestiges of our homestead dream, which had been largely overtaken by the reality of 300 acres and a herd of beef cattle, coupled with Jack's enthusiasm for more and bigger everything. When tired and stressed, I felt that he'd stolen my fantasy. But I knew I'd been a partner in that crime. We'd bought a working farm that had an agenda of its own, and both of us were struggling to keep our heads above water and to realign the fantasy with that reality.

Jack came in for lunch, sunburned and dusty; Galen was sleeping, and Erica and Robin were playing together outside. Together. A miracle. Jack took off his broad-brimmed hat and long-sleeved shirt; fair-skinned and bald, he couldn't do field work without them. He scooped out a finger-full of the heavy-duty hand cleaner beside the kitchen sink and lathered up. I put fried egg sandwiches on two plates, slathered his with mayonnaise, mine with ketchup, and poured tall glasses of milk from the glass jar in the fridge.

"The goats destroyed the apple tree this morning," I said. "They'll be out again this afternoon. We can't keep them in, and I just can't take it anymore." I peeked in on Galen in his little nursery beside the kitchen, then sat down and bit into my sandwich. Ketchup dripped off the bottom onto my t-shirt; I wiped it with my hand and said, "Maybe you're right. Maybe we should sell them."

Jack nodded. I waited for him to say "I told you so," but he didn't. "You know I think it makes sense. But they're really more your thing."

I nodded. "I suppose we could milk the black cow. She's half Holstein."

"Just think about it for a while." Jack drained a glass of milk, goats' milk, poured another, and bit into his second sandwich.

Two weeks later, the goats were gone.

"Why do we have to sell them? I love them!" wept Erica. I loved them too, but managed not to weep as they headed off in the back of a pick-up, on their way to feed someone else's fantasy.

Experienced farmers must have wondered what our problem was. It's perfectly possible to fence both goats and cows; we couldn't seem to do either. It wasn't just our inexperience, though for a few years we used that as an excuse. The crack that eventually widened to a chasm was already appearing on the façade of our farming experience. Jack thrived on the field work, the seasonal pressure to work against the deadlines for planting and harvesting. I settled comfortably into the daily routines: the barn chores, the garden, the "putting down" of food. That left a whole range of mid-level tasks largely ignored or half-heartedly tackled: fencing, barn-cleaning, equipment maintenance. Too big to slip easily into my days, too small to warrant Jack's enthusiasm. The goats were the first to slip through that crack.

One day not long after the goats left, I answered a knock at the door to a man I'd never seen before.

"I've been noticing that bus of yours behind the barn," said the stranger. "Are you lookin' to sell it?"

Out of sight and out of mind, the bus was an almost invisible reminder of an earlier enthusiasm, its brightly painted exterior largely hidden by overgrown burdocks and thistles.

"We'll never have time to camp," said Jack that evening.

Enthusiasms come, enthusiasms go.

The man wanted to use it as a movable hunt camp. We sold it to him for a song. He painted it drab green.

• • •

I began milking the black cow. The first time I brought her into the barn for the night, we listened to hours of distressed mooing and bawling as she and her calf called to each other on opposite

206

sides of the barn wall. In the morning, I placed a pan of dairy ration, a sweet-smelling mixture of grain and molasses, in front of her and settled onto the three-legged milking stool. Since the days of milking B-fub and Mama Cow, I'd acquired a pair of hobbles that attached to the cow's back legs to prevent kicking. So, she didn't make contact, but not for lack of trying. She danced back and forth in the silly, mincing steps the hobbles allowed, and swatted my head with her tail. I managed to claim a quart of milk, then let her back outside to her calf, who rushed toward her and finished the job.

The next evening, I gave her some dairy ration as soon as she settled into her stanchion. The calf stayed by the barn door, but stopped bawling after a couple of hours. In the morning, Big Black danced again while I milked, but this time I emptied her udder — nearly a gallon — before letting her back out with the calf.

Within a few days, she came eagerly to the barn in the evening to eat the sweet grain, and her calf barely acknowledged her departure from the herd. For the rest of the summer the family and the calf shared her milk; he had access all day, we had what she produced overnight, and everybody had all they needed. My summer-time evening chores now consisted of a walk to the pasture to bring her to the barn, sometimes with Galen in his little Snugli pack against my chest, sometimes leaving him in the house with Jack or one of the summer helpers, sometimes with Erica or Robin skipping along.

She needed a name. "Big Black" said Robin. Perfect. A perfectly descriptive name for an animal I wasn't sure I could love.

But I soon learned I could bond with a cow as well as with goats, pressing my body close to her flank, listening to the munching of grain and the swish of her tail, smelling the day's sunshine mixed with the faint aroma of warm milk. Not in tall prairie grasses like Laura, but close enough. I milked her every day until

Christmas that year. She was due to calve in April and needed few months' rest prior to giving birth.

On a freezing cold morning in February, I was stirring the breakfast oatmeal. Galen sat in his highchair chewing on a piece of dry toast. Erica and Robin hadn't come downstairs yet, and Jack was just returning from the barn. I heard him stomp the snow off his boots on the back porch before opening the kitchen door and called out "Coffee's ready!"

He came into the kitchen quietly and hung his barn jacket on the hook on the kitchen wall. I looked up from the stove. "What's wrong?"

"Big Black. She's gone," he said.

She'd seemed fine until a week or so ago when I noticed a discharge from her nose and a heaviness in her breathing. I'd been giving her penicillin injections for several days, but she wasn't eating and barely drinking. Yesterday morning, she'd refused to stand up.

I wiped tears from my eyes as Jack moved quickly to the practical problem of a dead cow.

"She's in the middle of the barn. I don't know what we're going to do with her. I can't get the tractor in there."

"Can you and Morley lift her?"

"No way. I think I'll try to hoist her with the manure bucket and roll her out the back."

There wasn't a chapter in *Grow It* about what to do with a 700-pound dead milk cow on the barn floor. We were on our own.

Jack's plan was to remove the manure bucket itself and use the pulley system to hoist Big Black's body off the barn floor, then push it outside on the track where he could lift her up with the tractor's front-end loader. But then what? We couldn't leave a dead cow lying outside the barn until spring, but with three feet of snow on ground that was frozen several feet below the surface, we could hardly bury her.

"I guess I'll have to take her to the dump," said Jack, spooning oatmeal into his bowl.

Erica and Robin came thumping down the steps.

"Oatmeal again," said Erica. "Why do we always have oatmeal?" She looked at her bowl and made a face.

"It's good for you," I said. Then, "Big Black died last night."

"I thought you said she'd get better. I thought you were giving her medicine?" Erica wailed.

"We were, but it didn't help."

Robin slid down the steps on his bottom and skated across the kitchen floor in sock feet. "She wasn't breathing right. I heard her yesterday. Snuff, snuff. Boogers in her nose."

When Jack had gone to work and Erica and Robin had climbed onto the school bus, I put Galen back in his crib with a few toys, pulled on my rubber barn boots, and ran out to the barn. There I stood, looking at the black corpse that had been Big Black, larger in death than in life. I walked close to her and tentatively put my hand on her flank—that warm, soft, breathing flank that had pressed against my forehead as I milked, now cold and stiff. I wiped my eyes with the back of my mittens and ran back to the house. Galen was standing in his crib, just beginning to cry at being abandoned. I lifted up his warm body and gave him a hug.

The next day, Jack lowered the front-end loader with its stiff cargo into the back of the pick-up truck and drove away, the rear end of the truck riding dangerously low to the ground.

Some weeks later, a newsletter arrived from the Township. Among announcements about dog tags, figure skating classes, hockey teams, and fund-raising pancake suppers, these words leapt off the page:

Attention Township Residents!!
It is against the law to dispose of dead livestock at the township dump. Residents are responsible for disposing of carcasses on their own property.

Anyone found in violation of this law will be reported to the Provincial Police. Please refer to the Dead Animal Disposal Act, which is available at the Township Office.

There was a Dead Animal Disposal Act? Apparently so.

"Um...was anyone else at the dump when you took her?" I asked Jack.

"No," he said, his brow furrowed. "I didn't know. I just thought it made sense."

"Was she the only dead cow there?"

"I think so..."

As it turns out, the Dead Animal Disposal Act spells out quite explicitly the options for disposing of dead animals. Hauling them to the municipal dump in the back of a Datsun pick-up isn't on the list.

Just as a matter of curiosity, I asked Morley, what *were* we to do with a dead cow in the middle of the winter? Morley had little patience for arbitrary rules and regulations. Sure, he said, in warm weather, dig a trench and bury the body. That just makes sense. But in the winter, drag the carcass into the bush, where wolves or coyotes will make short work of it.

That's not in the act, either, but I nodded. How much more dignified an end it would have been for Big Black than the dump, where wolves no doubt found her anyway, among the discarded tires and empty soup cans.

• • •

The morning mist had almost burned off the fields when I returned from the barn on a late August morning. Just a faint, grey-white stripe hung low in front of the hill. Heavy dew weighted down spikes of grass and clung to tiny spider webs stretched between them. A flock of geese that had settled on the back field for

210

the night was beginning to stir; they called to one another, rose tentatively, then landed again, preparing for their day's journey. Two sandhill cranes flew low, croaking in their prehistoric voices, then rose to fly over the hill into the next valley where they gathered by the dozens for their flight south.

The summertime helpers had all gone home and we were moving into that prolonged, quiet evening of the year, after the rush of summer, before winter closes in. Jack, briefcase in one hand, cartons of fresh eggs for colleagues in the other, gave me a quick kiss at the kitchen door. "Gotta go. Meeting with Tom at nine. Sorry, I didn't change Galen." And he was gone.

Galen toddled across the kitchen in his bare feet, his wet diaper drooping almost to his knees, and clutched my legs as I set the milk pail on the floor. Erica was still sleeping; I heard Robin moving around in his room.

I pulled the rectangular, blue-and-white granite roasting pan filled with yesterday's milk off the top shelf of the fridge, placed it on the counter, and slid a shallow ladle along the surface. Spoonful by spoonful, thick glob by thick glob, I filled a bowl with the dense, yellowish cream, exposing a stripe of bluish-white skimmed milk with each pass of the spoon. When only small bits of cream remained floating on top, I emptied the skimmed milk into a gallon jar, screwed on the lid, and put it back in the fridge. Then, I washed the roasting pan, attached a clean piece of cheesecloth with clothespins on all four sides, and poured the morning's fresh milk through it, capturing a few stray bits of hay, then put the pan back in the fridge for the cream to rise until I repeated the operation tomorrow. One of many small daily rhythms within the larger drumbeat of the seasons. Tomorrow I'd have enough cream to make butter.

I paused and looked out the kitchen window at the dark, late-summer green of the hill rising above the bright new growth on the recently cut hayfield. Here and there, a precocious maple had already begun to turn red. The stripe of mist was gone now, and the sun was already above the window, its journey from sunrise to sunset well underway. Even now, two months after the longest day, it rose before seven and didn't set until almost nine.

I pushed my bangs up on my forehead, shook my newly cropped hair, and felt the air moving on my neck and the tickling of my earrings swinging against it. Jack hadn't wanted me to cut it, but my Lady Godiva days were over. I felt lighter, fresher. I hoped the dangly earrings compensated for my shorn locks.

By the time I'd fed breakfast to the kids and was hanging a load of diapers on the clothesline, the thermometer read twenty-seven Celsius. Eighty Fahrenheit. And muggy. Good cottage cheese weather, Gloria said. Maybe I'd try.

I looked up from the clothesline to see Erica running toward me from the barn, her blond hair gathered in two ponytails under bangs that almost hid her eyes, her t-shirt covered with bits of straw. She'd been brushing Bill, the pony that had replaced Karma earlier in the summer. I hadn't ridden Karma more than a few times since we'd come to the farm, and Erica was old enough for a pony of her own.

"Something smells dead in the barn, Mommy."

It crossed my mind that an eight-year-old shouldn't recognize the smell of death.

"I can't deal with it now, Erica. Can't you see I'm busy?" I'd been to the barn earlier; in the coolness of the morning, I hadn't noticed.

"But maybe it's Gasman," she wailed. "I don't know where he is." Gasman, the old black cat that had been with us since our student days at Grinnell. Despite the many unplanned deaths we'd experienced—Shastek, Ranger, an un-named calf, Big Black, and two of last year's new-born goats—losing animals hadn't gotten any easier for Erica. It had become troublesomely easy for me, I thought, as I looked at her stricken, tear-stained face.

212

In fact, I hadn't seen Gasman for several days and he had been growing increasingly frail. I sighed, picked Galen up from where he sat on the grass, and headed with Erica to the barn. Robin left his trike in the middle of the yard and ran along, chanting, "Gasman's dead, Gasman's dead."

"Shut up! Mommy, make him shut up!" wailed Erica.

"Enough, Robin. Can't you see your sister's already upset?" He stuck out his tongue and raced into the barn. At five he was almost as tall as Erica, all tanned legs and arms in constant motion.

The barn was pleasantly cool. The acrid smell of pigs mingled with the sweetness of fresh hay; the four south-facing windows filtered sunlight through a film of grime, illuminating dust particles in the air. Bill stood patiently in a stall, waiting for Erica to finish brushing him. The pigs began squealing the moment we opened the door, expecting a second breakfast.

"Forget it, Male. No more this morning, Chauvinist," I said to the two pink snouts poking between the boards of their pen. In fact, I didn't know which was which; pigs were all the same to me.

Erica stood trembling in fear of what we'd find. "Let's look in the mangers," I said. Robin dashed from manger to manger, audibly sniffing. I walked along the aisle between stalls, sniffing more tentatively. Galen squirmed on my hip as I tried to ignore the spreading dampness.

"Here!" shouted Robin. "It really stinks here!"

And there he was. In an unused hay manger, the old black cat had made a nest for his final days. He did, indeed, stink.

I gave Erica a little hug. "I'm sorry, sweetie. We all loved him."

Erica shuddered and buried her face against my stomach. I let a few tears slide down my own cheeks, thinking about Gasman who had been with us since it all began and who had largely been forgotten in the midst of the farm menagerie.

"We'll bury him behind the barn," I said. "Can you find a shovel, Robin?" I put Galen down and wrapped the already-decomposing body in an old burlap feed bag. Robin charged toward me, waving a five-pronged pitchfork in the air.

"We can use this!"

I leapt to grab it from him. "Careful." It wasn't a shovel, but it would do.

I hollowed out a shallow grave with the edge of the pitchfork—Erica sobbing inconsolably, Robin more interested in hole-digging than in the loss of a cat, Galen standing in his bare feet at the barn door, still too wobbly on his feet to venture out. Erica and I marked the spot with a small stone. Robin ran out of the barn to remount his trike. I scooped up the wet baby and left Erica to mourn by the gravesite and return to brushing her horse.

Back at the house, I picked up where I'd left off. The cat had already become a footnote to a day that would move from the clothesline to the kitchen, from the kitchen to the garden, and back again. Cucumbers to pickle, corn to freeze, a few ripe tomatoes if I was lucky, maybe a loaf or two of zucchini bread. The year's first frost could be only a couple of weeks away. Perversely, I looked forward to it, to the shortening days, the chilly mornings, and the gradual shrinking of responsibility. Just last night, Jack, ever the enthusiast, had mentioned building a frame to cover the tomatoes.

"We've only had a few ripe ones. This way, we could eat tomatoes into October," he said.

"No," I said. "I've had enough," not really referring to tomatoes. Then, with a nod to a divine purpose that I didn't really believe extended to my garden: "When the garden is meant to die, it'll die."

• • •

One day in the early fall, I arrived home with a sheep in the back of the station wagon. It was destined for the freezer, but by the time I'd wrestled it into the car, it was too late for the abattoir; I had to take the animal home for the night.

214

"Oh, please! Can't we keep her?" Erica begged. She had never forgiven us for the sale of the goats, and she was looking from me, to Jack, to the shaggy white animal with a black nose and black feet that had just lumbered down from the back of the station wagon.

"Erica, we don't need another animal. The barn is full enough." I was brushing hay off the knees of my jeans, still damp with manure from my tussle with the sheep.

"I'll take care of her. I really will. Oh, please! Why does everything have to die? I don't want her to die! And I won't eat her. You can't make me! I won't! Never!"

Jack and I exchanged glances. I shrugged. He closed his eyes and sighed.

"Yes!" said Erica. "I can! I can! Oh, I love you! I love you!" I turned to accept her exclamations of affection only to find she had buried her face in the sheep's side and was murmuring sweet nothings into the oily fleece.

She looked up and smiled. "Her name is Mae."

I shook my head and looked at Erica with a combination of amusement and admiration. Was she really smart enough to realize that I could never eat a mutton chop named after my own mother?

We made a deal. Jack or I, whoever did morning chores, would look after Mae in the mornings. But Erica now had regular evening chores, including hay and water for both Mae and her pony, Bill. She also fed the pigs in the evenings, standing on her tip-toes to dump grain into their trough.

Several months after Mae's arrival, Erica came rushing back from the barn. "Mom! Mom! She has babies. Two babies! Come see!"

We should have known. But the ewe's tangled wooly coat obscured her tail end and udder, the usual indicators of imminent birth. There she was, nuzzling two kinky little bodies standing on their still-wobbly legs and miraculously locating the udder under the shaggy growth of wool.

"One is a boy and one is a girl," Erica announced. "Their names are Charlotte and Alexander."

"Not Chop and Stew?" I asked, smiling in resignation.

Erica glowered at me. "I will never, ever eat them."

It was only a few days after school started the following September that I glanced out an upstairs window and saw two pale shapes lying on the field where Mae and her lambs, now almost as big as their mother, had been grazing. I headed out reluctantly, with Galen in tow and Strider rushing ahead. We'd just passed the corner of the barn when I spotted him — a grey wolf trotting from the bush toward the carcasses, which I could now see clearly were Mae and Charlotte. The wolf had obviously made his kill some time earlier and, perhaps frightened away by some barking dog or passing car, was now returning to the feast. My mother's name meant nothing to him.

Strider barked and charged toward the carcasses. I scooped up Galen and called the dog, not knowing what the wolf would do. Strider turned his shaggy white head toward me, back toward the wolf, then hesitantly came back and stood by my side. With my free hand, I grabbed him by the collar. The wolf stopped, looked around with ears forward, and slowly turned back toward the hill; I didn't see him again.

As the afternoon dragged on, I rehearsed my message to Erica. In the end, I just blurted it out. "A wolf got into the field and killed Mae and Charlotte," I said, giving her a hug. "Alexander is fine. He's in the barn."

"No! Oh no!"

I held her close, but there was nothing I could do to ease her pain. She'd loved and cared for those animals, done everything she'd promised to do, and still...

"It's not fair!"

216

"No," I said, echoing my own mother and every mother I've ever known. "Life's not always fair." How feeble. How true.

The tragedy left Erica with a lone ram. What choice did we have but to buy her two new ewes?

• • •

Looking back in time, and back through these pages, Erica appears too often grieving for lost animals. That's no accident, no memory glitch. She connected with animals on a level no one else in the family reached.

Over the years, our menagerie grew to Old Macdonald proportions, but it was the cow-calf operation that paid the bills to the extent that anything did. That operation relied on sending young animals to their deaths and delivering them later, cut and wrapped in brown paper, to customers eager for our lean, grass-fed beef.

"You've got a good-lookin' crop of calves this year," Morley would say to Jack, as though they were a field of corn.

Erica became Jack's reliable helper in the meat delivery operation, lugging boxes of steaks and roasts to freezers in basements all over Sault Ste. Marie. This didn't appear to trouble her. It was harder for her to think of her lambs as a crop.

"I still won't eat lamb," she says to me, more than twenty-five years after she—and the last of her sheep—left the farm. "Remember the contract?"

I'd forgotten. After the wolf tragedy, when we agreed to buy her two new ewes, we drew up a written agreement. She agreed to be responsible for their care and to sell their lambs for meat. She also agreed to purchase hay from us from her profits, working off some of the value by doing her share of barn and field chores. And, we agreed not to serve lamb at our dinner table.

"I'm sure I was the only kid in grade four with a business contract," she laughs.

217

"It worked," I say. She paid her first year's university tuition with the proceeds from her sheep business. But we both know I mean more than that.

"The boys both grew up on the farm," I muse. "But you were invested in it in a way they weren't."

She agrees. The sheep, of course. The horses, too. "I loved the animals. More than people for a lot of years."

"Do you ever wish you were doing it now?" I ask, looking out the window of her suburban living room, in a house chosen because it backs onto a farmer's field. Shades of home.

"No. Not the farm. But I wish my kids could have had the freedom we had. Even the freedom to screw up." Her two boys are young adults now. She pauses, letting an emotional moment pass.

"I loved the farm. But in a way, it wasn't real. Like, when I got to university and realized I didn't have any street smarts. None. I just wanted to walk everywhere alone, at night. Because I always had. My city friends thought I was insane. They scared me so much that I became afraid of everything."

I nod. I remember that, the frightened phone calls, the feeling that our competent, independent daughter was lost. "No. I guess we didn't teach you to be suspicious. But in the end? Would you have had it different?" I need to know.

She shakes her head. "No. It was a wonderful way to grow up."

I look at the row of home-canned peaches, shining yellow in jars on her kitchen counter and think of her freezer, filled with local produce. Her little garden. Her commitment to full-time mothering, at some personal cost. Her dog and three cats. No. Not the farm. But she carries a passion for the hands-on making of a home. I gave her that. I think she's grateful.

CHAPTER 14 • ACCORDING TO THE SEASONS

Art returned for a second summer, and then a third. During his second year Jack's niece, Jenny, his brother Pete's oldest daughter, joined him. Jody continued to work for us during the summer months, sometimes with his younger brother, Tim. After a few years, Art's younger brother and Jenny's younger sister took their places. City kids looking for a farm experience provided a full crew on the hayfields and a summer-camp feel around the house — screen doors banging, good-natured teasing and taunting, occasional sulks, pies and cakes devoured at a single sitting, laundry on the clothesline every day, and a raucous crowd of teenagers around the supper table. Erica and Robin tagged along much of the time, feeling like members of the crew, calling their dad "Jack" like the big kids, and gradually learning to be a real help.

With extra help on the field and a toddler in the house, the division of labour, which had already veered sharply toward the conventional, became even more entrenched. I did most of the milking, all of the cooking and cleaning, all of the gardening, freezing and canning, and most of the childcare. Jack spent long hours on the fields, built and mended fences, cleaned the barn, and repaired equipment. Oh yes, and held down a full-time university teaching job. Both of us crossed the line into the other's territory when the need arose, but that happened less and less often as we settled into our comfort zones. The voices of feminism notwithstanding, that was okay. Although I was fulfilling neither the dream of homesteading nor the dream of professional excellence, I was no longer apologizing for being "a farm wife." More and more, I was seeing that "women's work" was only trivial because it was trivialized. By choosing to farm, we had chosen a home life that depended on women's work as much as men's, and neither of us ever exhausted our to-do list.

• • •

Walking back from the barn one early July day, I stopped and sniffed. On this shining morning, when the summer smells of cut grass and peonies should have filled my nostrils, I was smelling sewage.

"Too many people for the system," said Jack. Jenny was with us, as well as Art's brother Dan.

I grimaced. "The Whites had nine kids. That can't be it."

We hitched the tractor to the Whites' old outhouse, a dilapidated little building that used a pail under the seat instead of the usual pit, and dragged it close to the house. I painted it white and yellow, put a toilet seat over the hole, placed a pail of lime on the floor with an empty soup can for sprinkling after each use, and announced that the outhouse was to be used by anyone who was already outside. Every few days Jack carried the bucket out into the field, where he dug a hole and buried the contents. Men's work, I was pleased to note.

When, in spite of the outhouse, bath water and sewage continued bubbling to the surface, we reserved the bathroom for small children and full-grown adults, threw dishwater and wash water outside, kept soap and shampoo by the river, and called a guy with a backhoe to put in a new septic system.

On a Thursday morning several weeks later, the day before Jenny's parents were due to pick her up, the backhoe guy finally chugged into the yard, to Robin's delight and my own more ambivalent response. I was already heavily into image management, anticipating the arrival of Jack's brother Pete and his wife, Lucy. They were staying overnight in a hotel in the Sault but would spend some time visiting us on the farm. The backhoe hadn't been part of my image. But then, neither had seeping sewage.

I'd enlisted Jenny for the day. While the backhoe worked outside, she and I moved from room to room, tidying, dusting, and polishing. She bewailed her imminent return to a life of perpetually clean floors, clean fingernails, tennis lessons, and the rules and expectations of her conventional, successful, urban parents.

"That's not how I wanna live," she said. "I'm gonna have a farm like this. With horses. And chickens. I want chickens." She was scraping dried cookie dough off the counter while I ran a damp mop over the narrow, maple floorboards. "I don't care so much about a perfect house. I'd really like to be like you." It felt good to have a fan, but at the moment I was focused on how to make a good impression on her parents.

Late that afternoon, someone picked the backhoe operator up in a car and drove away, leaving the big yellow machine in our yard.

"I'll finish this up tomorrow," he promised as he left.

After they tired of climbing on the backhoe, Erica and Robin began playing a game of "flood", which involved filling a toy swimming pool with water from the hose, throwing various toy animals into the deluge, and rescuing them with a fishing net, shouting "Flood! Flood!" and "Save me! Save me!" at the top of their lungs. Jenny took care of Galen while I walked to the field and brought Gypsy, the new Brown Swiss milk cow, in for the night. The flood game continued. When we saw the last load of hay coming in from the field, Jenny and I set the table for eight. Jody and Tim had been working on the field with Jack and Dan.

"Seven hundred bales," said Jack, shovelling a forkful of pot roast into his mouth and nodding approval at his young crew. "These guys worked hard. Tomorrow, we'll take a break. It's Jenny's last day. Pete and Lucy will be coming in the afternoon. We'll want to show them around, have a nice supper before they leave."

"Way to go!" shouted Dan. "I'm watching the late show tonight and sleeping 'til noon."

"Me, too," said Jenny.

"Can I?" asked Erica, inching her chair closer to Jenny's.

"Nope. Just the big kids," I said.

"I'm big," said Robin.

After supper, the three boys and Jenny jumped in the river with bars of soap, splashing and shouting until the last glimmers of sunlight disappeared over the river. Jody and Tim headed home in the dusk. By the time Jenny and Dan came in, our three were asleep and Jack and I were in bed. We heard the TV turn on in the living room.

I snuggled against Jack, who still smelled of sweat, dry grass, and sunshine. He tickled me with his beard. "Tired?" he asked.

"Yeah. But mostly, I'm really nervous about Pete and Lucy coming," I whispered. "The whole septic thing. The outhouse. The place just isn't…" He didn't let me finish.

"It's fine," he said. "We've got a little plumbing problem, so what? Why do you care so much what other people think? It is what it is."

I closed my eyes and turned over. I wasn't sure why, but I did care, I always cared, and Jack didn't. An old story. No point in talking about it.

The next morning, when I turned on the kitchen tap to make coffee, nothing came out.

"What?" I screamed. "We're out of water!"

"Huh?" Jack muttered, zipping up his pants as he came into the kitchen. "Quiet down. You'll wake everybody."

"What's going on?" I didn't care who I woke.

We walked outside together. The newly dug hole for the septic tank was a muddy lake; the trenches for the tiles were moats; the untouched grass, a swamp. The hose lay beside the kids' plastic pool where all the plastic animals floated like so many dead bodies. The backhoe had sunk into the mud.

"What the hell happened here?" Jack asked. He wasn't muttering anymore.

I slumped against the deck, dropped my head to my knees. "It was a game. Called flood. They didn't turn the water off."

The thousand-gallon holding tank was drained dry; it would be two days before our slow-flowing well built up enough water to prime the pump. In the meantime, we had no running water in the house, a yard filled with muddy water, an outhouse with a bucket half-full of shit, foul-smelling sewage still oozing out near the old septic tank, and Pete and Lucy due in a few hours.

"It is what it is," said Jack. His stoic wisdom was even more annoying than his psychology professor punditry.

"Very profound," I said. "What are we going to do?"

The backhoe guy swore when I called, and made it clear that we'd be charged a daily rate for the equipment until the yard dried out enough for him to return.

I filled two big glass jars and the canning kettle full of drinking water from a neighbour's tap; Jack emptied the outhouse bucket, scrubbed the floor and walls as well as he could with Pinesol and water from the river, and we each carried two buckets of river water to the bathroom for flushing.

As the hour approached for her parents' arrival, Jenny announced that she was going to work on cleaning the barn, a job that always fell between the cracks.

By our third winter on the farm, despite the manure bucket and track that he'd thought would make barn-cleaning so easy, Jack had convinced himself that letting manure pile up under the yearlings all winter kept them warmer. Instead of cleaning daily or even weekly, we heaped dry straw on top of the accumulated manure and left the major cleanup for summer when the barn was empty and we had helpers.

Jack looked at Jenny in surprise. "You're what?" Nobody ever volunteered to clean the barn.

"Not a good plan, Jenny," I said. "Your mom and dad will be here soon."

"Yeah? So?" She shrugged and gave me a half-grin.

"So. You'll be a smelly mess. There's no shower." Another shrug. I was pretty sure I understood.

When Pete and Lucy finally showed up in their spiffy-clean Buick station wagon, wearing golf shirts tucked into belted Bermuda shorts, and sporting golf-course and tennis-court tans, Jenny emerged from the barn, pitchfork in hand, her jeans splattered with straw and manure, her long brown hair pulled into a tangled pony-tail under a feed-store ball cap, damp bangs clinging to her forehead, a sweat-stained tank top proudly advertising her farmer's tan.

"Hi Mom," she said, tossing the pitchfork aside and running toward Lucy with a wide-mouthed grin, arms outstretched. Lucy flinched. "Jenny." She gave a little laugh. "Look at you! I'll give you a hug after you've cleaned up."

"There's no water, Mom!" she said. I'd hoped to break it more gently.

Pete reached over and gave her an arms-length pat on the back. "This little brother of mine has turned you into a farmer."

"Tried my best," said Jack, shaking Pete's hand and giving Lucy a quick hug. "Welcome to the homestead. We're under a bit of construction and having a plumbing crisis. You know, country living!" he said, waving a dismissive hand at the outhouse and the water-logged trenches.

Jenny couldn't contain herself any longer. She blocked their way as they moved toward the house.

"Oh, Mom! Dad! You have to see! The cows! The barn! The hay! The river! The garden! The hill! Just look!" They looked, but they didn't see what Jenny saw; I could tell from their fixed smiles.

They saw a grimy teenager; a yard filled with muddy trenches; a barnyard dappled in cow pies and cluttered with equipment. I know, because that's what I saw, too, looking through their eyes, and for a long moment I wished it all away.

Then, I followed Jenny's gaze, past the flooded yard and the makeshift outhouse to the fields and the cows grazing against the backdrop of the hill. I put my arm around Jenny and pulled her close, breathing in the mingled smells of sweat and manure.

"We've enjoyed having her here so much," I said. "Now, Jenny. Go jump in the river! You stink!"

• • •

Seasons became years. By our seventh summer on the farm, we were no longer novices, and I no longer had the excuse of a baby in the house.

On a July day, I straightened my back and smeared the sweat from my face onto my t-shirt. Before I could stretch my shoulders back, another bale catapulted from the baler onto the wagon. More than a thousand bales worth of hay lay on the ground, and the weatherman was calling for a thunderstorm. All hands were on board to get the hay in before the rain. I'd sent Galen down the road to play with a friend so I could join the crew.

I bent down, looped my fingers under the taut twine that held the 50-pound rectangle of hay, and heaved it up two tiers to Erica, who shoved it snugly against the last one. She grinned, loving the fact that she was really part of the crew. Before we finished this day, four or five more loads would be stacked on wagons, then un- loaded, bale by bale onto the elevator, and finally stacked in the haymow. Dan was driving the tractor; he now was a lanky 16- year-old, clad in a long-sleeved cotton shirt and a broad-brimmed hat, with a red kerchief around his neck. Robin, old enough and big enough to be a real help, was working with Jody unloading bales from a full wagon to the elevator, leaving Jack, as always, with the hottest, heaviest job of all, picking the bales off the elevator and packing them tightly into place in the haymow. When they weren't packed snugly enough, we stumbled dangerously on them all winter.

The sun was high in the sky, the temperature in the high eighties, and the work relentless. I gazed across the field at the foot-wide windrows of freshly raked hay snaking across at 10-foot intervals, creating fluffy, pale-green stripes that stretched a quarter of a mile from the road to the edge of the bush. Round by round, the baler was erasing the stripes, leaving a field of short-cut grass that looked like a vast, well-manicured park.

Idly, I did the math. At 50 pounds a bale, 120 bales a load, we were talking three tons. Three tons of hay stacked on the wagon. The same three tons moved from the wagon to the elevator. Then again, stacked in the barn. Nine tons worth of handling per wagon load. And that didn't count feeding them a few at a time throughout the winter.

Another one shot onto the wagon.

Seven years. Seven years times nine tons times…

Another bale. Erica reached down from the first tier to grab it from me, it slipped onto the wagon floor, I pushed it back up to her, grasping it by the strings and hoisting it with my right knee just in time to turn around and pull the next one off the baler. The sharp edges of cut hay etched painful scratches into my forearms, and chaff mixed with sweat clung to my skin.

When I tugged on the twine of the next bale, the bundle of hay fell apart into thin wafers of at my feet.

"Stop!" I shouted. Dan pushed in the clutch and disengaged the baler, but not before it spit out another untied bale onto the chute between the baler and the wagon.

"Run and get Jack! Tell him the knotter's gone again."

I leaned back on the hay and enjoyed the slight breeze cooling my face and neck. Erica sprawled on the top of the half-built load. I should have felt dismay, not relief; there was a lot of hay to bale before the storm, and this would slow us down.

Jack hated mechanical breakdowns, which was too bad, since we'd learned that farming was about equipment as much as about land and animals. Fred White's original tractor, the W4, had seized up behind the far barn and was replaced by a newer Russian model, a Belarus 610. We'd ditched two ancient manure spreaders that Jack couldn't repair, and a small bulldozer sat rusting in the barnyard.

Jack was peering into the back of the baler. "It's the fu..." he glanced up at Erica, who smirked. "It's the friggin' knotter again." I already knew that. He was speaking in that front-of-the-mouth way that meant he was about to explode.

"You might as well head back to the house," he said. "We're not doing anything until I get this damned thing fixed." He looked at Erica and softened. "Then maybe Erica can drive, Dan can rack, and you can help with the unloading when the wagons come in."

"I can drive the baler?" Erica's eyes bulged with excitement. She was eleven. It was time. She'd already driven disks, harrows, the hayrake.

Halfway to the house, I looked back at Jack who stood beside the baler, looking smaller than usual, defeated. I thought of Morley's comment a few weeks earlier. He was helping Jack with a tractor repair when he looked up and said, "You're a professor. You're supposed to be so damned smart. Why can't you see how this works?" He couldn't, though. He wasn't smart in that mechanical way.

Back in the house, I was happy to escape both the heavy work and the sour mood. Unloading wasn't easy work, but at least gravity was on my side most of the time. And it took less time than building a load on the field, which let me juggle it with stuff in the house, including some secret down time.

I phoned the weather office, then emptied an ice cube tray into a big glass jar, filled it with water, and handed it to Erica. "Take this to Dad, and tell him they're calling for rain by seven or eight o'clock. And have fun driving."

The screen door slammed behind her, and she headed to the field, hugging the cold jar against her t-shirt — but not before taking advantage of the opportunity to taunt her brother.

"I'm gonna drive the baler. Too bad you can't," she shouted over her shoulder, tossing her shoulder-length blond braids for emphasis.

"Mom, why can't I drive too? I can steer better than Erica!" It was probably true. At nine, he'd begun driving the tractor with the hayrake. A few days earlier, Jack and I had stood by the edge of the field watching him make his first rounds alone. He was bursting with pride, and showing a natural comfort with the equipment. But the baler carried more status, and Erica had the advantage of both age and judgement.

"Because you'll be helping me unload the hay when the wagons come in."

"I want to drive." The screen door slammed again, and I saw Robin running across the field toward the baler. No big deal. He could help on the wagon until it was time to unload again.

I ran hot water into the milking pail, sniffed the sour cheese-cloth strainer from the morning's milk and tossed it in the garbage, then started loading the dishwasher, a recent acquisition that had only briefly pricked my back-to-the-land conscience. Looking up I saw the tractor framed in the kitchen window, moving again with Erica at the wheel, a smile animating her whole body, and Robin helping Jack on the wagon.

When the wagon was full, heading off the field with Erica and Robin riding on the top tier, I left the kitchen and began walking toward the barn to do my stint unloading just as the neighbour's car pulled into the driveway. The back door opened, and Galen came running toward me.

"Hi, Mommy. I'm home. Jen and I found a bear. It came to their house. It wasn't really a bear, it was a dog. They might keep it. Jen is going to name it Bear. It's brown. But maybe her dad won't let her. Because they have two cats. Can I go on the hay wagon now? Daddy said I could."

I gave my little blond chatterbox a hug—Happy Mouth, Erica had dubbed him. "Yes, you can come up on the hay wagon, but you have to be careful and stay out of the way. Can you do that?"

"Yes. I can help too. I can push the bales down." He was jumping from one foot to the other.

"No, pumpkin. You can't push the bales. But you can count them. That would be a big help."

"I can. I can count to 100. One, two, three, four…"

"Good stuff. Let's go."

"Seven, eight, nine…"

We walked the rest of the way to the barn together while Jack maneuvered the wagon into position. I boosted Galen up on the wagon; Erica scrambled up over the draw-bar; the unloading crew was ready.

"Seventeen, twenty, twenty two…"

Later, while everyone else worked to put the last wagonload in the barn, I walked to the pasture to bring Gypsy in. Dark clouds began to gather, but we'd beaten the rain.

When, sometime after ten o'clock, I finally turned to the supper dishes—my final task of the day—I found myself staring out the kitchen window yet again. The sky had cleared after the storm, the fields were fading into darkness and the hill was a shadowy shape in the background. A few clumps of grass missed by the baler shone pale in the fading light. If the weather cooperated, tomorrow would be much like today. Jack would head out early with the mower to cut another field. Later in the morning, the rake would begin its rounds on the field he'd cut this morning, followed by the baler. Around and around the field. Day after day. This was July on the farm.

I sighed. Exhaustion. Resignation. Contentment. All three.

Jack came up behind me and put his arms around my waist. "Leave the dishes 'til morning," he said. "Come out and look at the moon."

• • •

By the early 1980s, the nieces and nephews had cycled through and were now holding down summer jobs at home, no doubt sharing tales of farm work in the wilds of northern Ontario. But our own children were not quite old enough to be full farm hands.

Jack came in the house after his last teaching day in April and dropped his briefcase on the kitchen floor with a thump. "Another school year gone. Time to get moving around here now." His eyes lit up, anticipating the frenzy of summer.

Over pork chops and applesauce, he said, "Laura Jensen asked me today if her boys could work on the farm this summer. They're fourteen and sixteen. I said I'd think about it." Laura was one of Jack's mature students at the university. "It could solve our problem for haying season."

"Mom! Robin's making faces," said Erica.

"Am not." He blew a raspberry at her.

"Stop it, both of you," I said, and Erica assumed her smug big sister face.

I finished cutting pieces of pork chop for Galen, then turned back to Jack.

"Do you know these kids?"

"No. Laura says they're big and eager to work."

"Sounds familiar," I said, thinking of Art's first year.

"Mom, what's this meat?" asked Erica, stabbing her fork into a chunk.

"Pork. It's a pork chop. I'm trying to talk to Dad now."

"But is it from the pigs?" she asked. "Is it Oink? Or Squeal?"

"One of them, yes. Now please let me talk to Dad."

She put the meat down and took a bite of applesauce. "I don't really like pork."

Laura's boys arrived the first week of July. Chuck was a strapping seventeen-year-old whose hobby was archery. He carried a bow and arrow around with him much of the time, taking aim at random targets.

"You can't use that here," I said. "Too many kids around."

"I'll be careful," he was aiming his arrow at a fencepost.

"Not here. Not ever. Period."

"Yeah, okay, whatever." He stabbed the arrow into the ground.

His younger brother, Brian, was an overweight fifteen-year-old with B.O., a bad case of acne, and hair that hung over his forehead in greasy brown strings. He sulked through supper and rarely joined in the lively repartee that had become standard fare at mealtimes.

"Did you see those mosquitos? Look at these." Chuck was stuffing his second sandwich into his mouth with one hand and holding out his arm to reveal a series of red bumps. Badges of honour.

"Heck, those are just summer mosquitos," said Jody. "You oughta see the spring ones. They're as big as birds."

A late morning rainstorm had cancelled fieldwork for the day.

"What's on for the afternoon?" asked Jody.

"Firewood. We'll be in the bush. With the mosquitos!" said Jack.

"I'll drive the tractor," said Chuck.

"No, I will," said Jody, who claimed seniority among the summer workers.

"I don't really like doing firewood," Brian grumbled. "Do I have to help?"

"Only if you want to stay here," said Jack. He turned to Erica and Robin. "You two will be helping this afternoon, too. Let's get this job done."

"Can I drive..."

"I'll drive the tractor," said Jack, cutting Brent off before he could continue. Everybody else can ride on the wagon. "Erica, you can ride Bill if you want."

"My mom said it would be fun here," said Brian. "She was wrong."

His mom was also wrong when she told the boys we'd be paying them working wages. We did pay Jody and other local kids an hourly rate, often supplemented by a government grant. They came after breakfast, went home before supper — except on haying days — and slept in their own homes, where presumably they dropped their dirty clothes on their own bedroom floors. The kids who stayed with us became part of the family and received an envelope of cash when they left. That's what Morley did. That's what the nieces, nephews, and cousins expected. Nobody ever asked for more. Until Chuck and Brian.

In fact, their mom should have paid us. Chuck's aggression and fits of temper disrupted the household and interfered with the camaraderie of the farm work. Brian was not only a sulker, he was a bed-wetter — which I learned when I found several damp, reeking sheets bunched under his mattress.

"What the hell?" I said to Jack. "It's not as though I don't have enough to do around here. There are six people living in this house right now, eight for meals. Help for you. Do you know what it means for me? Couldn't she have said something? Does she think because you're a psych prof, we're a treatment centre?" I slammed the basket of laundry on the deck and started filling the clothesline, reeling it away from the house and watching the sheets flap in the breeze.

Jack ignored my outburst and rubbed the side of his face with his finger, leaving a trail of grease on his beard. "It seems there's quite a bit she didn't say. According to Chuck, neither one of them wanted to come here. That's probably why she told them they'd get good money. I think she just wanted to be rid of them for the summer."

A week later, Jack drove Chuck and Brian back to their mother's home in the Sault with an envelope of cash for each of them. Within days, word was out around the university: Jack Dunning was using slave labour on his farm, enticing kids to do grueling work for no wages. We were heartsick.

"I should never have agreed," he said that night as we were climbing into bed. "But she seemed so desperate for the boys to have this experience. She lied to them. She knew we didn't pay wages. If they'd been working for wages, they'd have been fired after the first couple of days."

"What are you going to do about the rumours?" I thumped my pillow and turned to face him.

"Nothing. What can I do? It'll just have to blow over." He reached over for me. "Look at the bright side," he said. "With all this experience, we'll be prepared when our own kids are teenagers."

Looking on the bright side never came easily to me.

• • •

The intensity of July faded into the gentler rhythms of August. Time to harvest the garden, mend fences, bring in firewood, but also time to relax a bit, swim at the beach, camp at the lake, and go to the fair. A break between July haying and September plowing.

We stopped farming a long time ago, but these rhythms still beat on around us.

On this September morning in 2015, Jack and I are sitting on the deck with our morning coffee, watching Ed plow the field closest to the house. Ed was one of the neighbourhood kids who sometimes helped us on these same fields thirty years ago; now he is one of the few active farmers around, and he rents our land to provide hay for his herd of beef cattle.

Plowing is an exercise in geometry; it depends on straight lines and careful division of the field into even segments, or "lands". The result: unbroken crowns and furrows stretching across the field, end to end. "Unless," says Jack, taking a sip of coffee and looking a bit wistful, "you've mistaken a tree on the far side for the midpoint stake, in which case you're fifteen feet off and you correct it halfway across the field and nothing will be straight from then on."

It's been more than twenty-five years since either of us plowed a field, and Jack is helping me remember the details.

You work outward from the centre, he reminds me, so the second pass creates a hump by flipping over on top of the first. I remember now. After that, it's smooth going, as each brown ribbon of earth flips over and leans against the last one, leaving a fringe of green along the top. Drive to the end. Lift the plows. Turn left. Drive past the last row of freshly turned earth. Drop the plows. Begin again. Look up at the changing leaves, down at the cloud shadows, over your right shoulder to keep the line straight. If you've measured and paced carefully and lined up your first pass accurately, you will create a deep, broad "dead furrow" where the crowns of abutting lands flip away from each other.

"Or," says Jack, "you create a dead furrow on one end that turns into a huge unplowed triangle at the other end that you have to try to patch up. And you hope that's the end away from the road where no one can see it." More than anything else, a freshly plowed field announces your farming skill to all who drive by.

Aside from the aesthetic challenge they create, traditional moldboard plows, which haven't changed much since oxen pulled them, have two disadvantages. They trap most of the decaying organic matter beneath the surface where new growth has trouble reaching it. And they create a slick, impenetrable layer of hardpan that interferes with drainage in wet years and with root development in dry years.

So in the mid 1980s, after a decade of following tradition, Jack decided to shift methods.

"More book stuff," Morley scoffed.

A shiny new tractor-mounted Howard rototiller, with its bright orange casing and silver blades, announced to the neighbourhood that the Dunnings were about to break the rules. Even George slowed down to watch the rototiller in action as it churned across the field that fall, leaving a path of clumpy soil mixed with chopped roots and grass.

"We'll go over it once in the fall instead of plowing, then twice more in the spring before planting," said Jack after reading the extensive instructions inside the orange manual. "No need for the discs or harrows. And it goes deeper than the hardpan, breaks it up."

That spring, our seedbed was finer than it had ever been and the fields freer of weeds. The neighbours lined up to get Jack to rototill their gardens. He took a break from the fieldwork in May and drove up and down the road, preparing vegetable gardens and cementing friendships, with one exception.

Bob Lewis was an old-timer. His family had cleared land in the valley. They had farmed summers and logged the nearby bush in the winters for several generations. Bob worked in the bush with his brother in the winter, sold firewood and pulpwood, and did a bit of farming in the summer. A few cows. Some chickens.

"I was wonderin'," I heard him say to Jack at the back door, "if you'd be able to till up my field, there."

"Sure," said Jack. "Glad to. Gonna plant a crop?" We'd never seen him plant a crop.

"Naw," said Bob. "I'm gonna sell the topsoil. Only thing the place is good for. Figured that machine of yours'd be the best way to ready it up."

As he backed his dented, un-muffled pick-up out the driveway, I said, "Selling the soil? Are you gonna do that?"

"No," said Jack. "I don't think I can. But what can I say?"

"You can say 'no.'"

"Yeah. That'll get around. But I can't be part of chopping up the valley and trucking it away."

It did get around. We didn't care.

• • •

On the deck thirty years later I ask, "What made you decide on the rototiller in the first place?"

"I read about people using chisel plows to break up the hard-pan, improve drainage. But I knew we couldn't use one on our clay soil. Too heavy. That's what led me to the rototiller."

"People thought we were nuts, you know."

"Yeah. For a while. But it worked. I never plowed again. And even though you'd never know it around here, moldboard plow-ing is on the way out." This morning, Ed is pulling a six-furrow moldboard plow, making short work of the field, turning straight, even furrows

Jack looks at me with a half-grin. "Truth is, I was never any good at plowing. Couldn't get the depth adjusted right. Couldn't get the rows to flip over evenly. Couldn't run two parallel lines at that distance, then ended up with crooked dead furrows. I always hated the way our fields looked."

236

"Compared to Morley's?" I ask.

"Compared to anybody's."

"You really cared that much?" I suddenly remember how he always went back across the hayfields with the baler to pick up loose clumps he'd missed, just to leave it tidy. And, because it's a nice day, and I'm feeling generous, and it was a long time ago, I don't say anything about muddy floors and dirty bolts on kitchen counters.

"So, you did it for your reputation?" I ask.

"Well. Not only. But it's better to be quirky than incompetent."

CHAPTER 15 • HAVING IT ALL

Sometimes during these middle years, I still found myself dwelling on the roads not taken. Alumni newsletters arrived regularly with announcements of advanced degrees, promotions, faculty appointments, and good works abroad. Guitar-playing protesters were going on to become doctors, teachers, even—God forbid—company managers. The party-girl with the bouffant hairdo who lived down the hall my freshman year was now a human rights lawyer. My friend Carolyn had completed her Ph.D. and kept me posted on her career progress. I dreaded opening her letters because I knew days of self-doubt and what-ifs would follow. On those days, I envied the river its ability to flow back.

• • •

One day when Galen was still a baby and I was feeling content with my life as a farm wife and mother, I sipped tea at Elda's kitchen table, cluttered with the remnants of our lunch. Galen sat on my lap, playing with a spoon, while Elda hovered over Robin's head with a pair of scissors. Elda was the official barber among the Sylvan Valley Crowd. Free haircuts, mushroom soup, and sandwiches. It was a good deal, as long as we didn't mind everyone having roughly the same haircut. She gave home perms too, so the women could choose straight or curly.

I was here for Robin's haircut, but something else was on my mind. Erica was in grade two, and she was coming home with stories about the "Bible teacher." I'd kept my peace about the born-again kindergarten teacher, feeling too new in the community and assuming she was an anomaly. Now I was beginning to wonder. Elda had grown up here, but she was one of "us". I was sure she'd agree with me.

"I can't believe it. She's proselytizing seven-year-olds," I said.

"I don't see it that way," Elda said, snipping dark curls from around Robin's ears. "Look down, Robin… She's just telling Bible stories."

Miss Grey represented the Canadian Bible Society and volunteered at local public school classrooms for half an hour each week, lugging her picture books and felt boards. In fact, she did a lot more than tell stories. After a mind-expanding trip to Japan, she explained to the children that Buddhists were heathens and destined for hell. Erica came home terrified by the Passover story; as the first-born and not Jewish, would she be killed? Could we maybe become Jewish? And Miss Grey routinely asked for a show of hands by those who loved Jesus. Of course, everybody loved Jesus.

"It's a public school," I said to Elda. "Religion doesn't belong there. And the kids are too young to make sense of the stories. Erica's not even seven, for god's sake." I shifted Galen on my lap. "Robin, sit still so Elda can finish."

"Miss Grey's been doing this since I was in school," said Elda. "It's a tradition, and most of the parents love her. If you don't like it, I'm sure you can ask to have Erica leave the room."

That didn't satisfy me; neither did assurances from the principal that he used the strap "only as a last resort" and "only on the back of the hand." That fall, my name appeared on the ballot for school board. To my surprise, no one opposed me. Why, I wondered, when everyone else in elected positions carried a local pedigree? Certainly, it wasn't because of my opinion about Miss Grey or the strap.

The answer arrived at the end of my driveway one snowy December morning when I was shovelling the heap of snow the plow had dumped. The mail lady stopped to put the day's envelopes in

239

our mailbox. We exchanged greetings, and then she said, "We're so lucky to have a teacher on the school board. You really understand how the system works." Aha. So it was a case of mistaken identity. She meant Sheila, who was also newly elected to the board, or maybe Carol, who'd served for the previous term. Both of them were teachers. I wasn't, and as a new Canadian, I hadn't a clue how the system worked.

• • •

I attended my first school board meeting as a trustee in January, 1977. I stood solemnly beside my chair, swore allegiance to Canada and the Queen (yet again) and promised to uphold the province's Education Act, which I had never seen. Jack was waiting up for me when I got home, close to midnight. "How'd it go?"

I shrugged. "Okay, I guess. They're a pretty stodgy bunch of old men—twelve of them. I expect they're all over fifty. And Sheila, of course. And it's more about money than kids." And so it seemed as my first year on the board unfolded: provincial grants, local taxation, equalization factors, teacher salaries, budget approvals. Miss Grey and the strap may have been top of my mind, but they didn't appear on anyone else's agenda.

As months past, I began to see those stodgy old men as individuals with their own sets of priorities, and I began to develop respect for their deep connections to and understanding of the communities they represented, a string of small villages along the north shore of Lake Huron between Echo Bay to the west and the town of Thessalon to the east. They were farmers, businessmen, one retired principal, good-hearted men who spoke with the voices of experience.

One night after I'd been on the board for almost a year, I came home late from a meeting to find Jack already asleep. He opened

240

an eye when I crawled into bed and mumbled his usual half-asleep greeting: "How was the meeting?"

"Okay," I said, too keyed up to leave it at that. "We're getting ready for negotiations with the secondary teachers. They're asking for the moon."

Jack was awake now, and seemed to be listening.

"If they get what they want, we have to raise taxes or cut staff. If we raise taxes, people will be pissed. If we cut staff, people will be pissed. Of course, the old guys don't say 'pissed.'" I tugged at my share of the covers.

"Interesting," said Jack. "Very interesting." I looked at him. Was he kidding?

"You just said 'we.' Not 'they.' It's the first time." He rolled onto his side and went back to sleep.

I lay awake thinking. Yes, this was working for me. The school board was satisfying what Sheila referred to as my "illusions of grandeur", and I was beginning to see that its decisions did, indeed, make a difference to kids in schools; the daily and seasonal routines of the farm were creeping into my bones; my circle of friends was broadening and deepening; the neighbourhood was feeling like home turf; when I shopped at Buchanans, people greeted me by name — usually my own.

I drifted off to sleep to the sound of a late fall rain hammering against the house. By morning it had turned to snow.

• • •

Though I had often imagined — still sometimes imagined — myself on a different path, I didn't want to leave the one I was on. But as Galen approached school age, the self-doubt I'd put to rest for a few years began to re-emerge. The river notwithstanding, I knew I couldn't go back. But I was determined to have it all somehow.

Summers continued to be hectic, driven by weather and the pressures of a short growing season, but for much of the year farm work consisted of necessary but brief forays to the barn twice a day. The school board filled, at most, one or two evenings a week. The fantasy of rural life had become a reality with staying power, but it was no longer a mission—just a life, and one with too many aimless days.

I wasn't alone. Everyone was changing. Carol had gone back to teaching full-time; Bonnie had left her husband and was living in town; other members of the Sylvan Valley circle who had dabbled in farming were working as teachers or nurses. Sheila was still farming seriously and now had five children, two still toddlers at home; but her marriage was on the rocks, and even she was looking, reluctantly, toward a return to teaching. Of that crowd, only Elda still stayed at home full-time. And me. Of course, Gloria continued in her role as farm wife and mentor, never appearing to question its worth. I envied her that, but it wasn't in my nature.

What to do? Should I return to university for a Ph.D. or some saleable qualification? Teacher? Counsellor? Librarian? All the options for further education meant leaving Jack, the kids, the farm, and the school board for an extended period. I couldn't do it. I considered writing; I'd always thought of myself as a writer-in-waiting. I pulled out my old typewriter and banged out some paragraphs about the farm, about Lake Superior, a dozen or so pages before concluding I hadn't waited long enough. Maybe sometime later I'd give life to that fantasy. For now, I needed something that looked outward, not inward.

A muffin franchise, at first glance, didn't seem to be the answer. But it had its appeal. By borrowing money against the farm, I could buy myself a small business, drive to town in clean clothes every morning after the chores were done and the kids left for school, spend several hours overseeing the operation, and return home in time for the school bus or, in the summer, in time to help with the field work. The muffins were healthy; the coffee good; the image wholesome; the prospects for profit excellent. Not the professional life I'd envisioned, but the more I thought about it, the more it seemed like a good way to fill the empty spot without giving up the life I valued. Maybe I *could* have it all.

I spent a week in Toronto, in the city's busiest subway station, learning the ropes: mixing muffin batter in huge tubs, baking dozens upon dozens of muffins, and watching them fly off the counter as the commuters rushed by and the cash poured in.

Back in the Sault, I ordered supplies, hired staff, studied operational manuals, and watched the shiny kiosk and kitchen spring up in a corner of the food court in the city's largest mall. Three days before opening, the huge yellow and blue sign went up over the curved plexiglas counter: *Mmmarvellous Mmmuffins*. The same day, Gino—a small, wiry guy who oozed something that may have passed for charm in some circles but just seemed oily to me— arrived from the head office to assist with the opening. He coached me on promotional strategies, ordering procedures, bookkeeping, franchise expectations.

I was filling out an employee schedule sheet for the first two weeks, half-listening to Gino explaining to the bakers how to soak raisins before adding them to the bran muffin batter, when the phone rang.

"Good afternoon, Mmmarvellous Mmmuffins," I answered, hoping I sounded cheerfully competent, professional.

It was Jack. Could I come home now? *Right now.* Erica's dog, Curry, a two-year-old collie, had been caught in one of the Trotter's beaver traps and killed. Erica was hysterical and needed me.

"Oh my god! You're sure she's dead?" I said into the phone. No question. Her neck had snapped.

Gino hovered. The young bakers stood with mouths agape.

"I'll be there as soon as I can," I said, reaching for my jacket and car keys as I hung up.

Gino didn't understand. If it had been the child, maybe. But it was a dog. And this was a business.

"It *is* a child. It's my daughter. She's heartbroken, and I'm going home. I'll be back tomorrow. We still have two days before opening. Time enough."

Gino shook his head as I rushed off.

By the time I got home, Erica had retreated to her bedroom where I found her sobbing into her pillow. "The stupid Trotters," she said, her voice muffled by the pillow. "They shouldn't be allowed to set traps."

"Where was it?" I ask.

"Over near Whites'. Beside the creek."

Of course, the Trotters had every right to set traps. They had a license and had done nothing wrong. It was Curry who'd been wrong—on the loose, away from home. But this wasn't the time to reason with Erica.

"We're all going to miss her," I said.

"Everything dies here," she said. She'd shifted position and was sobbing against my shoulder. "The goats. Mae and Charlotte. Gasman. Big Black." She was going back years.

The next day, though the pall of grief still hung over the house, life assumed a new normal. The kids climbed on the school bus. Jack drove to the college. I drove to the muffin shop.

On opening day, Gino tried his best to teach me the basics of marketing. I was a reluctant student. When the local newspaper arrived to interview me about this new enterprise, Gino stepped in and lied about the number of employees. Ten, he said. I tried to correct him. I scolded him when the interviewer left. Seven, not ten. And mostly part time. He scolded me back. "You have to make it sound more impressive. That's how business works."

When muffins didn't fly out at the rate we'd expected for opening day, Gino decided we had to draw attention to the place. He wandered into the middle of the mall to "create a scene." He

244

bumped into a garbage can and knocked it over with a crash, causing a commotion just outside the shop. I cringed behind the cash register — or, as Gino called it, the "Jewish piana". People stopped and looked, but they didn't rush to buy muffins. What had I got myself into? Well, I'd run it my way when he went back to Toronto in a couple of days.

By the end of the first week, I already knew: I really didn't care if people ate muffins. In fact, when — rarely — customers crowded around the counter, I became claustrophobic and annoyed. I wanted to shout, "Shoo! Go! Buy a donut!" But maybe it would grow on me. In the meantime, I'd have to put in a week or two of long days to get things running smoothly, whether I liked it or not.

I was tucking Galen into bed on Friday night. My hands smelled like cinnamon, and seven dozen muffins sat on the kitchen table, leftovers for the pigs; franchise rules prohibited me from selling day-olds. After I'd read *In The Night Kitchen* twice, a story featuring baking, dough, and a naked little boy falling through the air, Galen asked, "Will you have to go to the muffin store again tomorrow?"

"Yes, for a while. Not for all day."

"But, it's Saturday tomorrow." His face fell. "I thought you would be home."

"I know," I said, running my finger along his fair cheek, still faintly freckled from a summer in the sun. "But Saturday will be a busy day there."

"I knew it would be bad," he said, tears inching down his cheeks. "But I didn't think it would be *this* bad." My heart sank.

Mmmuffins didn't grow on me; it didn't grow at all. The kiosk looked clean and fresh; the muffins, displayed in wicker baskets, were delicious; I baked in small batches all day to keep the aroma fresh to entice customers. But at the end of the day, the numbers never lived up to the promises. I packed up extra muffins, sometimes dozens, for the kids' lunches, for friends, for nursing homes, for the pigs. By mid-January 1980, Canada was deep in recession. After paying for supplies, paying employees minimum wage, paying rent to the mall, paying the franchise fees, and making a monthly payment on the business loan, the books barely balanced. Nothing for me. I tried to cut back on staff, but not very successfully since I insisted on being home until the school bus left in the morning and back again by the time it returned, leaving employees to open in the morning and close at night. It wasn't just about me, I told myself. The young people working for me needed the money more than I did.

That Christmas, Mom, Dad, and both of my brothers drove from Pennsylvania to spend the holiday with us and to deliver Gylden, a Golden Retriever puppy for Erica. Pictures from that Christmas show Erica snuggling the puppy; Mom smiling as she unwrapped a candle from Galen; Dad wearing a too-snug rust-coloured vest I'd knitted; Robin unpacking a Star Wars model kit; Galen, grinning a toothless grin and twisting a Rubik's cube; and me, posing for the camera in an over-sized baker's hat—someone's idea of a joke. Jack, as always, was on the other side of the camera. Photography had become his latest enthusiasm.

What the photos don't show is that I was once again wishing I could reverse the current and find another way to have it all.

• • •

As months at Mmmarvellous Mmmuffins dragged on, I established a tolerable routine: up with the kids, barn chores, shower and dress for work, arrive at the shop mid-morning in time to give the morning staff their breaks, leave mid-afternoon, after giving the afternoon staff theirs, arrive home in time to meet the school bus. In the meantime, I made decisions about how much to bake, paid bills, ordered supplies, and tried to pretend this had been a good move and that I was a professional woman.

246

Sometimes, the afternoon baker called me at home. "We have two dozen apple cinnamon, six oatmeal raisin, and two dozen pineapple bran. The mall is dead. Should I bake more?"

How the hell should I know? But I had to answer.

"Well, maybe a dozen blueberry. They sometimes sell in the evening." The next day, I picked up the leftovers: eight apple cinnamon, two oatmeal raisin, eighteen pineapple bran, and eight blueberry. Bad call, again. Happy pigs.

• • •

One February morning, after the rest of the family had left for the day, I opened the barn door to a cold gust of wind instead of the usual warm, moist air. The door of Erica's sheep stall stood wide open, the ewes — now four — milled about in the aisle, and wind rushed through the back barn door, which hung ajar on its hinges. No sign of Alexander, the ram.

I herded the ewes back into their pen and tied the door closed with baler twine. Then I yanked the back door shut. It would need major repairs, but for the moment I found a hammer and fashioned a latch out of a spike and more baler twine. Then I went in search of Alexander.

I found him in the barnyard, among the cows. In all the years we'd had him, Alexander had never reconciled himself to his ram status; he dreamed of being a bull. In the summer, he wriggled out of the sheep yard to graze on the big pasture with the cows, waiting for them to come into heat. When that happened, he became a miracle of self-delusion, following the fertile cow about, ever hopeful, making lovesick, baaing sounds and rolling his eyes. He spent hours trying to mount her, only to be pushed away by the cow herself, or by the irritated bull, who always won in the end, of course.

Now, on this frigid, snowy day, he had abandoned his fellow sheep in their warm pen to stand outside with the cows. But he wasn't his usual audacious self. His head hung down, and he was taking small, stiff steps. I approached him from behind and saw a large part of his intestines protruding from a hideous wound in his side. A sharp object had obviously punctured his abdomen, almost certainly the horn of a cow that had lost patience with his uninvited attentions.

First, I called the vet. Then, I called Mmmuffins to explain. I wouldn't be coming in to work because our ram's insides were hanging out. They'd have to manage without me. Bake lots of raisin bran and order more coffee.

By the time the vet arrived, Alexander had slipped into a state of shock. He remained standing but did not respond to our prodding. Together, we moved him into a stall in the barn.

"He's in bad shape," said the vet. "I'd put him down if I were you."

I heard Erica's voice: *Everything dies here.*

"He's my daughter's," I said. "I want to try."

"It's going to cost you more than he's worth, and there's no guarantee he'll make it."

He was a farm vet, a practical man, not the sort of vet who urges you to brush your cat's teeth. But how could he know what Alexander was worth? I looked at the wooly head that had bashed through fences, gates, and barn doors for the past four years and shook my head.

"I know. I'll risk it."

Reluctantly, the vet pulled a bottle of disinfectant from his bag and began to scrub up for surgery. "He's too far gone to risk anesthesia. You'll have to sit on him."

We stretched Alexander out on some fresh straw. I straddled his neck, sitting gently back on his head and putting most of my weight on his shoulders. With scalpel and scissors, the vet enlarged the puncture, tucked the protruding intestines back where they belonged, cleansed and disinfected the whole lot, and stitched him up again.

"What a brave sheep," I said in my "weren't you a good boy at the dentist" voice.

The vet looked up from his work, apparently feeling some obligation to set the record straight. "Sheep have brains the size of a pea," he said. "You could do open heart surgery without being noticed." I nodded, thinking of the number of times this particular pea-sized brain had outsmarted me.

"If he makes it through the afternoon," the vet continued, "he'll probably be okay. Just keep him quiet until the wound is healed, give him half a syringe of antibiotic twice a day for a week, and don't let him in with the cattle again." The first two I figured we could manage.

By the time the school bus deposited the children at home that afternoon, Alexander was on his feet and eating grain — more docile than usual, but Erica had been spared another tragedy. And I'd had a mmmuffin-free day.

Chapter 16 • Grey Days

It was an exceptionally wet, dreary spring. When finally, in late May, Jack got on the field, the tractor sank in the mud. I roto-tilled the garden during a brief dry spell, only to have it drenched by ten days of rain before I could finally "muck it in"—poking peas, beans, and corn into their muddy rows with my index fingers. Sheila hosted a Noah's Ark party, which provided a brief note of humour; Jack and I dressed as a pair of water buffalo.

On most days, our moods matched the weather. Erica had become a sulky adolescent who slouched to and from the school bus, made good marks and few friends. She spent much of her time communing with Stardust, the larger, friskier horse that had joined Bill in the horse shed—sitting on him bareback, her face nestled against his mane—and with Gylden, her Golden Retriever. "They understand me better than you do!" When she was in the house, she buried herself in a nest of blankets in her bedroom, wrote stories of the life she would live if only she had different parents. Royalty would have pleased her, though she lacked the finer social graces for it.

Robin, now twelve, spent as much time as he could out of the house, often in the equipment shed dismantling strollers, bicycles—anything with wheels—to construct dune buggies and other strange vehicles. Whenever all three kids were together, tempers flared. *Robin's making faces. Don't touch me! Get out of my room! Mom! Robin's sniffing again...gross...make him stop. That's mine. Give it back! Mom!*

"What are we doing wrong?" I asked Jack, after Robin had shoved Galen to the floor for no apparent reason. "Why must everything be a battle? I don't want to live like this, someone always angry, someone always being bullied or picked on. And he's only twelve. Other people's kids aren't like this. Where will it end?"

"You're catastrophizing again, Paula," he said. "He's a boy. Almost a teenager. Teenage boys can be difficult, you know. Some more difficult than others."

I rolled my eyes. I hated it when he used his condescending psychology-professor voice. But he went on.

"You don't get that upset with Erica's moping around, which is more what girls do. She whines about him, and then you blame him for acting out. And Galen. He can be pretty sneaky, and he knows exactly how to set Robin up. Yeah, you're right. Robin's a difficult kid sometimes. You know we have to set firm conditions, and we're not very good at that."

What he really meant, of course, was *you're* not very good at that.

"Are you finished? This isn't a textbook, you know. This is our kid!"

"I know he's our kid, for Christ's sake. Did you think I'd forgotten that? Maybe you need to think about what he's feeling."

I swallowed hard. Jack continued.

"He's trying to carve out a niche for himself in a family where he doesn't think he fits very well. Erica's got the brainy, goody-two-shoes niche. Galen's got the cute, clever little brother niche. Robin's going for the only niche he thinks he can fill: tough — and nothing like the rest of us. Maybe we aren't the best parents for him. But we're what he's got."

Okay. I'd try harder. I ordered a book about getting along with your adolescent children. It urged me to avoid direct conflict and respond to their moodiness and rebellion with helpful interjections that affirmed their moods, like "I see you're feeling sad today," and "What can I do to make you feel better?" and "You're angry; I

251

wonder why." I tried. Robin called me a stupid idiot. Erica glared and skulked away. Galen was cheerfully oblivious.

Jack was having a rough time, too. He'd been denied a promotion because, after the conflict with his adviser years ago, he'd never finished his Ph.D. He was angry and bitter. He applied for a two-year position in Papua New Guinea and waited dejectedly for a response that never came. The next fall, he celebrated his thirty-eighth birthday by buying a brand new Toyota Celica, an impractical extravagance that seemed both frivolous and ostentatious to me, and didn't do much to improve his outlook.

I trudged reluctantly through my daily obligations at Mmmuffins, in the house, and on the farm, convinced that I'd thrown my life away. I hated the business, and spent as little time there as possible. Of course, it did badly. I wanted out, but the country was still deep in recession, and no one was buying struggling businesses. Every little bit of profit it realized went to pay others so I wouldn't have to deal with it.

Only Galen seemed content with who and where he was, and his perpetual cheeriness annoyed us all.

• • •

The school board continued to be a bright spot in the gloom. At the beginning of my third term, I was elected chairperson. Okay, chair*man*; I didn't make a fuss. But when Miss Grey's annual request to continue her Bible classes came before the program committee that year, I was ready. So far, although I'd repeatedly voted against her presence in the school, I'd watched the rest of the board vote in favour and accepted the loss. This time, though, I'd gathered stories from several parents who objected to her presence. I knew I spoke for a minority — a tiny minority — but I was going to speak.

The motion was rapidly moved and seconded.

252

"I'd like to speak to that motion." I shuffled a few papers and began reciting my meager list of complaints. A Jewish parent who objected to her fundamentalist Christian teaching; a parent whose child had come home frightened by Abraham's willingness to sacrifice his son; another whose child explained that, according to Miss Grey, praying would cure her grandmother's cancer.

Other members shook their heads and shared their own opinions. A good woman. Loved by the community. Donates her time. Simply teaches from the Bible. I wasn't going to win. But I'd known that. On to Plan B. I was learning.

"Do we ever see her curriculum ahead of time?" I asked.

Heads shook. Never.

I moved that we approve her presence in the school, ask her to be more sensitive to the fears of young children, and require her to submit her curriculum to this committee for approval.

Reluctant nods.

I wasn't quite done. "I'd also like to move that parents be informed in writing of her activities in the school and offered the opportunity to withdraw their children...*and* that those children be given some alternate activity. Not just sitting in the hall."

My motions passed, barely. A small victory that fell flat at home. My own children refused to let me withdraw them from Miss Grey's class.

"I don't wanna leave the room. And nobody pays any attention to her anyway," said Erica.

Miraculously, Robin agreed with her. He didn't want to leave his friends.

Happy Mouth, for once, had no opinion.

• • •

One frigid winter morning, with the thermometer reading minus 30 Celsius, I scraped frost from the front window of the house to watch all three children climb onto the school bus in the near dark. This was the last year they'd be on the bus together. Erica was fourteen; next year she'd be on the high school bus, which arrived even earlier. She was wearing leg warmers above her snow boots and a green and yellow ski jacket with a long white scarf wrapped around her neck and covering most of her face. Robin leaned against the pine tree with his jacket half-zipped and his hands and head bare. He'd left the house in running shoes again, despite the weather. Galen, now eight, was still willing to wear snow-pants. He stood with Erica, holding his blue plastic lunch box in mittened hands.

As always, as soon as the bus left, I began the day with barn chores. I pulled green barn coveralls over my jeans, topped them with a heavy quilted jacket and an orange woolen toque. Chores would be quick today; we'd stopped milking Gypsy as she approached her due-date. The back door scraped against the ice that had collected on the threshold. It was a perfect winter morning. The sun was just rising over the hills to the east. Pale shadows of the fence between the house and the barn angled toward me, phantom posts reflected on the rippled snow, connected by wavering squares of page wire and disappearing into the deeper shadow created by the snow banks beside the path. The dry snow creaked beneath my feet with each step, like a door hinge in need of oil.

I opened the stable door to a wave of warm air on my face; it formed a cloud of steam when it hit the sub-zero outdoor temperature. The dozen yearlings lumbered about in their several stalls, their moist breath showing white in the dim light, a reminder that the barn's warmth was only a relative thing. I headed straight to the watering hose, which had been carefully drained after its last use. But the moment I picked it up, I noticed the heat light was out in the insulated box containing the spigot. *Damn.* Coldest night of the year; of course, the water's frozen.

The dozen outside cows had seen me coming; they knew the routine and had already clustered around the old claw-foot bathtub, mooing and pushing against each other to be first in line for their morning drink. The inside animals were restless, too, because no water was flowing to their automatic watering bowls, a recent improvement over rows of buckets to be filled with the hose.

I lifted the lid off the top of the water box and screwed a new, 100-watt light bulb into the dangling socket. If it worked quickly, I'd have water by the time I was done here. If not, I'd have to leave it until I got home from Mmmuffins. If it hadn't thawed by then, Erica and Robin would have to help carry buckets of water from the house.

I could see it already: children protesting; water spilling onto the kitchen floor, sloshing out of buckets, freezing immediately as it hit jacket and jeans on the path to the barn; spilling again as thirsty animals shoved against each other for their share. I sent a silent prayer to whatever deity might be listening.

Climbing the ladder into the haymow, it was hard to remember the July days when the bales smelled of sunshine and the mow was a place of excruciating heat and hard labour. On this January morning, a sharp, cold wind blew through the cracks between the barn boards, depositing a skim of snow on the bales closest to the north wall. I tossed ten bales to the outside animals, who had given up on the water and were now milling about waiting for food. The moisture from their breath was re-freezing on their noses and the short hairs around their mouths, giving them all hoary goatees.

I forgot the cold for a moment as I swung from the top tier of hay, settled my left foot on the top rung, and let my arms briefly support the weight of my upper body as my right foot found its spot one rung down—a little jerk, pivot, and balance routine, the closest I'll ever to come to a pirouette, I thought. It reminded me, every day, that I was strong and competent. Even graceful.

As I descended, I flashed back to the three-year-old Robin at the top of the ladder. He was still at it. It seemed his job in life was to trigger the maternal terror-switch. Or the maternal anger switch. Could they be the same? As I hefted bales of hay and spread them among the inside animals, my mind spun in a dizzying circle of self-doubt. Was I angry because I was afraid for him? Afraid he wouldn't "fit" into the family, or the school, or the world? Afraid for me too, because if he didn't, I would be a failure as a parent? Despite Jack's attempts to reassure me, I was finding Robin's level of defiance more and more difficult to handle.

Love, fear, anxiety, anger. A potent cocktail of maternal emotion.

He's a good kid really, I reminded myself. Just last week some neighbours phoned to say what a fine boy he was; they'd hired him to stack some firewood and accidentally overpaid him by twenty dollars. He could have kept the extra money and no one would have been the wiser. But he didn't. Yes, I was proud of that.

And sometimes he showed a surprising sensitivity for his age. Just the other day, he'd come into the living room where I was staring out the window, looked at me, and said, "What's wrong? You look sad." No one else had noticed, but he could tell I was troubled.

"What's wrong, Robin, is that I'm worried about you," I'd replied. "The school called again. About the snowballs at recess this morning. And about pushing Charlie into the snow bank. Why can't you follow the rules?"

"The rules are stupid. Everybody picks on me, so I'm gonna pick on them back." He was kicking a ball against the sofa leg.

"Robin, you know that's not the best way to deal with it." I sounded feeble, even to myself. "Who's picking on you?"

"Everybody. Charlie, for one. All the teachers. I hate them all. They can't make me do anything."

So it seemed. And neither could I. I couldn't make him stop teasing his brother and sister. I couldn't make him do his chores. I couldn't make him stay away from the river. I couldn't make him change his underwear. At twelve, he was as tall as I was and twice as stubborn. I couldn't make him do anything.

I couldn't really make Erica do anything, either, I thought as I checked the water one last time. Still frozen. But she wanted my approval. He didn't seem to care.

Back in the house, I changed my clothes, and drove to Mmmuffins in time for the morning rush — as usual, there wasn't one — and arrived home again five hours later, just before the school bus. Happy Mouth came in the door first.

"Hi, Mommy! Guess what! I can read a whole book. I have it here and I'm going to read it to you. And I didn't finish my lunch because you gave me an orange and I couldn't peel it, but that's okay because Davey gave me his banana because he wasn't hungry. And tomorrow is hot dog day, can I get two?"

"Hold on a minute. Boots off at the door, please. I just cleaned up in here. Yes, you can have two hot dogs tomorrow. And I'd love to hear you read later. But get unbundled first and let me say hi to Robin and Erica."

Erica came in next.

"Hi there, how was your day?" I said.

"It was okay. But I have tons of homework and we have a French test tomorrow. Do I have to do chores tonight?"

"Yup, but you can do them early if you want, then you'll have all evening for homework. First thing, you and Robin will both have to help carry water to the barn. The pipes are frozen. So change into your barn clothes, and let's get it done right away."

She slammed her books on the kitchen table. "Why can't Robin do chores? I do everything around here. Why can't Robin do anything?"

"Robin doesn't have sheep and horses. He has other responsibilities. He shovels snow. He stacks firewood. You don't. And he'll be helping with the water."

"Yeah, sure." She tossed her school jacket and scarf on a hook on the kitchen wall and grabbed her barn jacket and coveralls.

We were off to a great start. Happy Mouth came bouncing back into the kitchen with his book.

"Later, Galen. We have work to do in the barn. You can help. You're not big enough to carry water pails, but you can manage the doors. Put on your barn coat and barn boots."

Robin finally came into the kitchen, hatless and gloveless with snow driven into his thick, dark curls.

"Hi there, how was your day?"

"Why do you always have to say that? 'Hi there, how was your day,'" he mimicked in a tone that I was certain did not resemble my own.

"Okay, then. Never mind your day. Barn water's frozen. I need you to help carry water to the cows."

"I'm not taking water to the stupid cows. They're not my cows. They're your cows, and I hate them."

For no reason that I could see, he stuck his tongue out at Galen. "Gaylord, Gaylord," he chanted.

"Shut up! That's not my name!" yelled Galen.

"Gay-boy, Gay-boy."

"Enough," I said, and started running water into pails. "Erica, let's go. The animals need water. Robin, change your jacket and take these pails to the yearlings in the first stall." I was playing it straight, hoping he would just take the pails and go.

"I told you I hate the stupid cows. I don't care if they have water," he said.

Erica grabbed the pails, stomped past Robin, and headed out the door, muttering under her breath, "You think cows are stupid? They're a lot smarter than you."

He stuck out his foot as she walked by, missing a major spill by just inches. "Idiot," he said.

"Enough. Both of you," I said, fighting back tears as a familiar leaden feeling settled into my chest. I tried to focus on Jack's words. *He's trying to find his niche.*

Erica came back to the kitchen as I was filling two more buckets.

"The water's thawed," she said. "I turned on the outside water, and the two front watering bowls are thawed too. The back one is still frozen."

I put my head in my hands and leaned against the kitchen counter. The relief I felt had nothing to do with the water and everything to do with avoiding an unwinnable battle with my son.

"What's the matter?" asked Erica.

"Nothing." I lied. "Thanks for turning on the water. I'll get supper ready while you finish up the chores. Put some water in that back watering bowl and it'll thaw before you're done in the barn. I watered the chickens and gathered eggs earlier, so you don't have to do that. And I checked the horses. They're fine, too."

I paused. "And Erica. Thanks for being helpful." Her own niche was upstaged too often.

She gave me a half smile, shrugged, and headed back to the barn. Robin disappeared into his bedroom. Galen was waiting in the living room to read me his book. The house was quiet again, but not peaceful.

I went upstairs and knocked on Robin's door.

"What?"

"Can I come in?"

"What d'ya want?" I opened the door and was greeted by the pungent smell of stale, pubescent male sweat. Clothes lay in heaps on the floor. Robin slouched on his unmade bed. His voice was angry. "Why does everyone pick on me? Even you."

"I wasn't picking on you, Robin. I was asking you to help out."
Think about what he's feeling.

"We all need to help out here. I do things I don't like, too. And you're the strongest one here when Dad's not home. Sometimes I need your help."

He looked at me and sneered. "Yeah. Girls can't do much." It wasn't the response I was looking for, but for once I didn't take the bait.

I closed the door, then opened it again. "I love you, kiddo," I said and felt a rush of tenderness for the boy I didn't understand.

"Mommy? Please? Can I read you the book now?" I wiped my cheeks with the back of my hand and rumpled Galen's blond fly-away hair.

"Sure," I said. "Show me how well you can read."

• • •

Now, I wonder if I've reconstructed this memory honestly. The barn, I have no doubt. Thirty years later, I can dance its choreographed routines in my mind without a misstep. But Robin, I'm not so sure. I hope I told him I loved him on that miserable winter day. I hope that rush of tenderness did sweep through me and neutralize the anger. It didn't always.

This afternoon, Robin — the adult, family-man Robin — has come to pick up his own twelve-year-old son, who gets on and off the school bus here. When I watch him dash down the driveway to meet the bus, long legs and dark curls so like his dad's, the last three decades disappear in a moment of recognition.

Robin sighs and leans his six-foot six-inch frame against the kitchen counter, watching his son gather his iPod, his back pack, his shoes, and he shakes his head. "The school called today. I guess I'll be getting what I deserve now. I know I gave you guys a hard time." He gives me a rueful smile.

As he stands here, remembering those troublesome years, I am finding it difficult to reconstruct a moment that justifies the frustration I so often felt. Perhaps there was no justification. Perhaps he was just a rebellious boy, an angry young man, frustratingly out of step with his parents and their expectations. Perhaps it was the burden of a hundred small moments of conflict. Perhaps he was just pushing my buttons, something he's still good at.

Robin has always known he was adopted. But how does that make sense to a child, I wonder? He has different intellectual strengths and different emotional set-points than the rest of the family. He understands that now; he's comfortable with who he is. But it must have been hard to understand growing up. No wonder he struggled to find his niche.

In the mid 1990s, the daughter Sheila had given up at birth contacted her, and I felt a resurgence of interest in knowing Robin's birth mother. I still imagine the encounter, the pride in sharing my—our—son with this woman who must, surely, imagine the same moment. It will not come; on this point, Robin is firm. "I've got a family," he says. "Why would I need another one?" Jack's words from long ago come back: "Maybe we aren't the best parents for him. But we're what he's got."

And maybe it was enough, after all.

• • •

One night toward the end of January, 1983, I came home late from a school board meeting and was surprised to find Jack up and waiting for me. Before I could take off my coat and put my papers on the table, he reached out and hugged me. This wasn't passion.

"Your mom phoned. It's your dad." His voice cracked; my heart pounded. "Cancer"

An earlier bowel cancer, presumably eradicated, had metastasized to Dad's liver. The prognosis was grim.

261

Chapter 17 • End of an Era

It was our eleventh summer on the farm, the third summer for Mmmuffins, my fifth year on the school board, my eighteenth year as a wife, sixteenth year as a mother, and thirty-eighth year as my father's daughter. I plowed, planted, baked, deliberated, and parented in the shadow of Dad's illness. He began having chemotherapy and radiation treatments in the spring, although the doctors didn't hold out much hope. But during the summer, his condition stabilized, and in early August, after the hay was done, we took the family to Niagara on the Lake to meet Mom and Dad for a weekend of theatre-going. Dad was excited about seeing a production of *John Bull's Other Island*, a rarely produced Shaw play he particularly liked. He seemed himself, chatty and thoughtful. But I had to force myself to look at his body, always thin but now emaciated and fragile, as he lounged in the sun by the hotel swimming pool.

While the children swam, and Dad and Jack chatted in lounge chairs, Mom took me aside to tell me Dad had decided not to undergo further treatment.

I was stunned. "But why?"

She had tears in her eyes, but she spoke without a break in her voice. "The treatments are hard on him, Paula. When he made his decision, I said, 'Warren, you're shortening your life,' and he said 'I'm shortening it by two days a week now with the chemo.'"

Time stopped while the last fragments of hope drained away.

"That's how he feels," she said. "It has to be up to him."

Back on the farm, I harvested the garden, Jack prepared for another teaching year, we camped for a few days on Lake Superior.

Galen won first prize at the Laird Fair for his kitten, Monster, who, he assured the judge, could actually speak. Robin won first prize for the most imaginatively sculptured zucchini. Erica won second prize for the best school lunch and rode Stardust in the western competition. My carrot cake took first place. None of it mattered.

In November, we drove to Pennsylvania for Thanksgiving. Dad was up and about, but using oxygen occasionally. The cancer had moved to his lungs. When he passed the turkey-carving ritual to my brother, I knew he couldn't last much longer.

In January, I made my last visit to him. His world had shrunk to bed, chair, and bathroom; his body to a skin-covered skeleton. We watched Penn State football and talked politics — Trudeau (whom I admired), Reagan (whom we both detested). I couldn't say what I really wanted to say, so I sat at his typewriter, in the study he could no longer use, breathed his lingering, familiar scent, and wrote the things I couldn't speak:

"Although we are a loud, relaxed, talkative family," I wrote, "we have never been much given to emotional displays — overactive tear ducts notwithstanding. We have to be facing a life crisis before we can simply say 'I love you.'"

I shared what I was feeling about my own life, though as I read it now, more than three decades later, I sense a false cheeriness: "I am basically content with my life," I said. "I love this place. It's a good place to raise children and the farm is a healthy focus to our lives … As you know, I am not terribly happy with my decision to go into business — in fact, I may soon be able to report that the business is sold; we are in the process of putting it on the market."

And I concluded with the obvious. "What I am trying to tell you, Dad, is that I'm not a finished product yet, but you probably know that already. I always assumed you would be around to see the finished product, but in the natural order of things, that was hardly likely, was it?"

I placed the letter in his hands as I said my final goodbye. A week later, his response came in the mail, his always spidery handwriting even fainter, slantier, and less legible than usual.

"You are right about our reticence, yours and mine ... I like to think that our feelings toward one another are understood and shared at a much deeper level than the usual surface expressions, and your letter gave me assurance that this is so ... Of course I love you. But that threadbare expression seems so inadequate to express all that you have given us ..."

A week later, he died in his own bed with my mother beside him.

Mom didn't want a lot of commotion, so I decided none of the children would go to Pennsylvania for Dad's funeral. Robin stayed with Sheila and Bill; Galen stayed with Carol and Gerry. Erica was on a French exchange program, living with a family in Montreal for the winter. She was angry to be left alone with strangers, and she was right to be. I've made a lot of mistakes as a parent, but that was one of the biggest. Until Dad died, I didn't know how mourning worked; I didn't realize how tears and laughter would meld and help to heal, and how the inevitability of death that I'd come to accept on the farm would begin to become part of the family fabric, too. Dad's grandchildren should have been there.

That spring, on a rare evening when the kids were all at the supper table and all getting along, we talked about planting a tree for Dad in our yard. But our success with trees was spotty. The Pappy Tree planted in honour of my grandfather several years earlier had already died, and we were lying to my grandmother regularly, sending her pictures of a different tree, a volunteer poplar that had sprung up in the side yard and seemed certain to survive. She would never know. But if a tree planted in Dad's memory died, Mom would know, and so would I.

Then we started remembering all the things Dad had done during his visits to the farm. After the fiasco of chasing cows in the early years, he stayed clear of the animals. But he always busied himself with some small project: replacing panes of glass in barn windows, staining the deck, building a gate to the horse yard — an ungraceful but sturdy construction, made of rough-cut lumber, that hung on huge hinges and was held shut by a wire loop over the adjacent post.

"That's it!" I said. "The Warren Sylvester Smith Memorial Gate." Without plaque or ceremony, that's what it became until, more than a decade later, we dismantled the horse yard fence.

• • •

I finally unloaded Mmmuffins for less than we'd paid for it, just enough to pay off the remaining loan, but I wanted out at any cost. Jack resigned himself to the financial loss. He stared at the purchase agreement spread out on the kitchen table and shook his head. "It's no worse than buying a brand new Cadillac, not bothering to insure it, and driving it into the river," he said.

"We lose money on the farm, too," I said, feeling both relieved and defensive. But I knew it wasn't the same. For all my grumbling and self-questioning, I loved the farm. I didn't give a damn about muffins. Or Mmmuffins. Never had. So, in early August, 1984, the last of the summer's hay went into the barn and I ended my business career. To celebrate, we headed north.

For several years, we'd made a practice of camping for the last two weeks of August — after haying, after the Fall Fair — at Agawa Bay in Lake Superior Provincial Park, a place where the same glaciers that created our farm had left spectacular rocky headlands and just enough soil to support the mixed boreal forest that creeps to the edge of the lake. There, along the water's edge, stunted trees wrap their roots along the surface of rocks, reaching into the smallest crevices to derive what little nourishment they can. There, on the rocks' surface, arctic lichen thrive in a micro ecosystem close to the cold water of Lake Superior. And there, by some magic, we managed to leave behind the family tensions and squabbles that come with changing priorities and adolescent children.

We took hikes along trails through the forest, or climbed the rocks along the rugged shoreline, where wave action filled giant "bathtubs" with water, warmed by the sun, perfect for lounging and bathing. Back at the campsite, Erica curled up against a log, reading. Robin rode his bike up and down the campground, happy, making friends, exploring—even, at times it seemed, contemplative. I lounged at the campsite, walked on the beach, picked blueberries with Galen, watched him swim, canoed with Jack, and leaned against giant driftwood logs, turning the pages of a book and allowing myself the luxury of daydreaming between chapters. Two weeks of campfires, s'mores, sunsets over the lake.

"What an amazing place." I said, poking a stick in the dying embers of the campfire on our last night, watching the kids on the beach. Robin and Galen were trying to skip stones, Robin towering over his little brother. Erica was throwing sticks into the water for Gylden. Her pigtails were long gone; blond hair cascaded over her shoulders, and as I watched her I realized that my awkward adolescent daughter had become a young woman. She'd be starting her last year of high school in two weeks.

Jack dug into the bag for a marshmallow the kids had missed, put it on a stick, and dangled it over the embers. He nodded.

"If there's a God, he lives right here. On those rocks," I said, looking at the headland jutting out into the lake, just a few yards from our campsite.

"Mishibishu," said Jack. Spirit of the Lake. We'd seem his image at the Ojibway pictograph site at Agawa Rock just that morning.

"I used to feel this way about the farm. You know? That it was just too wonderful to be true. Now, I hardly notice—except when other people say something."

"Yeah," he said, turning his marshmallow stick slowly. "It's not quite the same anymore."

"It's the same. We're different."

"I guess," he said, He popped the marshmallow into his mouth, leaving a sticky glob on his beard, and stood up to get his camera. "Gotta get that sunset."

"Lake Superior sunset, photo number seven hundred and three," I said, stretching my legs out toward the fire, staring across the water at the red sky, suddenly remembering the nineteen-year-old boy who'd leapt to his feet twenty years ago, returning with a beer and a hand-writing test. And the eighteen-year-old girl, who'd scoffed at his enthusiasm, but played along.

Well, maybe not so different.

• • •

Back at home, another school year begun, the sun was rising over the hill, promising a clear, fall day. The house was quiet except for a terrific clanging sound that seemed to be emanating from the hill itself. Jack came into the kitchen, picked up his brief case and a bag of egg cartons, and approached me for his morning kiss.

"What's that noise?" I muttered into his beard. It smelled like coffee.

He stood still and listened. He knew immediately; his dad had been in the sand and gravel business. "A crusher."

"Well, I hope it won't be there long," I said, taking another sip of cold coffee.

"No chance," said Jack. "If they've brought in a crusher, they're serious. And they'll run it 'round the clock to get their full value from it."

They were our neighbours, the same neighbours who had approached us shortly after we moved to the farm about turning the hill into a ski resort. Now it seemed they were turning it into a commercial gravel pit.

Most of the farms in the valley have small gravel pits in the hills behind the fields, where the glacier left piles of tiny, smooth stones and sand close to the surface. Landowners haul their gravel out with tractors and use it for small projects like laneways and drainage ditches. Our own pit is in the Rocky Pasture, alongside a spring-fed creek; it's a shallow indentation, rarely used, now filled in with grasses and small shrubs. For years, the kids insisted it was really a dinosaur pit, thoroughly convinced that Tyrannosaurus Rex had wallowed in our own back forty.

"But it's awful! We won't be able to hear ourselves think!" I was on the deck now, looking toward the hill.

For once, Jack did not accuse me of catastrophising.

"Yeah," said Jack. "And that's not the worst of it. Where do you think the gravel deposit ends?"

I looked at him blankly.

"They can go right through to our side of the hill. We don't own the top, remember."

We weren't alone in our dismay. Several neighbours joined us to protest. At full tilt, it wouldn't take long for a gravel operation to demolish the dominant geographic feature of the Echo River Valley. It would take even less time for heavy equipment and trucks of gravel to wreak havoc on the road and change the nature of this quiet community along the river. We knew the township was eager for a new source of gravel for road maintenance and construction, and that they would probably approve an exemption to their own recently-passed municipal plan that had zoned our area "rural and agricultural". But there had been no application for exemption, no public notice, no due process. Just a crusher running night and day, and dump trucks of gravel travelling from the hill, along a laneway just a few yards from another neighbour's house. When a crack appeared in his foundation, he approached Jack.

"I've been talkin' to Keith and Nelson. We figure, you being a professor, you'd be the best one to take this on." And so, Jack and I became the de facto leaders of a challenge to the legality of the gravel pit.

For the fourteen years we'd been on the farm, I'd continued to pay my membership dues to the Women's Institute and attend their monthly meetings, partly out of loyalty to Gloria and partly because I'd become fond of these kind, conservative, traditional women.

I went to the next meeting as usual.

"Keep us, O Lord, from pettiness," I chanted with the ladies. "Grant that we may realize it is the little things that create differences; that in the big things of life we are at one."

We didn't talk about the gravel pit; we didn't need to. It lurked unspoken beneath the Pennies for Friendship, the singing of "God Save the Queen," the salmon salad sandwiches and date squares.

"It was a great garden year, wasn't it?" I said during a lull in the conversation.

Gloria glanced at me. "Yes."

Then she turned to Helen. "When are you and Don going to visit Bruce?" *Et tu*, Gloria?

Helen replied, and the conversation gravitated toward her.

"So, how many grandchildren do you have, now, Helen?" I asked.

"Three," she answered, then turned to Elsa. "Elsa, tell us about your horticulture course." Elsa. Even Elsa Jones in her flashy pink blouse out-ranked me in the conversation. Without saying a word, the ladies of the WI made it clear: they stood firmly behind Helen's family and their gravel pit.

The next day, I drove down to Gloria's for tea. We hadn't been visiting so much lately, but I needed to talk to her. She put teacups out on the same oilcloth tablecloth I'd sat at a hundred times.

"It's not about friendship, you know," I said. "It's the principle of the thing."

She poured the tea. No cookies.

"I know you don't agree with us. That's okay. I mean," I was stammering now. "Friends don't always agree."

Gloria pursed her lips, and I felt the weight of her disapproval. "Three generations of that family have lived in this valley. They've earned the right."

I stirred a spoonful of sugar into my tea. "Well, still, they should have followed the rules. Otherwise, what are the rules for?"

I stopped there. No point launching into my spiel about citizen equality and blind justice and the rule of law. For Gloria and the ladies in the WI, it was about a different set of principles, built on longstanding relationships and a sense of entitlement based on ownership and belonging. We would never close that gap.

We eventually won the gravel pit battle, but the community never felt quite the same afterwards. The ladies of the WI were growing older; several had already died, and others were moving to live with their children or into care facilities in the city. The new families moving in weren't interested. The handful of remaining members agreed to call it quits. I heard about the last meeting months after it happened.

"The end of an era," Gloria said, standing in my back yard. She was here on an errand of mercy; an elderly neighbour had died, and Gloria was taking up a collection for his family. "This WI knitted socks for the men in both wars."

I thought about the ladies gathering in homes every month for all those years—young women, then. I thought about Irene's smile, Helen's frown, Elsa's too-tight blouses, old Mrs. Trotter's stern judgments, and Gloria's controlling energy. I thought about

Christmas cookies for bachelors, Pennies for Friendship, "God Save the Queen," salmon sandwiches, bread-and-butter pickles, and the Christmas sleigh rides. I remembered about the nude and the gerbils, and I smiled.

The opening words of the WI prayer played back to me, in the droning voices of the assembled ladies: "Keep us, O Lord, from pettiness. Let us be large in thought, in word, in deed."

Sure, I thought as I gazed past Gloria and across the valley at the rock-faced hill beyond. But the question is, what is petty and what is large?

• • •

Jack and I sat on the back deck and looked past the road to the river, where a speedboat was cruising toward Echo Lake. It was the first really warm day of May in 1988, before the lawn had to be mowed, before the fields were ready to rototill, before the garden could be planted. Jack's classes had just ended. The cows with their new calves were already on pasture; Stardust was poking around in his yard finding the first bits of green grass; the daffodils were almost in bloom. I was thinking that it would be a good afternoon to work up the driest corner of the garden and plant some lettuce and spinach. It was the kind of day I loved to be exactly where I was.

Jack started to speak. Then stopped. Another boat sped by.

"See those guys on the river?" he said. "Sometimes when I'm on a tractor, I think—what's the difference? They're just bumping along on the water; I'm just bumping along on the field. But one is work. The other is play. And we probably lose as much money on the farm as they spend on their boats. More."

I chuckled. "Oh well. It's never been about money."

"No. But sometimes I'm not sure what it *is* about anymore." He leaned back, put his feet up on the railing, and clasped his hands behind his head. "I'm just not ready for this summer."

I looked out at the fields. Tender green shoots peeking above last year's stubble painted the fields a delicate green on a brown canvas. The poplars and maples on the hill were showing a blur of yellowy-green and red, more texture than colour, against the dark, almost-black green of the evergreens and the grey of the rocks. I was in my comfort zone.

Jack wasn't ready for the summer, wasn't sure what it was about anymore. These were my lines. It made me uneasy to hear them from Jack. "What do you mean?"

He straightened up and stretched. "Oh, I'm just tired. Haven't made the switch from school to farm yet, I guess."

"You'll perk up," I said. "You always do."

He nodded absently. "I guess so. But I'm getting tired of the routine. I don't know how someone like Morley can keep it up all his life. Really," he said as he stood up and headed for the kitchen door, "how much more is there to learn about shoveling manure?"

It dawned on me then—after twenty years of living with this man—that Jack's idea of the perfect life would be a learning curve that never peaked. Mine would be to snuggle into a comfort zone and never leave. I was finally there. He was ready to leave.

• • •

Summers had changed. Erica was home from her second year at university, working as a tour guide on the all-day tour train into the wilderness north of Sault Ste. Marie. She still took care of Stardust and rode him occasionally, but we didn't expect much more of her. Robin was working too, driving his own clunker of a car to the Sault where he had a job as a grease monkey. That left me, Jack, and Galen, now thirteen, to do most of the summer farm work alone. The pace was slow, and Jack missed the camaraderie of a crew of workers. At the same time, I realized how accustomed I'd become to playing a bit part in the fieldwork. I was used to pitching in when needed; now I was needed most of the time. Taking my full share of the heavy work taxed my strength and my endurance—and my commitment to the process. It seemed my comfort zone depended on other people doing the bulk of the heavy work.

That summer, Jack crawled reluctantly out of bed on July mornings to cut hay. I got up with him, and we had a quiet cup of coffee before any of the kids were moving. He hadn't perked up.

"The weather looks good for the next few days," he said one morning. This should have been good news, but his shoulders slumped, and he sighed. "I should cut at least a third of the big field this morning. And we have ten acres to bale this afternoon. We'll get started around two. Obviously, I'll need you and Galen."

I stared into my coffee cup. I knew he worked much harder than I did. I couldn't complain. Not out loud.

The day progressed more or less as Jack had outlined in the morning. I drove the tractor with the baler sometimes; Galen drove it sometimes; Jack never did. He built the load on the hay wagon, and then stacked the bales in the haymow while Galen and I unloaded, always taking the heaviest work for himself.

The river still sparkled, the fields still stretched from the road to the hill, the hill still rose at the back of the land with its mosaic of greens and outcroppings of grey. But I wasn't seeing them anymore.

Later that afternoon, when the baling was almost done, Robin came home and joined Jack and Galen on the field. At sixteen, he towered above Jack and enjoyed demonstrating his strength and stamina, as well as his understanding of equipment which was already greater than his dad's. I sighed with relief when I saw him crossing the field toward us.

I left them and walked out to the pasture where Diamond, the milk cow, grazed with the rest of the cows.

We'd gone a couple of years without milking a cow. A lot of things about farming were becoming tiresome to me, but I had always enjoyed milking, and I'd missed it. When I saw an ad for a Jersey milk cow, we discussed it for a long time. In the end, we agreed: we would buy the Jersey, but she would be mine. Jack would help out some, of course. But milking would fall almost entirely on me.

Diamond was a beautiful tawny cow with a delicate body, huge brown eyes, gently curving horns, and a white diamond on her forehead. To our surprise, the owners threw in a single-cow milking machine that hung over her back with a strap. When the machine was plugged in and turned on, four suction cups attached to her teats and delivered milk into a covered, stainless steel pail. It was a miracle to use, and Jack preferred it. But it was a pain to clean, and I usually preferred to pull the old stool up to her side, press against her body, and milk by hand into an open pail.

Even after an exhausting day on the field, the walk to the pasture was a pleasure. I came up beside Diamond and began the usual slow chant: "Let's go, girl; come on, time to go ..." She began to separate from the herd while the others looked up briefly. They quickly returned to their grazing; they all knew the routine.

On the walk back to the barn, I led from behind, my eyes focused on Diamond's tan rump and tail, and on her full udder swinging from side to side with each step, making a gentle slapping sound as it smacked first on one leg, then on the other.

As we approached the barn, her pace quickened. I wasn't in a hurry, but Diamond was anticipating the sweet mix of oats and molasses she knew would be waiting. She stood aside as I unlatched the barn door, then stepped awkwardly over the ledge, front feet then back, and headed for the stanchion.

274

I left her in the stanchion and went into the house to check the roast in the oven. The phone rang; I answered it. When I returned to the barn, Diamond was dead.

I had left the pan of grain just beyond her reach so she wouldn't eat it until I got back. But she had other ideas. She'd stretched her neck to reach it and caught her horn on the side of the stanchion. She strangled trying to free herself.

For weeks, I tried to re-wind the tape. "Just milk her. Do your errands in the house later. Then she'll be fine." But, of course, you can't re-wind the tape.

It was summer, so we buried her in a back field, in accordance with the Dead Animal Disposal Act. I haven't milked a cow since.

• • •

That fall, before the cows came in for the winter, we hired a couple of kids to clean the calf stalls, which had been left until the last minute. By mid-September, we'd shipped off the yearlings and delivered meat to our usual customers, the barn was filled with hay, the grain crop was harvested, the stable was ready for winter occupation, and the freezer was filled with our own meat and vegetables.

Erica returned to university, Jack returned to teaching, and I shifted my focus to the school board and my newest professional endeavor, a writing and desktop publishing business that—finally—felt like me. Robin still lived at home; he was in his last year of high school, but we didn't see much of him. Galen was in his first year of high school, a lanky teenager whose real enthusiasms were the school basketball team and the Toronto Blue Jays. He did the evening chores after school; Jack and I alternated morning chores. We'd already sold the pony, Bill, to another generation of young riders. That winter, we finally sold Erica's beloved horse, Stardust, too. She agreed it made sense, but didn't want to be home when the animal who had been her best friend was led onto a trailer, en route to a new home. We still had her dog, Gylden, who had become the family dog in her absence, and an assortment of cats she had loved and whose names I have long forgotten.

Jack came home from school one winter day with an air of enthusiasm that I hadn't seen for awhile. He brushed the snow off his coat and hung it on the kitchen hooks. Rubbing the melting snowflakes off his beard, he said, "Let's have a glass of wine. There's something we need to talk about." He was trying to be mysterious, but I could tell it was something good.

"What's up?" I asked, after we'd settled in the living room.

"Doug called me into his office today." Doug was the college president. "He wants to start a co-op education project, and he wants me to get it off the ground."

Jack lapsed into an excited description of how co-op education worked, how Doug envisioned this changing the nature of Algoma College. He was waving his hands as he spoke, shifting from side to side in his chair. I suddenly realized how long it had been since I'd seen Jack the enthusiast.

"It's a work-study program. Kids get placed in workplaces that fit with their major, and they get some credit for those work terms. I'd have to work with employers and with the various departments at school to set up the program. He wants to get it off the ground for next fall. I figure the psych department would be a good start. I already have a list of possible placements."

He stopped abruptly and looked out the window, where a February storm was hurling snow against the windows. His tone changed.

"The only thing is, I don't see how I can do it with the farm. It's not a teaching position. I could take a few weeks off in the summer, but it wouldn't be as flexible."

I followed his gaze to the storm outside, and then looked across the room at him. Even as I ached at the thought of leaving the farm behind, I knew it was my aversion to change—yes, my basically conservative nature—that caused the ache more than a continued enthusiasm for farming itself.

"You should do it," I said. "We'll work something out. We don't have to move, you know. It can still be home."

The last photograph we have of fieldwork, from the summer of 1989, shows me on the tractor pulling the baler, and fourteen-year-old Galen alone on the hay wagon, building a load of hay by himself. It was a rite of passage he almost missed.

The last of the cows clamoured onto the livestock truck a couple of months later, leaving the barn and the fields empty for the first time since old Dave Barkley cleared the land.

CODA

I began this retrospective journey wondering how far I'd have to go back to find out where it all began and how I came to call this place home. That is, of course, an unanswerable question; you can no more unravel the strands of a life than a spider can unspin its web. Or than a river can continue to flow backwards.

I'll never really know where it began; it probably wasn't Laura, or baking bread, or reading Adele Davis. It wasn't Jack, either. If my life is a river, Jack is a fast-moving tributary that added its current to my meandering flow, kept me moving when I might have lingered in eddies, lost in reverie, trapped in circles of indecision. Although it hasn't always been true in real time, in retrospect I'm grateful for that; Jack the enthusiast, has led me to places I'd never have gone on my own.

But Jack's enthusiasms alone didn't lead us to this place; they could have taken him, us, in any number of directions. It was, instead, a confluence of circumstances — a generation determined to move against the current, a child allergic to milk, a rental agreement cancelled, a health food cookbook — that set the ball in motion and made an unlikely destination seem inevitable. And once the ball began to roll, it picked up meaning as it went, became a cause, a lifestyle, and finally a reservoir of memories that continue to define us. Our lives create us as much as we create them. Mine created a farm wife, yes. It also created an endless search for self-definition, a conflicted stay-at-home mom, a dreadful businesswoman, and finally, a wordsmith and a bemused observer of a river in search of its source.

● ● ●

It's the last week of September, 2015, and no frost yet. That used to be rare; now it's usual. But even in the warm temperatures, the garden knows it's fall. Spindly broccoli stems send their last heads up in a rush to turn them into tiny yellow flowers before it's too late. Tomato plants—unstaked again this year—sprawl along the ground doing their best to hide the ripening fruit under drooping, leafy stems. The wizened foliage of potato plants signals spots where potatoes still wait to be dug. Here and there, a stray lettuce plant that escaped August's culling stands tall, gawky, oddly spring-green, its tiny leaves bitterly inedible. Pigweed has taken over the spaces occupied by peas and beans until a few weeks ago. Kale and Brussels sprouts cluster on the late-fall edge of the garden. We'll be eating those until snow falls.

"What do you think?" I ask Jack. We are sprawled on deck chairs, enjoying one of the year's last warm afternoons, legs propped up on the railing. "Is it time to leave?"

He sighs. It's a recurring dilemma. "Some days, yes. Too much yard. Too much house maintenance. Too much driving. We're not getting any younger." He turned seventy last year; this year it's my turn. Erica and Galen think we should move to southern Ontario, nearer to them and their families. I don't think that will happen any time soon. We've been spending winters in a warmer place for some years now, but this corner of northern Ontario is still home. Robin lives nearby; he'd love to buy the place if we ever decide to leave.

We are both looking across the fields at the hill; the maple reds are already fading, leaving the muted gold and orange palette of poplar and birch, interspersed with the almost-black greens of spruce and pine. Jack turns and looks at his pottery studio, the passion that replaced the farm when he retired from teaching. Still the enthusiast. Still playing in mud. Farmer Jack has become Potter Jack. "I'm not ready to leave the pottery. Not just yet."

I nod. Some days, perhaps the days when my rational mind is working overtime, I think it's time to sell, move to the city. We have come close. But so far, the ties holding us to this piece of land refuse to loosen. And so, we continue to circle in the same eddy, knowing that there comes a point, even for a slow-moving, indecisive river like the Echo, where the urge to move on is irresistible.

"Maybe when the time comes," says Jack "we should sell the place, get a motor home, just travel around for a few years."

"Or," I say, "you could fix up an old school bus."

We laugh together. The river is barely moving in the autumn light.

Paula Dunning lives in Echo Bay, Ontario, with her husband Jack, on the property where they raised their family and farmed for fifteen years in the 1970s and 1980s. After their farming venture, she embarked on a career as a freelance writer and editor, providing communication services for the public and private sectors and serving as editor of *Education Canada*, the flagship publication of the Canadian Education Association. Since retirement, she has turned her hand to essays, memoir, and short fiction. Her essays have aired on the CBC's Sunday Edition and her short fiction has been published in the literary journal, *Agnes and True*.

www.embajadoraspress.com/index.php/paula-dunning/

pauladunning@embajadoraspress.com`